Unscripting the Present

SUNY series in Queer Politics and Cultures
———————
Cynthia Burack and Jyl J. Josephson, editors

Unscripting the Present
The Security Panic of Queer Youth Sexuality

TIMOTHY GITZEN

Cover credit: "Men Lying on Bed," Cottonbro Studio.

Published by State University of New York Press, Albany

© 2025 State University of New York

All rights reserved

Printed in the United States of America

No part of this book may be used or reproduced in any manner whatsoever without written permission. No part of this book may be stored in a retrieval system or transmitted in any form or by any means including electronic, electrostatic, magnetic tape, mechanical, photocopying, recording, or otherwise without the prior permission in writing of the publisher.

Links to third-party websites are provided as a convenience and for informational purposes only. They do not constitute an endorsement or an approval of any of the products, services, or opinions of the organization, companies, or individuals. SUNY Press bears no responsibility for the accuracy, legality, or content of a URL, the external website, or for that of subsequent websites.

EU GPSR Authorised Representative:
Logos Europe, 9 rue Nicolas Poussin, 17000, La Rochelle, France
contact@logoseurope.eu

For information, contact State University of New York Press, Albany, NY
www.sunypress.edu

Library of Congress Cataloging-in-Publication Data

Name: Gitzen, Timothy, 1985– author.
Title: Unscripting the present : the security panic of queer youth
  sexuality / Timothy Gitzen.
Description: Albany, NY : State University of New York Press, [2025] |
  Series: SUNY series in queer politics and cultures | Includes
  bibliographical references and index.
Identifiers: LCCN 2024039396 | ISBN 9798855801644 (hardcover : alk. paper) |
  ISBN 9798855801668 (ebook)
Subjects: LCSH: Gay youth—United States. | Youth—Sexual behavior—United
  States. | Sex in popular culture—United States. | Moral panics—United States.
Classification: LCC HQ76.27.Y68 G58 2025 | DDC 306.76/60835—dc23/eng/20241226
LC record available at https://lccn.loc.gov/2024039396

*For Hezekiah and Wyatt,
may your futures shine as brightly as the stars.*

Contents

Acknowledgments	ix
Preface: Of Futures and Presents	xiii
Introduction: Panic Scripting	1
Chapter One Securitizing Sex	33
Chapter Two Radical Presentism	59
Chapter Three Relationality and the Contractual Self	83
Chapter Four The Ascendancy of Queer Pleasure	111
Chapter Five The American Security Apparatus	137
Coda: World Ending	163
Notes	169
References	181
Index	201

Acknowledgments

This was a bit of an unexpected book for a cultural anthropologist, as the beginnings of this book emerged at the height of the COVID-19 pandemic. Everyone handled the pandemic differently; for me, I binge-watched the Norwegian show *Skam* and some of its European adaptations. I found the third season about the queer coupling of Isak and Even so compelling that I felt a strong desire to write about it. On the surface, the show was no different from other films and shows about queer youth I had seen, such as the 2018 film *Love, Simon*. But there was something unique about the details, about the dialogue and even the messaging, that felt revolutionary and hopeful. The deluge of scholarly writing about *Skam* since its airing validated that feeling. And so what is now chapter 2 began in those pandemic daydreams of revolution and hope that saw queer youth as the protagonist of queer theory.

Planning and writing this book carried me through some particularly difficult and turbulent times, the pages filled with a much-needed catharsis as a result. Having grown up in Florida, this book is partly driven by Florida's 2022 Don't Say Gay law, mourning the loss of protections of queer youth in Florida and throughout the United States. How can we expect our children to grow up when their current lot in life is precarious and their futures seem so utterly fucked? I choose to remain hopeful, however, not in adults' actions but in queer youth's resilience and survivability. They outshine us in so many ways, for even if they have not lived through the AIDS epidemic, Don't Ask, Don't Tell, and antisodomy laws, they fight tooth and nail every day to have some semblance of assurance as to their futures. Ultimately, they are the inspiration for this project, and I thank them. May you lead through kindness as you move every which way in this life.

Some folks who read and heard of the early parts of this book deserve profound thanks for encouraging me to write through the turbulence, to never lose my passion for writing. Ilana Gershon first encouraged me to write about popular culture at the same time I was watching *Skam*. I do not think she expected that I would write a book, however. A prolific writer herself, she has always encouraged me to write, and continues to support me and my career in rather magical ways. I have known Jennifer Patico for more than a decade now. I was once her student and advisee, and she is forever a mentor and friend, as she is always ready to help, read, advise, and encourage. She not only read parts of this book but also served as a sounding board for preparing my book and submitting it to publishers. Cassandra White also read parts of this manuscript and has always encouraged me with her kindness and willingness to read and engage with me and my work. We also share a common anthropological interest in ghosts and the paranormal that will no doubt come to shape future collaborations and interactions.

It is strange to think that my friend and writing partner, Elliott Prasse-Freeman, has heard extensively about the process and joy of writing this book and yet has actually read next to none of it. I'm not entirely sure why that is, but perhaps it is because this book is profoundly personal, and thus, I wanted to wait to share it with him once completed. Indeed, this holds true for many of my usual writing interlocutors. This book, my second and the ultimate passion project, comes from a place of love and kindness for the next generation of queers that could have been written only after my first book. In other words, I wanted to take what I had learned from writing my first book and implement it in this book, including both theoretical and rhetorical techniques housed within a writing that showed growth and reflected something deep within me. The support I have received from friends and colleagues in this writing journey has been immeasurable, including Elliot's sometimes snarky support.

My colleagues at Wake Forest University are especially appreciated for making the conditions for writing this book spectacular. Jessica MacLellan began this tenure-track journey with me and remains the best cohort mate, colleague, and friend I could have ever hoped for. Talking to her is so effortless that I often forget we have only known each other for a short amount of time. Julie Velásquez Runk is incredibly kind and supportive, and though she began at Wake Forest at the same time as me, her academic and life experiences have been an invaluable resource for someone just starting out. Always making me smile and feel loved,

Nisrine Rahal has been a supportive friend always ready to break down any situation into its parts and try to reassemble them in new ways. The Anthropology Department at Wake Forest is easily one of the most supportive places I have had the good fortune to be in. Each member has encouraged me during both the writing process and in my seemingly broad range of research interests. Margaret Bender, Sherri Lawson Clark, Steve Folmar, Karin Friederic, Andrew Gurstelle, Ellen Miller, Paul Thacker, Rosemary McCarthy, and Jeff Nichols: I could not have hopped for better colleagues. Across the university, I am thankful to have received support and encouragement from Julia Jordan-Zachery, J. Moisés García-Rentería, Kristina Gupta, Dani Parker Moore, Mir Yarfitz, Michele Myers, Monique O'Connell, and Tony Marsh. I am also thankful for my undergraduate research assistants—Nick Beckom, Annelise Witcher, and Anna Kalbas—for their help with sex education research. Finally, my students at Wake Forest have been inspirational in writing this book, particularly those that come early or stick around after class to chat, those that regularly come to my office hours, and those I have advised in projects and honors theses.

SUNY Press has been amazing to work with. Rebecca Colesworthy, in particular, has been an absolute rockstar during this process, showing great enthusiasm for the project from the start. Her encouragement and advice made the entire process enjoyable and affirming. In addition, Hannah Andrews, who read a part of a chapter that was published first in the journal *Critical Studies in Television*, along with Vilde Schanke Sundet and her kindness, are to be thanked.

Making friends as an adult is hard, full stop. I have been quite lucky, however, to have three of the most amazing best friends one can hope for. Jaewon Shin and I met rather randomly, first having pizza together and talking about god only knows. Since then, we have found a way to navigate gay life in two different countries together. Sam Porter and I often narrate our daily lives to one another, I'm not quite sure why, but I think we want witnesses to the fact that we survive each day, especially when the days are hard. Mathew Wachtor has been a constant fixture in my life since 2008 when we were both young, naïve, and somehow living in South Korea at the same time. Both Sam and Mat had babies while I was writing this book—Wyatt and Hezekiah—and yet still found time to keep me grounded, stable, and sane when it should have been the other way around.

Finally, if my friends kept me grounded, my family constantly reminded me of my core values and ethics, with a splash of chaos mixed in for good measure. My father, Steven Gitzen, and his partner, Martha Guerra, keep inviting me back home to visit, so I must be doing something right.

Parts of chapter 2 were first published in *Sexuality & Culture* in volume 26 (1766–1781, Springer Nature) in 2022 as "Minute by Minute: The Radical Presentism of Queer Youth." Parts of chapter 4 were first published in *Critical Studies in Television* in 2024 as "Pleasure's Ascendency: Against Queer Youth Panic" (https://doi.org/10.1177/17496020241241996, Sage).

Preface

Of Futures and Presents

The future is relentless. Some believe and hope that things will get better in the future, but I'm not as taken in by the lure of future thinking. The present requires far more attention anyways.

Panic about gender and sexuality is on the rise in the United States, found especially in debates over sex education, gender-affirming care, bathrooms, sports, and media. At the heart of these panics resides queer youth, faced with both a wellspring of opportunities and insurmountable discrimination that backs them into a corner. Such contemporary sex panics about queer youth rely on imagination to instigate fear, requiring us to imagine what might happen, what could happen, to the innocence of children and thus insisting that action be taken in the present to prepare for that potential future. This anticipation for a future that may or may not even transpire renders queer youth both a population to protect and a population to fear, for conservatives and proponents of such panicked discourse over gender and sexuality see queer youth as the epitome of the child's loss of innocence: already sexualized as queer before becoming an adult. There no doubt exists a double standard, for the heterosexualization of children multiplies, found in seemingly benign instances when parents interpret interactions between children of the opposite sex as being boyfriend and girlfriend. Yet the possibility that the child may be queer disrupts a specific maturation telos that assumes children will grow up straight and reproduce the family and nation. Contemporary sex panics are thus panics about the future: how will children grow up, how will they become adults?

Let me briefly abscond to Brazil and an instance that renders such panic especially fraught. In the first episode of the HBO Max Brazilian show *Teenage Kiss: The Future Is Dead* (2023), a rather spectacular thing happens. In the middle of school and following a secretive call to arms, the members of the group Teenage Kiss, or TK, begin to kiss each other. Some are kissing one person, others two, but all genders are kissing all genders. Protagonist Ariel is standing in the center of a stairwell watching the sight before them, teachers panicking as they ring the fire alarm, and the sprinklers begin showering the kissing teens with water. As the show progresses, we learn that TK members often share kisses with each other, some as couples, but some as simply greetings—kissing becomes a way to foster and manage relationality among these teens. The school scene breaks and the motto of TK and the show flashes across the screen: "Welcome to the Present. Say Goodbye to the Past. The Future is Dead."

The show, based on the comic book by Rafael Coutinho, takes place in a dystopian Brazil where the Amazon Forest was privatized for industrialization and adults, once they turn eighteen, are overcome by the illness "monochromatism," which depletes one of emotions and causes one to literally lose their colors. Throughout the show, adults are presented as apathetic and unemotive with only gray coloring, compared to teens and children who are vibrant and colorful, symbolizing perhaps both the immediacy by which they live and the deluge of contradictory emotions and feelings that mark one's teenage years. This juxtaposition between adults and teens is threaded throughout the series, as adults are critical of the immediacy by which teens live while teens dread the moment they turn eighteen. The future is understood as inevitable, but an inevitable outcome that must be secured. In the first episode, when students arrive at school, they are required to line up and sing along to a national video recording that repeats the phrase "future, homeland, and family." Public service announcements shown throughout the series on virtual billboards repeat a similar ideology, that citizens must work to keep the family and homeland safe and secure for future generations.

In the wake of this march toward adulthood, a group of teenagers yearn to forgo fixation on their future fate and instead live in the immediacy of the present. They form a popular clothing brand that acts as a front for a secret society, TK, for those teens with superhuman powers. Ariel is recruited because after they turned fifteen, they began vomiting colors, the telltale sign that a teen has powers. Particularly marking these teens are not only the plethora of colors they wear and mobilize but the queerness of their dress, behavior, and attractions. Ariel, for instance, shares their first kiss with a girl, Lin, but later shares their second kiss with Tomás, a TK member and model responsible for introducing Ariel to TK. Many of the characters are queer—Lin, for instance, is in a relationship with fellow TK member Vic—but Ariel is also portrayed by Brazilian actor Benjamín, who is trans.

That these teens are concerned less with the future, particularly given the inevitable monochromatism that awaits them at the age of eighteen and with the passage to adulthood, places more meaning on their present interaction. In the second episode of the series, Tomás is seen bemoaning his eventual monochromatism and aging out, as he is almost eighteen, and thus when an enthusiastic fan arrives to meet Tomás, the two escape to Tomás's room to have sex. For Tomás, the sex is meant to displace or supplant his own individual panic about his inevitable future and adulthood, a lateral movement in the immediate present that focuses on pleasure over panic.

Furthermore, stopping in the middle of school to make out in front of everyone—seen as an act of remembrance for a fallen teen who died at the start of the series—is also an act of refusal, refusal to let the future dictate these teens' present. Where this dystopian Brazilian society sees the future as quintessential to the security of both the homeland and the family, teens see it as the end of vibrancy, as the cessation of love and intimacy, and they thus take every opportunity—or create every opportunity—to embrace present relationality to stave off the future. Indeed, the future may be the stuff of security, but the present is for kids.

While the show *Teenage Kiss* may be a portrayal of a dystopian Brazilian potentiality, the emphasis the show places on the tension between the future and the present is noticeable in our post-9/11 security and sex-panicked landscape. Security has shifted temporalities and attention from wholescale prevention of catastrophe to the anticipation and preparation of catastrophe. The future is thus governable in the present, as security logics and practices work to anticipate, plan, and prepare for the future as a way to not necessarily prevent it, but to keep the system and the population alive. In other words, society is oriented toward the future and the uncertainty that resides there, while the present becomes the time and place where we plan for that future. As I explore in this book, the rise in contemporary sex panics focused especially on queer youth frames said panic through such security logics, mobilizing security in practices of banning, restricting, and controlling to preempt future exposure to corrupting influences that challenge children's innocence.

Yet captured perfectly in *Teenage Kiss* is the tension between adult control, security, and panic and teenage intimacy, affection, and relationality, that in the wake of such a dystopian security and panicked landscape oriented toward the future, teens—particularly queer teens—are refusing this orientation in favor of lateral movements through the present. The kissing in the hallway, Tomás's sudden sex with a fan—these are lateral movements that are meant to highlight not the act of growing up but of *being present*. The motto itself embodies this very notion, for it is welcoming us to the present, where we shall reside, no longer concerned with the past, and thus, by living in the present, the refusal to engage with the future marks it as dead. This motto, in many ways, perfectly captures the lateral movements taken by the popular culture representations of queer youth I explore throughout this book, for they shrug off the future and focus in on the here and now. Doing so renders a challenge to the sex panics that attempt to hold them down, and the security logics that work to inform them. But it also works to foster relationality between youth, to potentially break down the tropes of individuality in favor of something else, something more.

The future may be dead, but the present is alive.

Introduction

Panic Scripting

> We lack a safe space to talk about sex.
>
> —Carol Vance, *Pleasure and Danger*

> The biggest letdown about being abducted by aliens is the abundance of gravity on the spaceship.
>
> —Shaun David Hutchinson, *We Are the Ants*

A wave of book banning is sweeping the country. In Texas alone there are over eight hundred book bans across the state as of 2022, with Keller Independent School District (KISD) prohibiting school libraries from carrying books that refer to "gender fluidity" (Caraway 2022).[1] Parents had petitioned the school district to remove books they deemed "pornographic," with one parent emailing the school board to complain about books like *The Bluest Eyes*, *Gender Queer*, and *We Are the Ants*, writing that the school board should "protect" students from "inappropriate content." School board president Charles Randklev wrote back, "I am . . . shocked, disappointed, and appalled this content has made its way into our schools" (Caraway 2022). Each of the books mentioned include characters navigating their gender identity and queer relationships. While some queer young adult novels, such as *We Are the Ants*, are available at the high school level, "no discussion or depictions of gender fluidity are allowed across all grade levels" because, according to Randklev, "the State of Texas considers performing gender modification procedures upon minors to be child abuse . . . political subject matter like gender theory

1

and sexual identity are best discussed within families, as parents choose, rather than within the classroom setting" (Caraway 2022).[2]

These book bans are part of a much larger movement in the United States that focuses on the parents' rights to regulate what materials their children have access to, including books in school libraries and even course content. As former Speaker of the House Kevin McCarthy declared, "[I]t's about every parent, mom and dad, but most importantly about the students in America" (Bouie 2023). Florida's parents' rights movement "has empowered certain parents to remove books, films, even whole classes that threaten to expose their children to material that might make them uncomfortable" (Bouie 2023). The *New York Times*' opinion writer Jamelle Bouie (2023) points out that "'Parents' rights,' you will have noticed, never seems to involve parents who want schools to be more open and accommodating toward gender-nonconforming students . . . we never hear about the rights of parents who want schools to offer a wide library of books and materials to their children."[3]

Let's name it for what it really is: a sex panic.

Banning books featuring queer characters, queer relationships, or gender identity fall squarely within a larger contemporary wave of sex panics and fits within a well-documented history of sex panics that focus on the protection and innocence of the child (e.g., Levine 2003; Angelides 2019; Rubin 2011; Lancaster 2011). That Florida parents took to banning books, films, and entire classes demonstrates the mechanisms for sex panics: banning content. Protecting the innocence of the child from material that parents deem "pornographic" manifests a very particular relationship between the child, the adult, the material at hand, and the very notion of innocence. The invocation of "parents' rights" foregrounds the parent over the child while also eliding or erasing, forcibly so, the agency of the child and young people (Angelides 2019). Focusing on the protection of the child's innocence renders innocence an already existing state of the child, that not only are children susceptible to corruption from outside the family unit—thus meaning the family cannot corrupt the child—but that the family, and the family alone, is responsible for the child's innocence. Nonnormative sexual and gender identities and navigations are thus seen as corrupting influences, contained in the material parents work so diligently to get banned.

Sex panics are all-consuming, all-encompassing, and ever-present. They operate through fear, but fear of what, exactly? I argue that sex panics fear the future, even though they operate in the present. The future is brimming with potential, but that potential is so uncertain that the possibility for catastrophe is too great to ignore. This has been made even more apparent in recent years with the 2020 COVID-19 global pandemic and the promise by scientists and doctors that the next pandemic is on the horizon, if not already here.[4] That we have experienced one global pandemic makes all future pandemics more likely while also promising the potential for more—more quarantines, more layoffs, more sickness, more death. Catastrophe is on the horizon, and we are on the edge, on the cusp of whatever catastrophe befalls us next.

Contemporary American society is marked by a continuous feeling of uncertainty and precarity that works to wear people down, and slowly at that (Berlant 2011; Povinelli 2011).[5] The belief in the future's uncertainty manifests precarity in the present, where we feel the future's uncertainty through moments of wear and tear that do little to reassure a public that things will get better. They may, quite possibly, get worse. Our fixation on what is to come blurs our vision, makes us somewhat cross-eyed at the prophecies of catastrophe. It also renders what has transpired as data for interpreting, expecting, preparing, and even foretelling the future—if only we were truly clairvoyant, our feelings of uncertainty might then subside.

Alien abductions may prove useful here.

Shaun David Hutchinson's 2016 queer young adult novel *We Are the Ants* begins with protagonist Henry Denton's abduction by aliens that Henry calls sluggers. "I didn't waste time thinking about the future," Henry muses, "until the night the sluggers abducted me and told me the world was going to end" (Hutchinson 2016, 4). These aliens provided Henry the means to save Earth by pressing, essentially, a big red button. He had until the scheduled day that would mark the end of the world to press the button, otherwise the world would end. The remainder of the book therefore sees Henry, with the fate of all life on Earth in his hands, fluctuate between saving Earth and letting all life perish. He is continuously in two places and two time periods at once: in the future when the world is to end and in the present when and where he is currently experiencing intense bullying, a budding romance, and a troublesome family life, while mourning the suicide of his former boyfriend.

For Henry, only the prospect of the end of the world shook him into thinking about the future; he was perpetually living in the present, in his present trauma and violence. It is not that his alien abduction and the certainty of the world's end displaced his current experiences, but it invited Henry to intentionally think about whether his current experiences of trauma, violence, and potential love would carry into the future or not. Would he continue to be bullied? Would he ever get over the intense loss of his boyfriend? Would he be able to fully love his romantic interest, Diego? This is where the uncertainty over the future lies: Henry cannot definitively answer any of these questions—he is not sure, not certain, about his future, only that inaction leads to the loss of all life, not just his. We watch as Henry asks the people around him the hypothetical question: if they had the power to save all life on Earth, would they? Some find the question absurd, but everyone replies that they would, that life is worth it. Henry is not so sure.

Catastrophe is inevitable. For Henry Denton, catastrophe is a foregone conclusion, unless he—and he alone—intervenes. Perhaps *We Are the Ants* is an allegory for the eventual end of the world with which we are currently faced, whereby the big red button is a metaphor for action. But perhaps, in addition to being representative of the experience of trauma and suicidal ideation, *We Are the Ants* embodies our own fear and belief that catastrophe is inevitable. We are always faced with the end of the world—the mortal coil seemingly too arduous to bear day in and day out so that we, like Henry, ponder the sweet release of the end of it all. We also cannot be sure *what* the catastrophe may be: another global pandemic, nuclear holocaust, civil or world war, Gaia's revenge—we cannot be certain, but we know it is there, haunting us from its privileged place in the future.

The fear of the future that sex panics proffer may not seem as totalizing or destructive as these iterations of catastrophe, but I contend that they are and that they are meant to seem world-ending and catastrophic because sex, gender, and sexuality are earth-shattering and world-building concepts. While I explore in more detail other specific sex panics in chapter 1, the panic about gender and sexual identity in books contained within school libraries invokes this sex panic fear about not just the innocence of the child but also about how the child will grow up. That Randklev, the KISD school board president, claims that these topics are best left for the private life of the family indicates that families are responsible for how our young people grow up, a responsibility not necessarily given to schools. Innocence implies a time when one is no longer innocent, a transition from one to the other over a period of time.

Banning books like *We Are the Ants* assumes that such books will influence how children and youth mature, for as a parent who emailed the KISD school board with their concerns about certain books wrote, "I am an adult, with a mature brain . . . these kids are not" (Caraway 2022). This parent's distinction in mental acuity of the adult from the child supposes that the child, without a mature brain, will grow up to be an adult with a mature brain. It is this growing up, this orientation toward the future, that sex panics seek to govern through acts like banning books. Parents work to govern this future because growing up is not without risk, because what sorts of adults will children grow into? These sex panics are panics about the potential future catastrophe of children being queer and trans, a foregone conclusion if supposedly exposed to books that feature queer and trans (or gender nonconforming) characters, especially queer and trans youth. Yet the catastrophe or risk is also the lack of control, that once children become adults and their parents can no longer control that which the now-adult child encounters—the adult child can now read all the "pornography" the adult child wishes. It is the parents' hope via their actions in the present that through their childrearing, their adult children will make safe and, put bluntly, heterosexual choices as adult children.

There is quite a bit in common between Henry Denton's impending end of the world and what the catastrophe sex panics wish to avoid or manage. Henry's catastrophe is akin to the next pandemic, as both are concerned with security, for perhaps Henry's end-of-the-world scenario is a deadly virus that rapidly spreads without prejudice. The catastrophe of sex panics is far more personal, far more sexually motivated, and is focused on the growth of children, protecting their innocence for as long as possible so that parents can teach them the proper moral lessons for the children to grow up into normative adults. The similarity between these two catastrophes or panics is how they orient toward future destruction by taking action in the present to *prepare* for that future. Some actions may work to prevent the future, but most of these actions work to *preempt* the future, to imagine the catastrophe and act in the here and now that works to prepare for it while also working to mitigate its effects. Preemptive action, a hallmark of securitization, can forestall the future from happening, and may work to avoid that catastrophe, but it also assumes that the future will happen (even if it does not) and thus preparation for living through that future takes place now before it actually transpires. When scientists and doctors say the next pandemic is on the horizon or already here, they do not mean to say that we can prevent it but that we can prepare for it. We thus begin governing through these preparatory actions, using our reading of the future to organize our present (Lakoff 2017; Collier and Lakoff 2021).

Banning books works in a similar way, for fear lies in the possibility that children will be exposed to such books and the future implications of that exposure. Therefore, parents and school boards banning books imagine a future where children read such books and are influenced by the themes contained within them, and as such, they act in the present to avoid such a future from transpiring.

Fundamentally, to bring sex panics and securitization together is to recognize that sex panics operate through fear and anxiety—here, a fear about the child and their sexuality—that sex panics marshal fear and anxiety laden in the risk of sex/uality to both amass troves of supporters and proponents of renewed sex laws, including book bans, and to target queer youth. Marginalized groups like queer youth become targets given that they challenge and disrupt the heteronormativity of the family, society, and the nation. The securitization of sex shifts the scale of sex/uality practices from the personal and local to the level of the nation: sex panics are national panics because security is a national concern. The securitization of sex also renders sex panics a temporal construction, one that requires the future to be imagined and acted upon in the present.

Therefore, I refer to contemporary sex panics that work in this way as *security panics*, a fear about future catastrophe that gets actualized as panic in the present. Security panics are not exclusively about sex; fear about the next global pandemic is a type of security panic, especially when that fear drives people to take (sometimes drastic) action in the present to prepare for or preempt that future catastrophe. The key is panic, that one is panicked over a specific security concern and thus using such fear to mobilize action. I argue that interpreting sex panics through the framework of security is important for understanding just how deeply rooted the politics of fear, anxiety, and uncertainty are in contemporary American culture and society, and how concerns about sex—especially queer youth sexuality—are part of a broader set of security concerns. Similarly, drawing a connection between sex panics and security demonstrates how widespread security logics and practices have become in the twenty-first century and in daily life.

This temporal relationship formed within security panics elides the experiences and agency of young people. Hidden in the present are the lateral representations, experiences, and maneuvers of queer youth, glossed over by an intense focus on the future and the uncertainty of and possibility for catastrophe. This means that rather than adhering to a logic of "growing up," an adult-oriented security and heteronormative ideology, queer youth are making lateral movements that craft their sexualities through meaningful social relations in the present. *Unscripting the Present* is an exploration into representations of those lateral movements, the experiences that do not necessarily fit within future-oriented narratives or dispositions and instead focus intensely on the here and now. It at once illustrates how sex panics become security panics in the contemporary moment before interrogating the experiences of queer protagonists in popular culture media artifacts as a method for discerning how sexuality is crafted, how selves and social relations are managed, and how queer youth encounter both security panics and security writ large.

Sex and Children

In describing obscenity laws and "sex law[s]," Gayle Rubin (2011, 161), writing originally in the 1980s, notes that "the law is especially ferocious in maintaining the boundary between childhood 'innocence' and 'adult' sexuality . . . the amount of laws devoted to protecting young people from premature exposure to sexuality is breathtaking." Since the 1980s, antiobscenity laws and "sex laws" have only increased, focused especially on phenomena like sex offenders, sexual predators and molesters, sex work and sex trafficking, and pornography (e.g., Lancaster 2011; Barnard 2020; Halperin 2017; De Orio 2017; Mansnerus 2017; Bernstein 2017; Queen and Saunders 2017; Levine 2003). These "sex conflicts," as Rubin (2011, 168) also terms them, emerge out of what Jeffrey Weeks (1981) calls "moral panics," or "the 'political moment' of sex, in which diffuse attitudes are channeled into political action and from there into social change" (Rubin 2011, 168).[6] Roger Lancaster (2011, 23) defines moral panics as "any mass movement that emerges in response to a false, exaggerated, or ill-defined moral threat to society and proposes to address this threat through punitive measures: tougher enforcement, 'zero tolerance,' new laws, communal vigilance, violent purges."[7] Both Lancaster and Rubin frame the panic about sex and sexuality as moral panics, for as Rubin (2011, 168) writes, "[B]ecause sexuality in Western societies is so mystified, the wars over it are often fought at oblique angles, aimed at phony targets, conducted with misplaced passions, and are highly, intensely symbolic." But such panics "rarely alleviate any real problem because they are aimed at chimeras and signifiers" (Rubin 2011, 168).[8]

The book banning examples discussed above illustrate both Lancaster and Rubin's points about moral panics and sexuality. The mobilization of parents and school boards against books deemed "pornographic" or ill-suited for the immature and innocent minds of children no doubt exaggerates the material in books like *We Are the Ants*, which depict the physical and emotional precarity and trauma of daily life, particularly for marginalized communities. Laws, bans, enforcements, and purges—punitive measures, as Lancaster (2011) terms them—all mark these book bans and frame them as moral panics. What makes them sex panics is that many of the books banned involve queer romances and questioning one's gender identity—fear of nonnormativity renders these books as a corrupting influence on children that thus require regulation through bans and purges. Stated alternatively, these books are seen to be corrupting the assumed heterosexuality and cisgenderedness of the child, and the heteronormativity of growing up.

However, I return to Rubin's (2011) initial point from whence I started, namely that contemporary sex panics emerge out of the possibility of childhood innocence encountering adult sexuality, and by extension, that such an encounter with sexuality might very well corrupt the child's innocence. There are many ways adult sexuality may intersect with so-called childhood innocence, yet my focus in this book is on queer youth sexuality specifically, and youth or childhood sexuality more broadly. In other words, I am interested in the (queer) sexuality of children and youth—the consideration of children and youth having sexuality in the first place—and the subsequent laws and policies that are enacted to mitigate that sexuality or craft it into a normative sexuality. Banning *We Are the Ants* supposedly does this, for the book narrates Henry's budding queer relationship with Diego as he grapples with the trauma of his (then) boyfriend's suicide prior to the start of the novel. Exposure to queer relationships supposedly provides youth with corrupting ideas—or simply, the wrong ideas—that might shape their sexual development in nonnormative ways.

My focus on (queer) childhood or youth sexuality moves in two directions. The first is to interrogate the sex panics that take up childhood sexuality and queer youth sexuality as objects to regulate, control, and manage. Statutes like Florida's Don't Say Gay law that ban even the mention of nonnormative sexualities in public schools are demonstrative of a sex panic aimed at both the sexuality of the child and the possibility of queer youth sexuality, as simply mentioning nonnormative sexuality is to adversely affect children and youth. As Steven Angelides (2019, xiii) writes, "[S]ex panics often seem to be especially histrionic less in cases of forced, violent, or horrific sexual exploitation and abuse than when young people's sexual curiosities, desires, pleasures, motives, intentions, and willful actions—in short, their agentive and assertive subjectivities—are brought into the social frame." Rubin (2011) makes a somewhat analogous point in that consideration of the child's sexuality is fundamentally a historically situated question. The second direction is to take seriously the experience of youth themselves, to *not* "accept the teleology of the child (and narrative itself) as heterosexually determined" (Bruhm and Hurley 2004, xiv), and instead entertain the very real possibility—or foregone conclusion—that some kids are queer. This involves "rethinking stubborn paradigms that render childhood innocence a matter of common sense and that obscure the suffering of actual children" (Chinn and Duane 2015, 17). *Unscripting the Present* moves in both directions, discussing in the first chapter contemporary sex panic laws and policies before moving into four concentrated chapters on queer youth's experiences in popular culture media artifacts (i.e., television and film).

If my focus is on childhood sexuality and queer youth sexuality, then it is first necessary to theoretically situate the child, their sexuality, and their (potential) queerness. The child haunts adult existence because "the child is precisely who we are not and, in fact, never were" (Stockton 2009, 5). We tell stories of our childhood, perhaps not fully realizing that "the story of the child is a story about stories" (Sheldon 2016, 7). As Kathryn Bond Stockton (2009, 5) writes of the child: "It is the act of adults looking back. It is a ghostly, unreachable fancy, making us wonder: Given that we cannot know the contours of children, who they are to themselves, should we stop talking of children altogether? Should all talk of the child subside, beyond our critique of the bad effects of looking back nostalgically in fantasy?"

In reality, talk of children abounds, despite our inability to "know the contours of children, who they are to themselves." To consider children as entities unto themselves rather than as empty signifiers for our adult nostalgia and looking to the past makes childhood itself a queer sort of time and experience. While the child may exist within "reproductive (repro)-time," as Judith (Jack) Halberstam (2005, 4–5) writes, and a milestone along the "life cycle of the Western human subject," the queerness of the child—childhood itself as queer—emerges from disrupting the "life cycle" and telos of growth and development in favor of a moment of childhood reprieve: children as children and not future adults or adult's past selves. As Steven Bruhm and Natasha Hurley (2004, xiv) suggest, "[C]hildhood itself is afforded a modicum of queerness when the people worry more about how the child turns out than about how the child exists as a child."

There is a rhetorical move that both Stockton and Bruhm and Hurley make in drawing attention to the general queerness of the child, insofar as the time of children can involve queer relationships and interactions "as long as the queerness can be rationalized as a series of mistakes or misplaced desires" (Bruhm and Hurley 2004, xiv). Entertaining, however, the possibility of the "gay child spotlights the drama of children's darkness: the motion of their bodies around troubled words; also their propensity for growing astray inside the delay that defines who they 'are'" (Stockton 2009, 6). For Stockton (2009, 2016), delay is central to understanding childhood because adults determine when children grow up and what constitutes growing up. As such, Stockton (2009, 6) contends that "children grow sideways as well as up . . . in part because they cannot, according to our concepts, advance to adulthood until we say it's time." It is this sideways growth, or lateral maneuvering, that I wish to focus on throughout this book: instances when queer youth, in particular, eschew the forward-looking, future-oriented movement of growing up and instead dwell intimately and consciously in the present moment.

Understanding the child or youth in relation to time importantly indexes what Lee Edelman (2004) calls "reproductive futurism," the ways the Child represents the reproduction of a heterosexual and heteronormative future, projected forward in the process of growing up.[9] In other words, "[T]he child is the emblem of the future in whose name the totality of society is contracted, a precious resource governing the parameters of public politics and private sociality to secure the welfare of tomorrow in a stable form (reproduction), consigning queerness to the purely negative" (Gill-Peterson 2015, 182). While inspired by Edelman, Rebekah Sheldon (2016, 5–6) is far more concerned with the material consequences of the child-figure, "for it is not just the case that the child retro-reproductively forecloses the future but also that the figuration of the child as the self-similar issue of the present, the safe space of human prosperity and a return to a manageable nature, forecloses the mutational in the reproductive." For Sheldon (2016, 3), such biological materialism of the child-figure partially emerges from historically situated theories of physiological growth and development, theories that effectuate "the link forged between the child and the species helped to shape eugenic historiography, focalized reproduction as a matter of concern for racial nationalism, and made the child a mode of timekeeping." I am thus critical of marking the child solely through a developmental model or temporality, a point I shall return to below, because such a model or temporality abjures the role sociocultural construction plays in our (adult) understanding of the child (or youth) and thus biologically essentializes the very category of the child (or youth). And as Sheldon (2016, 3) astutely writes, such biological essentialism can be easily folded into "eugenic historiography" and "racial nationalism."

The queer child, however, "gets displaced grammatically into a different temporal register, a register that will allow the dominant narrative to consign the child to a cultural unconscious" (Bruhm and Hurley 2004, xix).[10] It is that temporal register that I am after, a temporal register, I argue, that locates queer youth within the present, in sideways or lateral movements, irrespective of their inevitable upward growth. To say that children grow sideways, as Stockton (2009) does, is to emphasize that *growth* takes place, that change happens even if that change does not contribute to adult-determined maturation of growing up. Queer youth become queer in these sideways growths—whereby becoming is a temporally delayed process—but queer youth *are queer* in their lateral maneuverings, as the former again assumes some sort of growth while the latter cares more about the present state of being, the present experiences one encounters. Both certainly can happen simultaneously, but in highlighting lateral maneuverings, I am giving queer youth room to be who they are in the present rather than presume that experiences they have will somehow contribute to who they shall *become*. As Jen Gilbert (2014, 23) opines, "[C]ould we instead give the child space and time to grow into whatever—to see her being as important as her becoming?" This is not to say that queer youth are forever stinted, never to grow up—they turn eighteen at some point and then legally become adults in the United States. But rather, my point is that accounting for the experiences queer youth have in constructing and managing their queerness, their sexualities, requires greater attention to unscripted moments, impromptu interactions and encounters that break the mold. I shall discuss this below.

Understanding childhood sexuality and queer youth sexuality in the midst of sex panics requires attention to both, I contend, and the recognition that they are intimately intertwined. As Angelides (2019, xiv) argues, "[T]he avoidance, minimalization, or neutralization of agency has now often become more a first-order aim . . . than an outcome or side effect of sex panics." Angelides's broader argument is that sex panics erase the individual agency—especially sexual agency—of children and youth. I move parallel to Ian Barnard's (2020, 112–13) work on the panic of queer kids insofar as while many of the queer theorists discussed above focus "primarily on representations of protoqueer children in texts composed for (and by) adults and/or in reading queerness between the lines of supposedly heteronormative acts," I instead interrogate "texts composed for (queer) kids and representing 'actual' queer kids as one way of countering the erasures" of queer youth sexuality. While Barnard interrogates specifically queer young adult literature alongside the film *Moonlight*, my concern in this book is with popular queer media artifacts, namely films and television shows, for the visual representation of queer youth (sexuality) enables both a departure from the so-called protogay child and a *witnessing* of the queerness of the teenage characters.

Security Panics

Roger Lancaster (2011, 2) begins his book *Sex Panics and the Punitive State* by musing "[W]hat, after all, could exaggerated fears of pedophiles have to do with the sorts of collective anxieties unleased after September 11, 2001? Quite a lot, I suggest." For Lancaster, the post-9/11 landscape saw not only a rise in fear but also a rise in anxiety about "cultural figures," such as sexual predators, that represent "other conditions of injury in the body politic." In other words, "in the wake of 9/11, sexual fear has colored the imagination of disaster in ways that reveal its misplaced, obsessive, and delirious character" (Lancaster 2011, 7). However, while Lancaster sees the post-9/11 landscape as engendering a type of fear and panic that have "a tendency to spread uncontrollably," I contend that a much more intimate relationship between sex panics and the post-9/11 security landscape emerges.

In their collaborative book *Trapped*, anthropologists Mark Maguire and Setha Low sketch out the hallmarks of securitization in the contemporary world. They write that "securitization refers to a nexus of 1) individuals searching for safety within an insecure state, 2) state militarization and production of fearful citizens, and 3) the financial securitization of mortgages and other monetary instruments to reduce financial risk" (Maguire and Low 2024, 50). As I elaborate in subsequent chapters, the focus on "individuals" is itself characteristic of a specifically neoliberal American ideology, one that imbues the American security apparatus with a propensity for individualism and self-responsibility. However, entire populations or groups of people—including marginalized groups like queer youth—are seeking that safety from or within not only an insecure state but also, following political theorist Wendy Brown (1995), an injurious and discriminatory state, one that targets them specifically as threatening. There is seemingly no alternative: marginalized folks are seeking protection from the very institution responsible for their continued insecurity.[11] Missing from Maguire and Low's definition of securitization is thus attention to the injurious and discriminatory state, and the way that marginalized populations like queer youth are targets of securitization and receivers of regulations and fear.[12]

I define securitization as a triparted assemblage: (1) individuals' and populations' search for safety from and inside an insecure, injurious, and discriminatory state *and* general population; (2) the active targeting of marginalized populations as threats to the security and coherence of the state *and* general population; and (3) the state *and* general populations' mobilization of fear to enthrall participation in securitization practices and to target those marginalized populations. My emphasis on both the state and general population is crucial, as it is not always the state that mobilizes fears, or security panics, and the state is not the only institution or body responsible for the targeting of marginalized populations. As I illustrate below, securitization also involves the management and mitigation of risk, a risk that is intimately tied to fear.

In the post-9/11 security and economic landscape, risk has become quintessential to understanding and interpreting the world and daily life. As Louise Amoore (2013, 7) suggests, "[W]hat has occurred is that society has come to understand itself and its problems in terms of risk management." A central way to manage risk is to mobilize anticipatory logic: "[I]t acts not strictly to *prevent* the playing out of a particular course of events on the basis of past data tracked forward into probable futures but to *preempt* an unfolding and emergent event in relation to an array of possible projected futures" (Amoore 2013, 9). Francois Ewald (2002, 296) terms this the *precautionary principle*, whereby "decisions are made not in a context of certainty, nor even of available knowledge, but of doubt, premonition, foreboding, challenge, mistrust, fear, and anxiety." As Amoore (2013, 9) summarizes, "[T]he precautionary principle authorizes decisions in anticipation of the uncertain future." Richard Grusin (2004, 28) terms this within the context of news media and cultural industries "premediation" to describe how these industries construct "as many of the possible worlds, or possible paths, as the future could be imagined to take." Yet Marieke De Goede (2008, 156) warns of the potential limits of the language of risk, arguing that "premediation simultaneously *deploys and exceeds* the language of risk . . . practices of remediation exceed the logic of risk calculation and self-consciously deploy imagination in their scenarios, worst-case narratives and disaster rehearsals."

I take De Goede's point seriously, that post-9/11 security is not reducible to risk, though it is also important to explicate risk, as much of the sex-panicked discourse does actively mobilize the language of risk even if it also "exceed[s] the language of risk." Such consideration of risk is particularly salient for understanding the collection of data. For Amoore (2013, 12), risk "enables the fractionation of ever-more finite categories of life—*degrees of* safe and dangerous, vulnerable and durable, mobile and restricted, identifiable and unidentified, verifiable and unverified, and so on." Elsewhere I refer to this as an "epistemological conundrum" because "the laborious accumulation of knowledge may be totalizing, but it is never total, as each marginal unit of additional information indexes the partialness of knowledge that then necessitates the collection of even more information" (Gitzen 2023, 15). This pairs with the precautionary principle in that "decisions are taken on the basis of future possibilities, however improbable or unlikely" (Gitzen 2023, 15). Security therefore engenders a different type of temporality, one that is less a move from past to present to future and instead sees the future imagined in the present by utilizing experiences from the past. The example of another global pandemic proves useful, for on the one hand, scientists and emergency planners mobilize past epidemics and pandemics—paired with global health data—to craft policies and plans for what seems to be an inevitable future outbreak. But on the other hand, a key aspect of the precautionary principle and anticipatory logic is to imagine the unimaginable, to make decisions based on fear and anxiety. And so, preparing for the next global pandemic is not only about mobilizing past data to make predictions about the future but also theorizing about what is missing, paying attention to the fringes, to the fear and rumors that may be circulating, and making plans in accordance with those data points. Yet as De Goede (2008, 157) rightly asks, "[H]ow is responsibility for present action displaced through a narrative of the future? What role do these imaginations play in bringing about the futures they are supposed to describe or preempt?" Asked another way, what or who do we sacrifice in the present in order to preempt an imagined and potential future?

To interpret sex panics through this understanding of security and securitization is to recognize that sex panics, operating through fear and anxiety—they are steeped in the affective residue of social uncertainty over sex—fit within my definition of securitization. Sex panics involve individuals and populations, marginalized and not, seeking safety from a state and general population that is ultimately insecure, injurious, and discriminatory. The fact that the state, in particular, is injurious and discriminatory not only intensifies the injurious and discriminatory effects of the sex panic, with practices such as book banning, but it makes the state the only body or institution that can resolve the sex panic. As I discuss in chapter 1, lawsuits are brought up against discriminatory laws like Florida's Don't Say Gay law that restrict what schools can teach about gender and sexuality, claiming that these laws are unconstitutional. Recourse is sought from the same legal system that enabled the law to be passed in the first place. Ultimately, however, it is the fear and anxiety about sex that manifests panic, a panic that is governable and actionable, a panic that targets marginalized populations especially—here, queer youth—as threats to the heteronormative foundations of both the state and the general population.

While sex panics may seem as though they are wholly concerned with the present world and the regulation of current access to sexual materials and interactions, we must not mistake method for goal. The goal of sex panics lies in the future, because parents and adults are concerned with how children grow up, "how they become 'good adults'" (Talburt 2018, xii). Childhood and youth are seen as transitory stages in the process of growing up. Adults thus attempt to imagine every possible future of the child, the imaginable and the unimaginable, and plan for those futures in the present (the method). While Sheldon (2016, 6) suggests that "the child comes to inform the rhetorical figuration of future catastrophe," I argue that the child *represents* and *embodies* both the rhetorical and material figuration of future catastrophe. This is the anticipatory logic of the sex panic, for it not only mobilizes past experiences with sexual materials and encounters—for instance, pornography debates, the AIDS crisis, divorce rates, STD data—but also operationalizes fears, anxiety, and uncertainty surrounding sex, the future of the family, and the (re)production of society in the present. The method involves both prevention and preemption, avoiding certain materials and encounters to prevent certain futures from unfolding, while also preparing for that future to transpire.

The use of fear and anxiety thus intersects with anthropologist Joseph Masco's (2014, 18) "national security affect"—"historically produced, shared, and officially constituted as a necessary background condition of everyday life"—for such fear about the security of the nation and society, the promulgation of both into the future, is felt in the present and used for governing daily life. A similar affect exists with regard to sex panics, and in particular, youth sexuality. Susan Talburt (2018, xii) refers to this as "public feelings" regarding youth sexuality: "[C]onverging and contradictory public feelings about youth sexualities[,] whether perennial anxieties or celebrations of youth, 'stick' [. . .] to youth, shift, and reassemble across contexts as new actors and practices appear." In short, "youth function as 'affective magnets'" for public feelings regarding sex and sexuality (Talburt 2018, xvi). Janice Irvine (2007, 8) makes an analogous point, observing that "failure to theorize the public feelings of sex panics makes 'the hysterical public' seem not only unified but also anonymous and inscrutable." She refers to these as "transient feelings" because "they are the product of a specific context; in its absence, they recede" (Irvine 2007, 8). Anxiety about how the future will unfold thus affectively manifests as anxiety about youth and their sexualities in the here and now. In short, the present becomes ground zero for fights over the future.

A Messy Primer

I am always uncomfortable when I seek to define or conceptualize the word "queer," in part because how does one define a word at the heart of a field now more than forty years on? Indeed, as David Eng, Halberstam, and José Esteban Muñoz asked in 2005, "[W]hat's queer about queer studies *now*?" (1). This question has been asked in multiple iterations by numerous scholars since then—"[W]hat is queer in queer anthropology *today*?" (Weiss 2016), "[W]hat is left of queer *now*?" (Eng and Puar 2020)—which makes me think: will we always be wondering what exactly queer is and does, especially in the *here and now*? Granted, "here" is relative given that queer theory in the United States ought to be different from queer theory "elsewhere" and transnationally (Mikdashi and Puar 2016; Chiang and Wong 2016, 2017; Weiss 2022). It is the "now" and "today" with which I am more intrigued and inspired to query how the present moment may in fact be instrumental to both our understandings and use of queer.

Recent trends in queer studies and queer theory seem to point us away from the present and toward the future, a response almost to Edelman's (2004) polemic that takes to task the future for being unobtainable for queers given that it is, for him, "kid's stuff." Muñoz (2009, 1) is perhaps most explicit in his own polemic about a utopic imagining of queer, stating that "queerness is essentially about the rejection of a here and now and an insistence on potentiality or concrete possibility for another world."

Muñoz is hopeful of the future, antithetical to Edelman's skepticism and seeming resignation that queers are slotted in the present. Anthropologist Margot Weiss (2022, 316) similarly notes how she had previously written that "queer indexes that desire to reach beyond theoretical or conceptual closure to an *elsewhere*, the frustration when one's desires are thwarted, and then the return and reopening of new horizons." The deference of queer, the looking for it elsewhere and otherwise, taps into the seemingly incessant need to query the queer in queer studies, theory, and even anthropology, rendering the journey to queer itself queer *enough*.

This deference is why I am continuously uncomfortable when trying to define "queer," for not only have scholars been contemplating this term for decades, but I do not quite feel satisfied that hope, potentiality, and horizons are the property of the future. *Unscripting the Present* is premised on lateral movements *in the present* because the future is, echoing Edelman, not for queers. But also, the present needs to be accounted for and managed *now*; we cannot procrastinate our current lot in life for the hope things *might* get better. I firmly believe that lateral movements are queer and incredibly hopeful, generative, and transformative in ways that explode consideration of the future by radically embodying the present. And yet, I also believe lateral movements to be potentially shameful and cringe-worthy, for how else can we account for when queers themselves fuck up? This embracement of the present is not quite the same as Edelman's (2004) attention to the present, for while queer youth must indeed navigate a precarious present moment, they are not necessarily stuck in place. Stated alternatively, Edelman does not account for the lateral movements that queer youth make because attention is still placed on the future, a foreclosed and unachievable future. For queer youth, the future is tomorrow's problem.

Therefore, queer for me is not one thing. At once I follow Halberstam's (2005, 6) understanding of queer as "nonnormative logics and organizations of community, sexual identity, embodiment, and activity in space and time." Queer is not meant to be an umbrella term for all forms of non-heterosexual identities. I do not use queer to talk about identity unless an individual character identifies as queer; I refer to folks or youth as queer not to draw attention to their identity but instead to indicate nonnormativity. Queer is a word that embodies practice in the present.

I also take seriously Barnard's (2020, 9–10) mobilization of Rubin to think of "queer as an epistemology for conceptualizing . . . the 'outer limits of sexuality' . . . even as a generous reading of the phrase 'outer limits' itself pushes queer to its limits (exactly when does sexuality begin and end?) and given that sexuality can never be separated from racial, class, gender, and other identifications and inscriptions." Yet even here, as Barnard also recognizes, is a tension in queer: "[H]ow, in seeking to move beyond sex, sexuality, and gender, *queer* often returns to them; and how, in seeking to center same-sex-desiring (and gender-transgressing) subjects, *queer* often finds itself otherwise" (Weiss 2022, 317). Tension is how I can best conceptualize queer, and it is not just one tension: tension between ideology versus practice, sexuality as object versus an otherwise object, present versus the future, growing up versus growing sideways (or moving laterally), hopeful versus shameful. This is why I am partial to Kadji Amin's (2017) call to deidealize queer studies and theory, as it does not set queer up for failure for being too hopeful. Sometimes queer is failure (Halberstam 2011), sometimes it is hopeful and even utopic, and sometimes it is icky.

Finally, my interpretation of queer must also entail some engagement with securitization. Security itself is a normative discourse and practice that is in the business of making threats out of nonnormative practices and peoples (Puar 2007; Gitzen 2023). In part, this engagement invokes the elsewhere and otherwise that some scholars elucidate as a current direction in queer studies (Mikdashi and Puar 2016; Weiss 2022), that queerness extends beyond gender and sexuality as well as the West.[13] Yet the interconnection of queerness and security also illustrates how "security functions as a palimpsest: beneath queer, trans, and feminist definitions of bodily autonomy and safe space, one invariably confronts histories of colonialism, slavery, and national security" (Ben Daniel and Berwick 2020, 129). This understanding of queer is particularly salient in chapter 5 when I discuss the American security apparatus, but with the securitization of sex, a queer reading directs us not only to *who* is most affected by such securitization practices but also to *how* these practices render those marginalized folks threatening and in need of regulation. In short, a queer critique interprets sex panics as security panics concerned with the management of those marginalized, namely queer, youth.

The other linguistic caveat that I must make is with my use of "child" and "youth." In many ways, I see these terms as potentially interchangeable. I favor the word "youth" in my descriptions and examinations of popular media artifacts, as youth affectively indexes the teenage years of one's life, after childhood. As such, "child," "children," and "childhood" all denote a younger version of the individual, before the individual is classified as a teenager. Most of the literature on the queer child imagines the child in proto fashion (e.g., Stockton 2009; Sedgwick 1991; Edelman 2004; Bruhm and Hurley 2004), as alluded to above, where they are wholly marked by innocence. Youth, though still thought to be clinging to innocence, are far more exposed to the seemingly corrupting influences of adulthood, namely sex, drugs, and alcohol.

In more materialist fashion, the distinction between the child and youth, or adolescence even, lies also with the development of the brain, body, and psychology of the individual. Different words mark different stages of development, for, as Gilbert (2014, 28) notes, "handled gingerly, theories of development can also be narratives about the psychical relations that create the adolescent." For Gilbert (2014, 27), adolescence and adulthood are both a "psychical relation," and thus opens up the seemingly stark distinction between the adolescent as a historical and social construct and as a "biological or physiological event." The result is that development "becomes either a description of adolescent experience or, more perniciously, a means to govern youth's bodies" that therefore "forecloses the more radical possibility that 'development' be understood as an effect of the contested relations between adults and adolescents, as well as the conflicts within the self" (Gilbert 2014, 27). Gilbert (2014, 28–29) is speaking specifically of sex education, calling for a "cautious theory of development in sex education," turning to developmental theorist Erik Erikson's argument that "when theories of development meet the imperatives of education, they move too quickly from tools for thinking to tools for measuring and correcting—a shift that critical studies of sex education rightly condemn."

I take Gilbert's polemic seriously, for the distinction between the child, the youth, and the adult is at once a developmental story of changing bodies and psychology, but the distinction is simultaneously a construction between two groups: the adult and the nonadult. The child and the youth are at odds with the adult, for "children" and "youth" are in part arbitrary designations and categories bestowed upon individuals under the age of eighteen by adults—they are categories of not-yet adults, often described as periods of transition from not-adult to adult. We need not look far to find the social constructedness of these categories, for age-of-consent laws differ not only from state to state but throughout the world: there is no universal agreement as to what constitutes a child, a youth, or an adult. Furthermore, Romeo and Juliet laws may permit teens under a certain age to have sex with one another, but they could be charged with possession and distribution of child pornography if caught sexting one another or sharing naked pictures of themselves with each other (Meiners 2016).[14] My point is that the more significant distinction is not between the child and the youth or adolescent; it is between the adult and the nonadult. This distinction matters because sex panics are adult discourses that imagine the child/youth figure as something very particular—a not-yet-formed adult, clinging to innocence as they are faced, on all sides, with adult corruption.

In practice, I primarily use the phrases "queer youth" and "queer youth sexuality" throughout this book, as I am primarily concerned with the experiences of queer high school students. The importance of high school and education is discussed in chapter 5, but I make mention here because the popular culture artifacts all take place among high school students and in the context of high school.

Unscripting: A Methodology

This book is an excavation of the present, less a genealogy of how we got here, and more of an inquiry into both what futures are preempted in the present and how queer youth maneuver amid and laterally to these security panics. This requires a few different methods. The first method involves critical legal analysis and discourse analysis, focused specifically on laws, policies, and practices like book bannings and Florida's Don't Say Gay law, in addition to responses to these laws and practices. The goal of this method is to not only think critically about these laws, practices, and responses but also to interpret them through the lens of security.

To address queer youth maneuverability in the present, I rely on the analysis of recent popular culture artifacts that feature queer protagonists, such as the film *Love, Simon*; the Norwegian multimodal show *Skam*; and the Netflix show *Sex Education*.[15] The majority of the queer characters I focus on are self-identified male primarily because many of the popular culture artifacts that focus on queer youth feature male characters. This is not to say that others do not exist—they do—but male characters still seem to saturate much of *popular* culture.[16] I recognize the limitation of only focusing on queer men, namely when I mobilize the word "queer."

The artifacts chosen are not meant to be an exhaustive list, or even fully representative, of queer youth sexuality but rather textually rich artifacts that I use to make broader theoretical arguments about queer youth sexuality. The chosen artifacts represent, to some extent, the material conditions that queer youth must navigate outside of the artifact's world—the queer representations of youth speak to the material realities in which queer youth reside. Broadly, the chapters include a set of artifacts that each speak to a different political or even legal context with regard to queer sexuality: relationality and shame, coming out and neoliberalism, queer sex and panic, and security and liberalism. While they may not all tap directly into a specific sex panic, these artifacts cauterize the wounds sex panics inflict, suture the social tears that separate queer and nonqueer folks, and perhaps provide queer youth with a life vest in a contextual sea of discrimination, marginalization, and securitization. These artifacts were chosen because they circumvented continued emphasis on shame spirals of queer folks—though shame is discussed—and the seemingly incessant need to foreclose queer happiness and hope. Unlike a promise for a happy and hopeful future, these texts reorient us toward the present in which queer youth reside and survive; these are artifacts of not only the icky, contentious, exhaustive, and even injurious but also of the hope, happiness, and silver lining of the present. As such, these artifacts, I believe, are potentially instructive in the daily lives of queer youth themselves, enabling queer youth to feel a modicum of hope in their perhaps murky and lonely present.

I do not limit my analysis to US-based artifacts, as I include numerous non-US texts. I include both kinds of texts to compare different representations and provide a theoretically nuanced interpretation of narratives of queer youth sexuality and the US sex-panicked context. In part, the US context is not all that unique. According to Human Rights Watch, since 2014, Brazil—home of the show *Teenage Kiss* discussed in the preface—has introduced over two hundred pieces of legislation that seek to ban "indoctrination" or "gender ideology" in schools (Human Rights Watch 2022). Anti-trans lawmakers and proponents are sweeping parts of Western Europe as well, though perhaps not as successful as those in the US. However, there is a more significant reason for including non-US artifacts in this book. By looking outside of the US toward other texts, I can throw into stark contrast US-based representations and contexts that enable further analysis and interpretation. In other words, making comparisons between US and non-US texts not only elucidates the intensity of sex panics in the US but also highlights how some of the core cultural values in the US—such as individuality and self-responsibility—influence these sex panics. At times, I repeat my interrogation of certain popular culture artifacts in multiple chapters to weave together the different arguments made in each chapter, thus contributing to a broader "narrative resonance" of queer youth sexuality (see Lepselter 2016).

It is important to note that representations of queer youth may not always align with actual experiences of queer youth. This becomes even more apparent when considering that the representations discussed in this book are created and written by adults—there may be some input from teens, as I discuss in chapter 2, but these are representations of queer youth from the perspective of adults. Yet I still find the media texts generative of a broader queer theory and politics, as indexical of queer youth narratives. My aim in this book is therefore a textual analysis of the archive of popular media artifacts featured in the subsequent chapters. Following Samuel Chambers (2009, 20), "I insist more on the importance of *reading* . . . [media] like one might read any other text" and that the media texts discussed herein "matter . . . because of the queer politics that can be drawn to light from particular readings of them." In other words, my focus on these media texts emphasizes what they "*can tell us about the world*" (Chambers 2009, 20).[17] As such, this book is fundamentally interdisciplinary, as I mobilize not only textual analysis but also queer theory, linguistic theory, media studies, anthropology, sociological theory, and feminist theory to interrogate queer youth sexuality and its representations.

My goal is to engage in a methodology I call *unscripting*, an orientation toward impromptu moments and encounters and the active descripting—doing away with the social scripts—of the present. Such a methodology is useful not only because the popular culture artifacts I analyze are themselves scripted by writers, but those scripts are also influenced by sets of social scripts. Sociologists William Simon and John Gagnon (1986, 98) argue that "scripts are essentially a metaphor for conceptualizing the production of behavior within social life." For Simon and Gagnon, these scripts are comprised of three levels: cultural scenarios, interpersonal scripts, and intrapsychic scripts. Essentially, culture, individual relationships, and one's sense of self are all scripted, and it is the interaction of those scripts—to various degrees—that generates one's behavior. Simon and Gagnon (1986, 104) are famous for introducing the notion of sexual scripts, where these scripts "view the sexual as becoming significant either when it is defined as significant collective life . . . or when individual experiences or development assign it a special significance." Sexual scripts enable an individual to discern when a situation is sexual or not; for instance, sexual scripts frame a visit to the doctor's office as not sexual, and thus the individual does not behave in a sexual manner.

Similar to Simon and Gagnon (1986), Ken Plummer (1991, 235) explores the sexual scripts that influence the child, noting that it is culture that "furnishes the child with scripts which help to define the who, what, where, when and why of sexuality." For Plummer (1991, 238), the child learns how to be a sexual being through socio-cultural scripts that "are assembled in a piecemeal fashion from a number of sources: from caretakers, from peers, from the media and wider culture, from the child's own slowly unfolding biography with its own set of earlier acquired meanings." Not surprisingly, many children must navigate their scripts with their friends, other peers, the media, or alone "in secretive and dark corners" (Plummer 1991, 239), particularly because, as I demonstrate in chapter 1, sex education is lacking and adults often sidestep conversations about sex as it would thus presume that the child is, as Angelides (2019) contends, a sexual subject.[18]

Even sex panics are scripted. Irvine (2007) names these "sex panic scripts" and they "denote affectively rich ways of talking" (18), whereby "virtually identical dialogue is often employed not only in different communities but across decades [. . . and] can be similarly routinized, as outrage, anger, and disgust" (17). The inclusion of time is important because sex panics and their scripts are not locatable in a single time period but move with the ebb and flow of historical and social contexts, affectively so. For Irvine (2007, 18–19), "[S]ex panic scripts stress danger and disease [. . .] encourage the production of feelings such as outrage and fear in community debates [. . . and] rely heavily on tales about sexual groups or issues that use distortion, hyperbole, or outright fabrication." Sex panic scripts, like sex panics themselves, mobilize fear through an insistence on danger and disease to engender an emotional response in people, whereby the emotions themselves are socially and politically relevant for the sex panic and its affects.

My use of scripts aligns with Irvine's (2007) conceptualization given that her focus is on language, on emotionally charged talk; a more literal interpretation of scripts requires closer attention to the language used in specific instances, for what is said indexes a much more complicated and interactional process of interpretation. I therefore suggest that scripts are like sieves or translation machines that take the complex mess of experiences and talk and interpret them. In anthropologist Paul Kockelman's (2017, 139) discussion of the ways sieves contribute to interpretation, particularly within the age of computation, he defines sieves as "mechanical devices that separate desired materials from undesired materials [. . .] norms and laws may sieve (accepting certain behaviors and rejecting others), as may price and infrastructure."[19] Language is a crucial mechanism by which sieves operate and interpret data for Kockelman, as language is an interactional tool that works to create meaning and foster relationality between people. As such, language plays an important role throughout this book, for as I elaborate in subsequent chapters, regulating what can be said mirrors the invocation for something to be said. Florida's Don't Say Gay law that limits what can be verbalized in the classroom, for instance, juxtaposes with the act of coming out, of revealing some*thing* about the self to others, and thus the regulation of speaking compared to a near compulsion to speak renders the speech act—whether uttered or not—itself a sieve that works to script individual moments.

Key to the sieve is that "separating substances is not just an end in itself, but often a means for further ends" (Kockelman 2017, 139). This means that what gets separated does something beyond its separation—separating culturally normative behavior from nonnormative behavior is done so that the individual, for instance, can be regarded as an upstanding, normative individual. Sieves can also be used to interpret security, for security operates like a sieve, sifting through the mass to identify suspicious or benign objects, whereby when data passes through the security sieve it renders an object a threat or nonthreat. Interestingly, sieves will often take on characteristics of that which passes through, just as that which passes through takes on features of the sieve: "[I]n sieving for a feature, the substances sieved may be affected by the sieving, and thereby come to take on features they did not originally have—in particular, features that allow such substances to slip through such sieves" (Kockelman 2017, 139).[20] This is an important aspect of the sieve because it means that there is an intimate relationship formed between the sieve and that which passes through insofar as the two affect one another and to the extent that undesirables may pass through the sieve.

To consider scripts as a type of sieve is to recognize the ways scripts work to distinguish between desirable and undesirable behavior, on the one hand, and that such separation is meant to do something more than the separation itself, on the other hand. In scripting normative sexual behavior in particular locations and at particular times, these social scripts work to distinguish the normative from the nonnormative, which then, in turn, is used to categorize people as normative or nonnormative. However, given that sieves are not without change or affect, because sieves "take on (and not just take in) features of the substances they sieve" (Kockelman 2017,

140), scripts are slowly changing without us necessarily noticing it, and as such, nonnormative behavior and individuals are able to pass through or maneuver within and through the sieving scripts.

While recognizing that sex panics are themselves a type of script, I am suggesting that sex panics operate by inflaming the sieving scripts of sex and sexuality, inflaming because sex panics work through fear and anxiety, sensationalizing daily life into an object of panic. These scripts thus become more scrutinized and even intensified insofar as attention to normative versus nonnormative morphs into a distinction between healthy and secure at one end and unhealthy, insecure, and even threating at the other. Sieving scripts that work to distinguish youth sexuality may certainly separate out children from (adult) sexuality, but it may also separate heterosexual youth sexuality from queer youth sexuality as well. In this act of sieving, however, queer youth sexuality is doubly rejected as nonnormative and not desirable. And yet, the fact that queer youth still exist—albeit insecurely and precariously so—illustrates that seemingly undesired objects still manage to pass through the sieving script.

I consider unscripting a form of what Halberstam (2011, 2) refers to as "low theory," a type of theory that looks for alternatives to "binary formulations."[21] Such low theory tries to "locate all the in-between spaces that save us from being snared by the hooks of hegemony and speared by the seductions of the gift shop. But it also makes its peace with the possibility that alternatives well in the murky waters of a counterintuitive, often impossibly dark and negative realm of critique and refusal." Unscripting attends to the alternative modes of living, the lateral movements and "in-between spaces" that circumvent the hegemony of growing up. Some of these alternatives may be "murky" or even icky and cringe-worthy. For Halberstam (2011, 2), failure works as a form of low theory given that "under certain circumstances failing, losing, forgetting, unmaking, undoing, unbecoming, and not knowing may in fact offer more creative, more cooperative, more surprising ways of being in the world."[22] This is another way of describing unscripting and the lateral movements that take place *within* the sieve, within and between scripts that may work to alter or even challenge the normative sieving scripts in the first place. The scripts that work to sieve the normative from nonnormative may slowly be changing by taking on features of the nonnormative. And if we recognize the influence of security framings for sex panics and sieving scripts, we can also consider that such lateral movements work to disentangle and quite possibly dismantle security's hold on sex and daily life.

Therefore, to queer the scripts of the present is another way to describe my methodology of unscripting, for at the heart, unscripting works to draw out the scripts—normative scripts at that—and aims to disentangle them from the present moment while also attending to the unplanned and impromptu moments that are themselves queer moments. These are moments that fly in the face of normative expectations, both in content and form, while also accounting for moments when plans or encounters go awry. As such, unscripting is a fundamentally queer methodology.

As a form of low theory attentive to failure, I contend that unscripting draws much needed attention to unplanned moments, impromptu encounters that exceed the expectations and scripts of the present. While the popular culture artifacts are actually scripted by writers, most are presented as unplanned encounters, intimacies, or moments. For instance, in the Netflix show *Teenage Bounty Hunters* (2020), female protagonist Sterling is working with classmate April on a school project, the two initially not getting along with one another. April eventually warms to Sterling, and while talking about the project, Sterling suddenly kisses April—her first kiss with another girl—before she begins to freak out and profusely apologize for the kiss. Yet rather than admonish Sterling or panic about the kiss, April locks the door before she kisses Sterling, much to Sterling's surprise. Exploring these seemingly impromptu moments draws much needed attention to times when plans may also be amiss, when the sieving scripts come under pressure from the suddenness of a moment as opposed to the daily trudge or expected encounters of daily life. Moments of sexual intimacy, as I explore in chapter 4, may be interrupted by a parent, by hesitation, or by panic—the best-laid plans can very well collide with the spontaneity and precarity of daily life. These moments when things do not go according to plan, in part because they were unexpected to begin with, are powerful scenes that work to challenge the dominant scripts of the present through the unscripted.

As a methodology, unscripting is a novel way to approach sociological, linguistic, cultural, and media scripts through anthropological and queer theory, attending specifically to not only the normativity of the script and the nonnormativity of that which is sieved out but also to how stuff might get *stuck* in the sieve (e.g., queers and queerness), and as such, that which is stuck can either widen the holes or change the inner workings of the sieve and scripts themselves. Unscripting does several things in the pages of this book. It at once draws attention to the sieving scripts that seek to govern and regulate the present moment. Given that the present is a battleground for future uncertainty and fear, the scripts that work to govern or regulate behavior become representative of the telos of the present. This requires examining speech acts, both those uttered and those not, and the ways sex panics attempt to create scripts that regulate what can be said while other kinds of sieving scripts compel individuals to say some*thing*. Such a speech act includes reporting on suspicious objects and persons, coming out, and queer sex talk. Unscripting also works to refocus attention on that which is changed by, or manages to pass through, the sieve undetected, as those are, I contend, the lateral movements of queer youth. As discussed above, queer youth sexuality is doubly braided as undesired and cast out, and so representations of queer youth and their sexuality exist almost clandestinely to the sieving script that generates normativity. Exploring those representations thus illustrates the ways queer youth sexuality may pass through the sieve (or grow up) while also recognizing the ways they exist within the sieve, within the present (of growing sideways or moving laterally). These moments also unscript the present by descripting or, perhaps, rescripting the present through queer youth experiences and representations.

Scripting the Book

Unscripting the Present is a diagonal journey through the present, an excavation of contemporary sex panics alongside an exploration of representations of queer youth's maneuverability in the wake of these sex panics. The two fundamental arguments this book makes—one about security panics and one about representations of queer youth's lateral maneuvering—manifest in the five subsequent chapters, both separately and, at times, intertwined. The arc of this book works inside out, moving from sex panics to securitization while also moving from securitization to sex panics. I begin with how the securitization of sex transforms sex panics into security panics before exploring how representations of queer youth in media artifacts move laterally to such panic and how queer youth find their own way of living and even resisting in the present. Moving through the book in this fashion illustrates at first the broader context with which queer youth must contend—a panicked context—to help frame and situate queer youth's response and maneuverability in the present moment. I end by returning to an explicit interrogation of securitization in high schools and of queer youth to demonstrate how queer youth are caught in the webs of the American security apparatus and the security panics that weave through contemporary American life.

In the first chapter, "Securitizing Sex," I situate the reader in the middle of contemporary sex panics sweeping the United States. I focus specifically on laws that ban what can be said in the classroom, such as Florida's Don't Say Gay law, and trace these contemporary laws to older laws that disallow the promotion of homosexuality in the classroom and even the US military's Don't Ask, Don't Tell policy that banned openly gay soldiers from serving in the military. I then tie these laws to the Department of Homeland Security's If You See Something, Say Something campaign that encourages citizens to report suspicious objects and activities to authorities, to utter a speech act for the sake of security. All these laws hinge on a speech act being said, or not said, and so I conceptualize these security panics through their language and query how what is said or not said are part and parcel of the securitization of sex.

I then transition to a series of chapters that shift focus to representations of queer youth and their sexualities. The popular culture artifacts mobilized in these chapters are not necessarily in response to the contemporary sex panics discussed in chapter 1, in part because at least half of the texts discussed do not originate in the United States. Rather, like the lateral movements discussed in these chapters themselves, these chapters exist diagonally to sex panics. My interrogation and textual analysis of these popular media artifacts and narratives of queer youth sexuality aim to provide theoretical insight into both contemporary US sex panics and queer youth sexuality. Panic and security are not missing from the following chapters—I revisit panic in chapter 4 and security in chapter 5—but my goal in the following chapters is to refocus attention to queer youth themselves, to move beyond a growing-up telos and future-oriented panic and offer different ways of interpreting narratives of queer youth sexuality in the present.

In chapter 2, "Radical Presentism," I provide a theoretical framework for understanding the construction of queer youth sexuality through the concept of radical presentism. By mobilizing multiple European adaptations of the Norwegian teen television show *Skam*, I explore how sexuality is "thingified" through speech acts by queer youth and understood in relation to existing circles of friends. This configuration of queer youth sexuality is legible only if considered from the present and a durational approach to temporality, meaning that one moves from minute to minute instead of making plans into the far-flung future. Such an approach eschews a future-oriented logic of "growing up" or hoping for things to "get better," and instead queer youth find ways to make do in the here and now.

In the third chapter, "Relationality and the Contractual Self," I extend my discussion of queer youth sexuality as a relationality to illustrate how queer youth sexuality in the United States, when compared to Europe, is individuated, and focuses on the responsibility of young queer people to self-manage their sexualities. A type of neoliberal self, or what I am calling a contractual self, manifests in the popular culture artifacts discussed, as queer youth are expected and obliged to behave and interact with others in ways that highlight their responsibilities to their individual queerness—that they alone are responsible for their sexualities—alongside their traits and skills that mark them as individuals. As such, I follow coming-out narratives in multiple media texts to trace how different narratives create different understandings of how queer youth sexuality operates, either as an individual truth or a relational construction. The former embodies a narrative of coming out that sees queer youth navigating their sexualities without input from others that result in coming out as a sexuality—the speech act of coming out renders sexuality an inner truth to be shared over a conduit—while the latter features queer youth mobilizing friendships and relationships to comprehend and identify themselves not only as a sexuality but as a partner in a relationship.

Chapter 4, "The Ascendency of Queer Pleasure," returns to the sex panics from the introduction and chapter 1 and contends that queer sex and pleasure has the ability to supplant panic. I survey multiple media texts featuring queer protagonists across the United States and Europe to show how the constructions of queer sex scenes are constitutive of broader understandings of queer youth sexuality. This chapter is particularly inspired by Lauren Berlant and Lee Edelman's (2014) notion of "sex without optimism," arguing that sex may not be about what happens in the future but instead intensifies present feelings and relationality. Mobilizing Jennifer Hirsch and Shamus Khan's (2020) notion of sexual projects, I interrogate how the sexual projects of queer youth in these popular culture artifacts work to rupture the security logics that inform contemporary sex panics. Doing so draws attention to the present acts of sex as not reproductive of a future but manifestations of queer pleasure and relationality. I do this by first drawing attention to the panic of talking about queer sex, as talk about queer sex is still considered awkward and taboo, before transitioning to an exploration of how the popular culture artifacts work to make queer sex among youth ordinary and mundane, if still nonnormative.

30 | Unscripting the Present

In the final chapter, "The American Security Apparatus," I return to the notion of security and explore moments when queer youth encounter, engage, or even participate in the American security apparatus. While the previous chapters speak to the contemporary sex panics saturating the US cultural and social zeitgeist, this chapter asks after LGBTQ+ inclusion and the spread of niceness, alongside broader pushes to diversify secondary schools and higher education. I argue that such inclusion fits within both a security temporality and the American security apparatus, but it also engenders an ambivalent feeling for many, what I call queer states of security. The second part of this chapter thus explores media artifacts where queer youth encounter or participate in security practices—from militarization to school shooting lockdowns—to not only interrogate the layers of securitization, racialization, and queerness found in the described scenes but also to examine the lateral movements queer youth take in the present during these security encounters. These are not always, if ever, expected movements and may work to infuse more ambivalence, or even cringe, into the scenes. In many ways, they unscript the security expectations and logics stitched into the present moment.

Alien Abductions

For the last eight years, I have been haunted by Henry Denton's experience of alien abduction. *We Are the Ants* sits with me, at times uncomfortably, perhaps because both Henry and I grew up in small Florida towns by the beach surrounded by a rather palpable toxic cocktail of masculinity, heterosexuality, whiteness, and ableism that saw neurodiverse gay boys as perennial fodder for bullying and even assault. Henry's admission that "the biggest letdown about being abducted by aliens is the abundance of gravity on the spaceship" reads to me as a wish for a different sort of context, a different starting point.[23] Henry continues his explication of gravity: "We spend our first nine months of life floating, weightless and blind, in an amniotic sac before we become gravity's bitch, and the seductive lure of space travel is the promise of returning to that perfect state of grace. But it's a sham. Gravity is jealous, sadistic, and infinite. Sometimes I think gravity may be death in disguise. Other times I think gravity is love, which is why love's only demand is that we fall" (Hutchinson 2016, 6). Gravity renders us both lost and found, for in our seemingly unconscious need to be weightless, gravity is that strong dose of reality that holds us down, that makes movement arduous and even precarious. We can climb, but gravity, like love, makes falling a greater possibility, painfully so. For Henry, gravity is sentient, or at least appears so, as it toys with us while we climb, whereto still undetermined and vague. Gravity is the embodiment of growing up, the force that holds youth to the temporal drudge forward that sees the future existence of the youth-as-adult in the present moment. It may restrict our vertical movement, but is that not one of the most common explanations of growing up, the difficult and arduous climb to adulthood? Gravity fixes our location and our humanness, but it also fixes our temporality and even our expectations (Valentine 2017).

Henry's disappointment in gravity's existence on the alien spaceship is also a disappointment in the linear pathway one must move, even in one's own alien abduction. He wishes for a return to weightlessness, a lateral movement through space and through time that confounds the restrictive capacity of both gravity and growing up. Indeed, *We Are the Ants* is a countdown to the end of the world, one that Henry is consciously making as he navigates his own precarious present, as he recognizes that the future is unforgiving. How do we navigate the future when the present is itself a fucked-up place and time to be in?

I don't know, Henry, but maybe we can figure it out together.

Chapter One

Securitizing Sex

[W]e fear the children we would protect.

—Kathryn Bond Stoctkon, "The Queer Child Now and Its Paradoxical Global Effects"

Sex education breaks a silence.

—Janice M. Irvine, *Talk about Sex*

There is a story that a growing number of states and conservative lawmakers are telling regarding sex. From the town halls to the chambers of state and national legislatures, these lawmakers weave together a picture of a parent's right to their child's education. Parents have a decisive say in what their child is to learn, what their child is exposed to, and what their child has access to with regard to their education. Parents' rights continue to fuel the expanding book bans throughout the country because merely having access to certain materials is deemed dangerous to both the innocent child and the heterosexual family dynamic. The same holds true for the type of sex education—if any—a child receives in school, for the child's exposure to material is even more dangerous than their potential exposure. There might be a difference between the child stumbling across *We Are the Ants* in a library and being sat down in a classroom and told about gender and sexual identities and orientation, but in both cases the object of threat is the same: the child.

Lawrence Grossberg (2005, 22) claims that the United States is at war with its kids, that "the sense of kids as risk and at risk is pervasive in our country." For Grossberg (2005, 22), there are multiple reasons for this supposed war, including increased violence among youth and economic precarity: "[T]he typical image of kids in the United States is that they are armed and violent, lawless, sex crazed, suicidal, drunk, and high."[1] Kathryn Bond Stockton (2016, 505–06) similarly notes in the epigraph that "'we' fear the children we would protect." Yet I contend that the war now being fought against kids is on the battlefield of sex and sex education, and it is waged in the name of parents' rights. Grossberg (2005, 15) refers to the child as "the enemy within," an apt metaphor for the treatment of children in this slew of contemporary sex panics. Let us follow Alice down the rabbit hole.

The family is considered by many, but primarily by the state, as the pinnacle heterosexual institution responsible for the reproduction of both the family and the nation in the Unites States (e.g., Rich 1980; Butler 2002).[2] Heterosexuality is a cornerstone of US exceptionalism, what Jasbir Puar (2007) also refers to as US sexual exceptionalism,[3] and thus must be kept safe and secure for the family and nation to stand firm and proceed into the future. The child is, as Lee Edelman (2004) contends, the symbol for that promulgation, the figure of reproductive futurism that embodies all the hopes and dreams of heterosexuality. If the child is so exceptional and quintessential to the family, nation, and heterosexuality, it seems to have become too big to fail. This is where the danger lies. For if Alice does fall down the rabbit hole of nonnormativity—if Alice stumbles upon *We Are the Ants*, for instance—the possibility that Alice brings those ideas and practices back to the family is perceived as a corrupting influence on not just the child but on the family institution as a whole.

The child's innocence is both what enshrines the child as the bearer of all our hopes and dreams but also poses the greatest threat: the child's easy corruptibility. Given that the child is never just a child but always an emblem and embodiment of our future, following Edelman (2004), then the possibility that the child quite literally fucks up throws the family, nation, and heterosexuality into potential disarray. Exposure to nonnormativity outside the family, outside the context of familial and national heterosexuality, is thus seen as a threat to both the child and the family, whereby the child is the enemy within, a carrier of nonnormative ideas and practices that introduces the family to outside corruption. Here the sex panic takes form, for fear and anxiety lie in the *potential* for this to happen, in the assumption that chances for exposure will lead to actual exposure and thus this potential exposure will corrupt the child and family.

Fear about potential exposure and outcomes is not a new fear with regard to the child or nonnormative sexualities. The 1993 implementation of the US military code Don't Ask, Don't Tell (DADT)—and even earlier precedents of racial segregation in the US military—mobilized a similar fear and anxiety about a soldier's exposure to nonnormative sexual behavior.[4] Don't Ask, Don't Tell stipulated that the military was not allowed to ask a soldier about their sexuality and that a soldier was not allowed to disclose their sexuality—nonheterosexual soldiers were not allowed to serve openly in the military, in other words. Key reasons for DADT and the disallowing of openly queer soldiers began with the assumption that "homosexuality was incompatible with military service" given that the existence of homosexual soldiers would "adversely affect the ability of the Armed Forces to maintain discipline, good order, and morale" that would lead to "security breaches" (Department of Defense cited in Sinclair 2009, 704–05). As such, "group cohesion and unity are paramount institutional needs for maintaining "discipline, good order, and morale" (C. L. Davis 1993, 24).[5] Don't Ask, Don't Tell relied on the potential for homosexual exposure to occur, whereby actual exposure would prove the rule, but given that actual exposure would be detrimental, the military had to mitigate potential exposure in the present to prevent actual exposure in the future.

At its core, DADT was a regulation of a speech act, one that foreclosed the possibility of saying gay in the military. Don't Ask, Don't Tell relied on an inverse to Althusserian interpellation, as one could not be asked or hailed and thus one could not be interpellated as gay; the speech act could not be uttered despite, as Judith Butler (1997, 104) contends, there being a doubling that takes place with DADT. As she writes:

> The term not only appears in the regulation as that discourse to be regulated, but reappears in the public debate over its fairness and value, specifically as the conjured or imagined act of self ascription that is explicitly prohibited by the regulation, a prohibition that cannot take place without a conjuring of the very act. We might conclude that the state and the military are merely concerned to *retain control* over what the term will mean, the conditions under which it may be uttered by a speaking subject, restricting that speaking to precisely and exclusively those subjects who are not described by the term they utter. (Butler 1997, 104–5)

For Butler, there is tension between the state and military controlling both the utterance of the term and its meaning, and the "public debate" over such regulation, whereby the term is spoken repeatedly. The iterative process of speaking the term thus challenges those instances or places where it must not be uttered. Such a regulation of the speech act, framed within the confines of the military and state, becomes a security concern as the speech act engenders disorder and chaos within the military unit. Simply uttering the word "gay" or "homosexual" renders the military and potentially the state insecure, and thus DADT worked to not only regulate a speech act but to also supposedly keep secure an institution and state under siege from the proliferation of talk.

That DADT was framed through a need for "discipline, good order, and morale" mirrors the justification for limiting sex education in schools and the wave of book bans that target books that discuss sexual orientation and gender identity. As Nathaniel Frank (2023), the director of What We Know Project at Cornell University's Center for the Study Inequality, writes, DADT "was sold as a way to *prevent* the culture wars from infecting a key institution of American society."[6] Frank compares DADT to Florida's 2023 Don't Say Gay law, arguing that the detrimental effects and even violence that emerged from DADT would no doubt befall students in Florida and other states with similar laws.[7] Yet Frank's point that both DADT and Don't Say Gay laws "prevent the culture wars" is telling, for culture wars include gender and sexuality identity and orientation. The focus on *preventing* culture wars involves imagining the culture wars happening in the future and taking steps in the present that work to prevent—or, in some cases, prepare for—those culture wars transpiring.

As laid out in the introduction, it is this future-oriented temporality that marks contemporary sex panics as security panics. Anticipatory logic (Amoore 2013) governs and manages risk, where risk here is defined as exposure to materials, ideas, and practices surrounding gender and sexual identity and orientation. Anticipated in these security panics is, as outlined above, the threat that the child and the child's potential exposure to corrupting material and experiences. Thinking of the child as a threat no doubt frames sex panics through security, for even if the laws and policies discussed below do not directly refer to the child as a threat, I will demonstrate how the language around the laws and talk of these laws indexes the child and materials as threats.

In this chapter, I move through laws and policies that limit the inclusion of gender identity and sexual orientation in public school sex education. Rather than survey different kinds of laws—such as bathroom laws or healthcare laws—I focus on sex education laws because they immediately impact queer youth in intimate ways. Sex education laws and policies draw attention to how these particular sex panics mobilize parents' fears and anxieties about the corruptive forces on their children. Throughout this chapter I untangle this relationship with the laws and policies discussed as method for interrogating security logics and practices woven through these laws and policies. Doing so, I argue, demonstrates how these sex panics surrounding sex education are forms of security panics.

Sex Education: A Commentary

Sex education means different things in different states and to different people. Educational standards, in general, vary from state to state, but "talk about sex in the public realm is consistently met with ambivalence and outright efforts to contain and silence it" (Irvine 2002, 4). In other words, sex is an incredibly taboo subject, for as Carole Vance (1992a, 436) writes in the introduction's epigraph, "we lack a safe space to talk about sex." Gayle Rubin (2011, 148) suggests that the most important ideology "whose grip on sexual thought is so strong" is sex negativity and a "culture [that] always treats sex with suspicion [. . .] sex is presumed guilty until proven innocent." To then construct and teach a curriculum around sex is to invite suspicion and doubt into education; it would be to render the education carried out (or attempted to be carried out) potentially threatening to the innocence of the child (Rubin 2011). As I continue to argue, the sex panics turned security panics I aim to dissect focus on the child and the child's innocence, that given the child's easy corruptibility because of their innocence, the child also poses a threat to the family and the nation *if* corrupted. Sex education becomes the field on which this battle is fought.

In sociologist Janice M. Irvine's (2002, 4) pathbreaking book *Talk about Sex* that addresses conflicts over sex education in the United States, Irvine writes that "sex education breaks a silence. It introduces talk about sex into the regulated public sphere of the school." This silence is an important object to consider, for as I explore below with different laws that regulate queer and trans inclusion, the speech act itself—saying LGBTQ—is a powerful act that is itself regulated and disallowed. As Irvine (2002, 132–33) deftly shows, critics of sex education claimed that "sexual speech . . . provokes and stimulates; it transforms the so-called natural modesty of children into inflamed desires that may be outside the child's control and thus prompt sexual activity [. . .] a version of the accusation that sexual speech produces sexual behavior was the charge that sexual speech constructs sexual identities." This is partly where the sex panics surrounding sex education lie, Irvine contends, in the very talk of sex, as it is believed to instigate behavior and even engender identity, two processes that can corrupt the innocence of the child. Irvine renders these sex panics as contributions to the so-called culture wars raging through the United States that pits conservatives and Christians against liberals and progressives (see also Kendall 2013).

Controlling and regulating what is said and not said through laws like Florida's Don't Say Gay law or even book banning—do not say gay, but also do not read gay—frames children themselves as objects of regulation and control. Jen Gilbert (2014) makes an analogous point by contending that sex education is based on a relationship and distinction between adults and adolescents.[8] To consider adolescents subjects means that "the adolescent becomes either a problem of social convention or an effect of an unruly physiology of psychology, and the adult escapes unscathed" (Gilbert 2014, 27). As such, following Donald Winnicott, Gilbert (2014, 34) argues that "there is no such thing as an adolescent. If you show me an adolescent, you certainly also show me parents, teachers, friends and peer groups, schools, police, the fashion industry, the media, the mall, and so on." Stated alternatively, "[T]he adolescent grows up through the parents' ambivalence toward their children and their own ambivalence toward their parents" (Gilbert 2014, 34). Gilbert's understanding of the adolescent in relation to the parent matters, not only in light of the explication of the child and youth discussed in the introduction but also because as a developmental narrative, adolescence is a period of risk, and as such, "sex education is steeped in the language of risks: risk groups, risk behaviors, risk reduction, at-risk populations" (Gilbert 2014, 37). Gilbert (2014, 37) notes that "it is almost impossible to convince people to see themselves at risk if they are invested in regarding themselves as safe and out of harm's way" whereby "safety . . . is a matter of perception."

Within the framing of sex panics, sex education works to speak sexual behaviors and identities into existence, but it also operates through a language and discourse of risk, not unlike security (Amoore 2013). These work together, for the language of risk enables sex education to label certain practices, behaviors, and identities as risky, as dangerous and insecure, and thus when made manifest through speech acts, these sexual behaviors and identities carry with them the mark of danger. In Cynthia Hunt's (2023) recent study of Ohio college students' retrospective description of their sex education experiences, students noted a sex-negativity and fear-based sex education curriculum, a finding that coincides with other studies (e.g., Irvine 2002; Kendall 2013; Fields 2008). That sex education promotes abstinence, in particular, and frames sexual activity and deviancy through discourses of risk, safety, and even fear ought not be at all surprising, particularly given the broader sex panics around children and children's sexuality that sex education fits within (see the introduction).

My point, in moving through this chapter, is to wed risk and speech act together, to think through the implication of the speech act as itself a risky and securitized practice. Focusing on the speech act (Austin 1975) in all the laws, policies, and practices discussed below invokes what is known as "securitization theory," a theory that "aims to gain an increasingly precise understanding of who securitizes, on what issues (threats), for whom (referent objects), why, with what results, and, not least, under what conditions" (Pedersen and Holbraad 2013, 10). In this way, security "is a particular kind of speech act that can be successful only under certain felicity conditions" (Pedersen and Holbraad 2013, 10). This definition also builds on my conceptualization of securitization that emphasizes the injurious, discriminatory, and insecure state and general public, contributing the linguistic component of security and securitization to underscore both the discursive nature of security and the material effects that flow from such discourse. According to political scientist Thierry Balzacq (2010, 3):

> [S]ecuritization [is] an articulated assemblage of practices whereby heuristic artefacts (metaphors, polity tools, image repertoires, analogies, stereotypes, emotions, etc.) are contextually mobilized by a securitizing actor, who works to prompt an audience to build a coherent network of implications (feelings, sensations, thoughts, and intuitions), about the critical vulnerability of a referent object, that concurs with the securitizing actor's reasons for choices and actions, by investing the referent subject with such an aura of unprecedented threatening complexion that a customized policy must be undertaken immediately to block its development.

Crucial to this definition is that there is a relationship between the individual who says or does something and the audience, that speech acts do not exist within a vacuum, but the "network of implications" is contingent on the audience. Balzacq mobilizes J. L. Austin (1975) to interrogate security speech acts, arguing that "securitization consists of practices which instantiate *intersubjective* understandings through the *habitus* inherited from different, often competing social fields" (Balzacq 2010, 2).[9] Security becomes performative through its discourse—speaking security into existence is to perform and participate in securitization practices and ideologies, as I explore in more detail in chapter 5. My interpretation and use of securitization theory hinges on a broader indexicality of security, whereby the speech act does not need to say "security" or "insecurity" or even "risk" to signal security. Rather, language that works to paint the speech act or practice—such as "saying gay"—as risky or dangerous or in need of regulation, control, or management to prevent something from taking place all instantiate securitization discourse and ideology.

To "say gay" is to expose children, critics claim, to seedy and seemingly "pornographic" perversion at an age when their development is crucial. It is to manifest the possibility of nonnormative behaviors, orientations, and identities in the symbol of reproductive futurism (Edelman 2004), the beacon of innocence that we adults pin all our hopes and dreams on in an effort to almost displace our own insecurities around sex and sexuality. Why work through our own problems when it is so much easier to transfer ownership of our insecurities to youth? Stockton (2016, 507) connects the word "gay" to the child in temporal fashion, noting that "the gay child was precisely ghostly because it could not live in the present tense, even though it often consciously, secretly had a relationship with the *word* gay—or with the word's vague association and connotations, without the word itself."

However, as I also explore in this chapter, such regulations and control of what is said ultimately renders queer youth themselves as a problem, as a threat in need of hiding and even regulation. Abstinence-only education, for example, erases the entire queer experience because as one gay teen noted prior to the Supreme Court's 2015 marriage equality decision, "I can't get married . . . so where does that leave me?" (Fisher 2009, 70). Another gay teen interpreted the message "to mean he was supposed to remain celibate because he was gay and could not legally marry" (Fisher 2009, 70). Countless studies demonstrate that, in general, sex education curriculum often excludes sexual difference and gender variance (e.g., Elia and Eliason 2010; Shannon 2016; Bible et al. 2020; Garg and Volerman 2021). Such a fact makes book banning and Don't Say Gay laws that much more panicked, for countless sex education programs are far from inclusive or comprehensive, and so what truly is the concern for proponents of these laws? The concern lies in the possibility of the speech act, not necessarily in the speech act itself. Risk here thus engenders a negative relationship with the future, for fear about what the future *might* bring, a fear about future uncertainty, is the same fear that frames security concerns. Sex panics as security panics therefore not only tap into the temporality of security but also into the objects of security itself: the family and the nation. As I explore below, there are multiple laws that pivot on the speech act as either a risk to or necessary for security. Aligning these laws together enables a more critical reading of the laws and policies that make up contemporary sex panics.

Old Laws, New Tricks

Before the advent of Don't Say Gay laws began moving through the country, multiple states had or still have what we could call "no promotion of homosexuality," or "no promo homo," laws on the books. These laws typically did not promote "homosexual conduct" and in fact actively discouraged it during sex education lessons. Some states even mentioned the criminality of such homosexual behavior given that several states had (and some continue to have) antisodomy laws in place. These antisodomy laws were made ineffective with the Supreme Court's 2003 *Lawrence v. Texas* decision that made these laws unconstitutional. However, some states have yet to repeal state antisodomy laws or revise sex education laws to reflect the 2003 Supreme Court decision.

Take Texas, for instance. In Texas, there are two iterations of the "no homo promo" law, one in the sex education statute and one in the AIDS education statute. Under the sex education statute, the school curriculum is required to include "emphasis, provided in a factual manner from a public health perspective, that homosexuality is not a lifestyle acceptable to the general public and that homosexual conduct is a criminal offense under section 21.06, Penal Code."[10] Yet the requirement to emphasize this transforms it into a declaration under the AIDS education statute, where the curriculum must "state that homosexual conduct is a criminal offense under section 21.06, Penal Code" (Hoshall 2013, 235). The slight change in wording is telling, not least of all because the necessity to declare homosexual conduct as wrong and illegal is framed within the broader AIDS education statute. Regardless of the 2003 Supreme Court decision, "it is apparently irrelevant that homosexual conduct is not, in fact, criminal" (Hoshall 2013, 235).

Yet what I find interesting is that such emphasis must be presented "in a factual manner from a public health perspective," not only indexing the AIDS crisis—particularly given that these statutes were instituted in 1991 during the height of the AIDS crisis—but the pathologizing of homosexuality (McNeill 2013). Alabama's 1992 sex education law pulls from Texas' law by requiring, in a way eerily similar to Texas, an "emphasis, in a factual manner and from a public health perspective, that homosexuality is not a lifestyle acceptable to the general public and that homosexual conduct is a criminal offense under the laws of the state" (Hoshall 2013, 222). Framing the discussion of homosexual conduct or homosexuality through the lens of public health renders homosexuality not only a concern of public health but itself an illness that requires active dissuasion. Moreover, homosexuality had historically been tied to HIV/AIDS as itself a homosexual disease whereby all homosexuals were considered to have HIV/AIDS. This dovetails into instances of HIV/AIDS criminalization and public health surveillance of HIV-infected individuals, particularly gay men, that further stigmatize both queer men and people living with HIV/AIDS (Strub 2017; Tomso 2017). Homosexuality must be prevented for the safety and *health* of our children. In this way, safety and health become synonymous, especially if we read these laws through the language of heteronormativity and the promotion of the family (McNeill 2013). This is particularly salient when considering Alabama's law's language, whereby public health and "the general public" are brought into relation and correlated with one another. Not only does the general public supposedly reject homosexuality as an acceptable "lifestyle," but it does so partly because homosexuality is a public health concern. Therefore, the general public determines what is an acceptable lifestyle—not the state—with regard to the health of the public. Stated alternatively, the general public is supposedly aware of homosexuality's alleged corrupting influence and sees it as a disease in need of management and prevention rather than a viable "lifestyle" in need of protection, tolerance, and acceptance (see Strub 2017).

No homo promo laws are typically framed through concerns for public health, usually with regard to HIV and AIDS. Arizona's 1991 law titled "Instruction on Acquired Immune Deficiency Syndrome; Department Assistance" states that during such instruction, no school shall "promote a homosexual life-style; portray homosexuality as a positive alternative life-style; [or] suggest that some methods of sex are safe methods of homosexual sex" (Hoshall 2013, 224). Unlike Texas or Alabama, Arizona's law does not require statements about homosexuality; in fact, it requires nothing be said about homosexuality. That such requirements, however, fall within an AIDS statute again frames homosexuality as a concern for public health and again symbolizes the historic tie between HIV/AIDS and homosexuality. Even if certain homosexual acts—"some methods of sex"—are considered safe, they must not be discussed because doing so might violate the first rule of not promoting a homosexual lifestyle. Arizona has since amended its sex education laws so that parents must *opt in* their students to sex education that involves "learning materials or presentations regarding sexuality" (Movement Advancement Project 2023).

These older no promo laws—including laws in Mississippi, Oklahoma, South Carolina, and Utah—act as both genealogical antecedents for newer Don't Say Gay laws and lay the foundation for how sex education more broadly has become central to contemporary security panics.[11] Historically, homosexuality has often been pathologized, especially given its earlier inclusion in the *Diagnostic and Statistical Manual of Mental Disorders*.[12] The concern that homosexuality supposedly poses to public health is not at all new—given that Texas and Arizona, for instance, make mention of homosexuality within AIDS statutes is indexical of a broader concern surrounding the AIDS crisis at the time, in the late 1980s and early 1990s. Framing homosexuality in these terms, as a concern for public health, makes it also a biosecurity concern, one that must be regulated to prevent its outbreak and spread (Gitzen 2023). It is not that homosexuality is only now a concern for or threat to security, particularly given McCarthy-era concerns about homosexuals working for the government, what was known as the Lavender Scare in the late 1940s and early 1950s. Rather, how security now operates has changed. Instead of rooting homosexuality out, Don't Say Gay laws, as I discuss below, work to preempt the possibility of nonnormative sexualities and gender identity by disallowing the mere mention of such notions. These laws *anticipate* the catastrophe and thus make plans in the present to stave off or prepare for that future.

New Laws, Old Tricks

Before signing the 2022 "Parental Rights in Education" bill into law, Florida governor Ron DeSantis remarked that "we will make sure that parents can send their kids to school to get an education, not an indoctrination" (Izaguirre 2022). DeSantis is drawing a direct correlation between gender and sexual orientation and identity to the broader "cultural wars" that conservatives claim are sweeping the country (Frank 2023). That gender and sexual orientation and identity are considered doctrines that are being imposed on Florida's youth in the classroom not only reifies the earlier language used in laws found in states like Texas and Alabama that refer to the "homosexual lifestyle" but frames gender and sexual orientation and identity as topics and notions to fear. The threat of indoctrination, almost cultlike, inscribes the experiences of gender and sexual minorities and the very concepts of gender and sexuality with a social and cultural anxiety about kids growing up to be anything but heterosexual. Indoctrination is thus a fearful possible future, whereby schools have the potential to indoctrinate students and thus actions must be taken to prevent, or at least prepare, for such indoctrination. As such, Florida's Don't Say Gay law becomes a way to address the anticipated risk of gender and sexual orientation and identity in schools.

Florida's Don't Say Gay law was originally signed into law in March 2022. As the bill states, "Classroom instruction by school personnel or third parties on sexual orientation or gender identity may not occur in kindergarten through grade 3 or in a manner that is not age appropriate or developmentally appropriate for students in accordance with state standards" (Izaguirre 2022). Parents are, in response, able to sue districts over violations of the law. The bill was expanded in 2023: sexual orientation and gender identity education may not take place from prekindergarten through grade 8 and must be age appropriate if provided in grades 9 through 12. Florida's Board of Education Rules from 2023 (6A-10.081), titled "Principles of Professional Conduct for the Education Profession in Florida," expands the law even further, and reads that educators "shall not intentionally provide classroom instruction to students in grades 4 through 12 on sexual orientation or gender identity unless such instruction is either expressly required by state academic standards . . . or is part of a reproductive health course or health lesson for which a student's parent has the option to have his or her student not attend" (Movement Advancement Project 2023). The choice for parents to opt their students out of any such discussion aligns with several states' opt-in and opt-out policies when it comes to sex education and gender identity and sexual orientation (Movement Advancement Project 2023). Yet my question becomes, who determines what is developmentally appropriate, especially given how intimately this is tied to social constructedness of children and youth (Gilbert 2014; Sheldon 2016)?

The expansion of Florida's Don't Say Gay law was part of four bills restricting queer and trans rights that DeSantis signed into law in May 2023. Part of these restrictions, in DeSantis's words, "makes sure that Florida students and teachers will never be forced to declare pronouns in school or be forced to use pronouns not based on biological sex" (Yurcaba 2023). One's pronouns are a speech act, according to DeSantis, that could potentially render not only confusion in a child or teacher but also an afront—a threat, even—to both the assumed sex assigned at birth and the heterosexuality of the child or teacher. The bill DeSantis signed requires that schools teach "that sex is determined by biology and reproductive function at birth; that biological males impregnate biological females by fertilizing the female egg with male sperm; that the female then gestates the offspring; and that these reproductive roles are binary, stable, and unchangeable" (Yurcaba 2023). That such a scientific explication of reproduction is used to justify the use of pronouns based on sex assigned at birth is an instance of cultural assumptions about gender and sex being brought down to the level of the body and biology as a way to naturalize such cultural assumptions and make them biologically given (Martin 1991, 1994). As such, the law disallows the requirement that students and employees must use preferred pronouns rather than pronouns that align with the sex one was assigned at birth.[13]

The other bills included those barring trans folks from using public bathrooms that align with their gender identities, and limiting drag performances in front of minors, performances that DeSantis and the bill refer to as "adult."[14] DeSantis also outlawed "the mutilation of minors" that would "grant Florida temporary custody of children whose parents provide them with gender-affirming care" (Yurcaba 2023).[15] The American Medical Association, American Academy of Pediatrics, and the American Psychological Association all oppose these types of gender-affirming care restrictions (Yurcaba 2023).

DeSantis is fearful, we discern from his words, of a future in which gender and sexuality are so fluid that not only are kids confused but the possibility that the "mutilation of minors" may occur rises as well. The very invocation of mutilation is a common trope when discussing gender-affirming care, as it not only indexes global concern over "female genital mutilation" but even broader concerns regarding bodily mutilation due to war and violence.[16] To thus refer to gender-affirming care for youth as mutilation is to infuse care with violence, with fear and anxiety that such care is not actually care but debilitating harm. There is panic in DeSantis's words and worries, a panic that suffuses the words of the newly minted laws that take aim at gender and sexual minorities and inclusive sex education. The blame for such mutilation and panic, House Republican representative Mike Johnson (R-LA) laments, is with liberals: "The Democratic Party and their cultural allies are on a misguided crusade to immerse young children in sexual imagery and radical gender ideology" (Finley 2023, 199).[17] That Johnson calls this a "crusade" again makes this a warlike issue, reducing the security of the nation and the family to the regulation of children's education and even bodies.[18]

In response to Florida's Don't Say Gay law, the White House stated: "This is not an issue of 'parents' rights.' This is discrimination, plain and simple. It's part of a disturbing and dangerous nationwide trend of right-wing politicians cynically targeting LGBTQI+ students, educators, and individuals to score political points. It encourages bullying and threatens students' mental health, physical safety, and well-being. It censors dedicated teachers and educators who want to do the right thing and support their students. And it must stop" (Finley 2023, 200). The invocation of "parents' rights" again reflects a growing debate with regard to sex education in particular: that parents have autonomy over themselves but also over their children. As such, children lack autonomy and agency, as their choices are determined by their parents and other adults. That the White House mentioned the effect such laws have on mental health and bullying is telling, and a topic I revisit below.

Other states are proposing and passing similar laws to Florida's Don't Say Gay law. In Arkansas, SB 294 (2023) was passed and disallows public school teachers, before grade five, from including in classroom instruction "sexually explicit materials, sexual reproduction, sexual intercourse, gender identity, or sexual orientation" (Movement Advancement Project 2023). Here we see Arkansas' law conflate different categories of knowledge, practice, and being, whereby sexually explicit materials and intercourse are categorized as similar to discussion of gender identity and sexual orientation, as though one's identity or orientation is somehow sexually explicit, pornographic even. Interestingly, the same law includes education regarding sexual abuse and assault and human trafficking prevention, but it allows parents and legal guardians to "exempt their child from the child sexual abuse and assault and human trafficking prevention program" (Movement Advancement Project 2023). The students that would likely need such education and prevention might thus be exempt from such education and prevention due to their parents.[19]

Kentucky has a similar law (SB 150, 2003) that "respects parental rights by ensuring that: Children in grade five and below do not receive any instruction through curriculum or programs on human sexuality or sexually transmitted diseases" (Movement Advancement Project 2023).[20] Kentucky, like Florida, is even more expansive in its restrictions, for it bars "instruction or presentation that has a goal or purpose of students studying or exploring gender identity, gender expression, or sexual orientation" (Movement Advancement Project 2023). Telling in the language of Kentucky's law is that the "goal or purpose" may not be the exploration of gender and sexual identity and orientation; students might be able to ask about sexuality, but educators are limited in their response. Are they simply answering a question—homosexuality is when an individual is attracted to the same gender—or is it a sustained conversation about sexual differences and what those orientations and identities mean?

Returning to book banning, an Oklahoma bill that was introduced focuses not only on the classroom but on books in school libraries as well. The bill disallows libraries from housing "books that make as their primary subject the study of lesbian, gay, bisexual, or transgender issues or recreational sexualization" (Finley 2023, 200).[21] Here, again, sexual intercourse or "recreational sexualization" is conflated with the ways one identifies or one's orientation, as if to have a nonheterosexual sexual orientation is to engage in so-called recreational sexualization. The sponsor of a similar Oklahoma bill, Republican senator Rob Standridge (R-OK), claims that this bill works to "protect students from oversexualization and 'grooming'" (Finley 2023, 200). The invocation of grooming implies a narrative of an adult befriending a child with the intention of then molesting the child. Such a framing is thrown around by conservative politicians and parents' rights activists to protest the supposed sexualization of the child by schools that include comprehensive sex education. As Michigan state senator Republican Lana Theis accused fellow senator Democrat Mallory McMorrow, "[P]rogressive mobs [are] trying to steal our children's innocence" (Block 2022). Innocence is something one has, Theis implies; it is something that can be stolen under the right circumstances, and those circumstances involve grooming. The discourse of grooming also has a long history of accusing queer folks of "recruiting" children to become queer or trans, which indexes the likes of pedophilia and sex trafficking, "conspiracy theories spawned by far-right extremists such as

QAnon supporters, propagated widely through social media and right-wing channels and spreading through mainstream conservative thought" (Block 2022). For instance, former Fox News host Tucker Carlson accused California teachers of attempting to "indoctrinate schoolchildren" regarding sexual orientation and gender identity: "They're grooming 7-year-olds and talking to 7-year-olds about their sex lives" (Block 2022).[22]

Do Say Gay

"The science is overwhelming," Frank (2023) writes. "Affirming young people's LGBTQ identity and providing them with supportive communities will help them thrive. Silencing or stigmatizing them will not." Frank reviews a series of studies that work to prove his point, including studies on negative social environments, gender-affirming care, and discrimination:

> Evidence also shows that hostile or negative social environments, especially in schools, cause or compound problems for L.G.B.T.Q. youth. One study involving more than 9,000 students found that L.G.B. students who experienced hostility and anti-gay victimization "reported higher levels of substance use, suicidality and sexual risk behaviors." Another study surveyed the social environment for more than 1,400 L.G.B. high school students in 34 Oregon counties and found that suicide attempts were "20 percent greater in unsupportive environments compared to supportive environments," stark evidence of the difference made by gay-friendly climates. (Frank 2023)

Cornell University's What We Know Public Policy Research Portal surveyed three hundred peer-reviewed studies that assessed "the link between anti-LGBT discrimination and well-being" and determined that 95 percent of those studies "found that discrimination is associated with mental and physical health harms for LGBT people" (What We Know 2023). Frank (2023) cites this same study and notes that "even just the *fear* of being stigmatized or mistreated has a measurable negative impact. Laws like the Florida bill will cause harm whether or not direct censorship takes place."[23]

Multiple studies and legal analyses of Don't Say Gay laws emerged in the wake of Florida's initial 2022 law. In conjunction with Clark University, the University of California's William's Institute conducted a survey of 113

LGBTQ+ parents about the law and their worries. They found that "many are concerned that the bill will not only result in restricted or nonexistent education about the existence of diverse sexual and gender identities, but it will result in a chilly or hostile school climate for LGBTQ educators, students, and families because it suggests that something is wrong with LGBTQ identities" (Goldberg 2023, 1). LGBTQ+ parents are worried, with 88 percent of parents indicating that "they were very or somewhat worried about the effects of the bill on their children and families" (Goldberg 2023, 1). The study's key findings also include that initial reactions from LGBTQ+ parents ranged from "fear to anger to disbelief" and some even thought of enrolling their children in private school; that LGBTQ+ parents were concerned that their children would not be able to speak freely about their families and thus would "negatively impact their sense of legitimacy" and encourage hostility in school among their children's peers; that children also expressed fear to their parents about living in Florida as LGBTQ+ youth; that LGBTQ+ parents worried about if they could be involved in activities at their children's schools; and finally, that parents with school-aged children in public schools expressed the greatest concern (Goldberg 2023, 1). The study also surveyed parents' experiences, where some reported that their children had experienced bullying and harassment because of their LGBTQ+ parents, that they were unable to talk about their families both in and out of school because their parents are LGBTQ+, and that they had general fears about living in Florida (Goldberg 2023, 2). As a result, 56 percent of respondents considered moving out of Florida and 16.5 percent had already taken steps to do so (Goldberg 2023, 1).[24]

In addition to social scientific studies that address the effects of these laws, multiple legal challenges have been made to Don't Say Gay laws. In addition to the law attacking and undercutting "the equal dignity of LBTQ people" that would result in stigmatizing LGBTQ+ teachers, students, and families, critics "note that the statute's broad and vague language . . . leaves crucial questions about the scope of its prohibitions unanswered" (Swidriski 2022). This vagueness includes the meanings of "classroom instruction," "age-appropriate," and "developmentally appropriate" in Florida's law. The law engenders several questions: "Is it a violation of the law for a school library to carry, or for a teacher to assign, a book featuring an LGBTQ+ character? If a student who has gay parents draws a picture of her family, can the teacher display it along with the other students' drawings? Is a teacher allowed to say anything if a student is being bullied because of their gender identity or sexual orientation?" (Swidriski 2022). Critics thus argue that this lack of clarity challenges not only free speech protections but "threatens basic principles of academic freedom" (Swidriski 2022).

The Southern Poverty Law Center filed multiple federal lawsuits in opposition to Florida's Don't Say Gay law (HB1557) in 2022.[25] The suits hinge on free speech and argue that the law "effectively silences and erases LGBTQ+ students and families, violating the right to free speech and expression protected by the First Amendment and the due process and equal protection clauses of the 14th Amendment" (SPLC 2022). As interim deputy legal director for the Southern Poverty Law Center's Children's Rights Practice Group, Bacardi Jackson, states,

> Children should not be the political fodder used to inflame hatred and bigotry for the sake of winning and holding onto power. But that's exactly what this unconstitutional law seeks to do. The real lives and identities of all of our children and their families are not words on a page that can just be edited out, nor should they be. All of us, and our democracy, are irreparably harmed when people, and especially children, are relegated, made invisible, and targeted for who they are or who they love. This law cannot stand. (SPLC 2022)

One plaintiff, student Will Larkins at Winter Park High School in Orange County, notes, "I am concerned that this law will eviscerate any hope of healthy and important discussions about LGBTQ+ issues or historical events, which are already lacking in our schools." Larkins continues, "Because of the vague language of the law, closed-minded parents are emboldened to become vigilantes to force their beliefs upon other people's children by suing the school district over anything they disagree with" (SPLC 2022). Other plaintiffs echoed the William's Institute's findings that the law would "force us to self-censor for fear of prompting responses from our children's teachers and classmates that would isolate our children and make them feel ashamed of their own family" (SPLC 2022). Similarly, plaintiffs Jennifer and Matthew Cousins were concerned that their four children would be unable to discuss "their older nonbinary sibling in the classroom for fear of their teacher or their school getting in trouble" (SPLC 2022).

These various studies, legal criticisms, and lawsuits all demonstrate the vicissitudes of LGBTQ+ parents, students, and educators, that more harm than good will result from these types of laws. Studies show, as Frank (2023) demonstrates in his editorial alongside the William's Institute and Cornell University's What We Know Public Policy Research Portal, that there is a correlation between restrictive laws such as Florida's Don't Say Gay law and parental and familial fear and concern for their child and the family's well-being. Increased stigmatization and even suicidal ideation arise, whereby positive messaging and acceptance yield positive results for LGBTQ+ students, educators, and families.

Therefore, Frank (2023) declares, "policies of equal treatment can help—even just by virtue of the affirming messages they send." As Frank concludes,

> We know so much about what hurts and helps LGBTQ youth. It is heartbreaking to watch lawmakers pass bills that are *known* to cause harm and whose only upside is scoring political points. Laws like these don't actually give parents any more rights than they currently have, while the damage they cause is already palpable, with students sharing more and more stories of censorship, isolation and fear. When combined with book bans and limits on transition-related care, along with a restrictive federal bill passed by the Republican-controlled House, the landscape for L.G.B.T.Q. youth looks grim. We know how to make these young lives better. We also know how to make them worse. The question is whether the adults actually care.

Laws that aim to protect might actually result in greater harm for social minorities. Yet Frank's invocation of adults pits them against youth, that the adults are the ones who make the necessary decisions that regulate and control the lives of youth. While Frank asks if adults actually care, the question is slightly misplaced because the impetus behind the wave of Don't Say Gay laws and parents' bills of rights sweeping the country is supposedly care. Parents and lawmakers care so much about their child's well-being that they will go to such extreme lengths to protect them. Frank might see this as rather ludicrous—that it is not care but harm emanating from these laws—but the framing of care and protection is important for understanding how these laws and policies operate. Care and protection here become technologies of the American security apparatus and quintessential to contemporary security logics and practices. As I explore below, dissecting these frames and panicked and sieving scripts demonstrates how security weaves through these contemporary sex panics about sex education.

If You See Something, Say Something: An Aside

The deluge of Don't Say Gay laws and the older no homo promo laws and even Don't Ask, Don't Tell all hinge on the restriction of what can be *said*. The restriction of the speech act renders what is potentially said as dangerous, as corrupting, and ultimately, as a threat. I wish to dwell briefly on the act of saying, on speech acts, as forms of security invocation and participation. To do so, I move somewhat laterally to another campaign of sorts: the Department of Homeland Security's If You See Something, Say Something campaign. The campaign encourages citizens to report suspicious activities and objects to authorities as a method of preventing acts of violence by supposed terrorists. It creates a form of "lateral surveillance" that empowers citizens with renewed responsibility for the safety and security of the nation (Reeves 2012; Gitzen 2023). As Joseph Masco (2014, 18) writes of national security in a post-9/11 landscape, "The goal of a national security system is to produce a citizen-subject who responds to officially designated signs of danger automatically, instinctively activating logics and actions learned over time through drills and media indoctrination."

According to both Masco (2014) and Deepa Kumar (2018), these security logics and the antecedents to If You See Something, Say Something emerged during the Cold War. Kumar refers to these types of campaigns, including Cold War–era practices like air-raid drills and duck-and-cover drills, as "security rituals." She defines security rituals as "the routinized and repetitive performance of security practices" that contributes as "a particular national ritual that sustains US militarism (Kumar 2018, 144). She continues, "The security ritual *as a form*, I argue, transcends the Cold War . . . it is central to the production and reproduction of a form of US nationalism that elevates security" whereby "the resultant security nationalism then creates a climate in which US militarism is normalized" (Kumar 2018, 145). For Kumar, these forms of security rituals enshrine US nationalism as the goal or "resultant" of said practices, but it also makes these practices themselves nationalist rituals, rituals that work to create and uphold the US nation.[26] In a similar vein, Simone Browne (2015, 137) refers to these types of practices, especially at airports, as "security theater," whereby theater is interpreted as a "military metaphor" and "must be understood not only as about the staging of security and the theatrical performance that passengers must successfully comply with in order to pass through screening zones, but also as reflecting the airport screening zone as a military theater of operations, a place where security in the domestic War on Terror is observed and upheld."[27] Bringing Browne and Kumar into conversation with one another demonstrates how the rituals are done in almost theatrical form, for not only do these rituals create and uphold US nationalism, but they also uphold a sieving form of segregation: who is a person of concern, and who is not?

The acts of seeing something and then saying something not only relies on the object or act under suspicion—that suspicion itself is a constructed state of being—but also the vigilance of the subject doing the seeing and saying. R. Guy Emerson (2022, 615) suggests, "Vigilance occurs prior to seeing something: it is apparent in the perceptual processes that ultimately allow for unusual items to be spotted. And vigilance occurs prior to saying something: it is apparent in the coming into thought that will eventually sustain decisions on how best to respond to danger. Vigilance operates in the formative processes that allow for vigilant subjects and risky objects; processes integral, and yet anterior, to the discovery of any securitized form." Such vigilance, according to Masco (2014), is part of a security education, one that often happens affectively and unconsciously (Gitzen 2023). Seeing something and then saying something is a dual process to the construction of vigilance, which is an "amalgam of seeing and saying something, of drawing a risky object from an uncertain field so as to ensure that what was unknown to authorities is made manifest" (Emerson 2022, 615). In short, the riskiness of the object does not exist *a priori* to the object or the subject seeing the object. It is "made manifest" in the act of seeing the object as risky and then telling the authorities about its perceived riskiness. The authorities become the arbiter of what actually counts as risky. Not all things one sees and says, according to Masco (2014, 28), are reportable, for multiple "objects" are rejected despite them being "quite capable of producing fear and terror: homelessness and poverty, decaying infrastructure and toxic environments, and extreme weather, to name but a few."

The security rituals and theater of seeing something and saying something extend into other more immediate forms of domestic terrorism, namely school shootings. In the wake of the December 14, 2012, shooting at Sandy Hook Elementary School that killed twenty-six individuals, including twenty children no older than seven, the national nonprofit organization Sandy Hook Promise was formed. One of the programs of Sandy Hook Promise is called "Say Something." This program "teaches elementary, middle, and high school students to recognize the warning signs of someone *at risk* of hurting themselves or others and how to say something to a trusted adult to get help" (Sandy Hook Promise 2023; emphasis added). The program does this by helping students "build essential SEL [social-emotional learning] competencies, including how to empathize with others and seek help when needed (relational skills) and how to identify problems and analyze situations, as well as solve problems in an ethically-responsible manner (responsible decision-making)" (Sandy Hook Promise 2023). Sandy Hook Promise refers to this program as a "proven, life-saving program."

In addition to education, the program also features the "Say Something Anonymous Reporting System" that allows individuals to "safely and anonymously surface *potential threats* before they happen" (Sandy Hook Promise 2023; emphasis added). While I discuss the notion of reporting bullies in chapter 5, I want to briefly dwell on the impetus and mechanism by which one "says something." The program's invocation of "surfac[ing] potential threats before they happen" is part and parcel of the anticipatory logic of security, where the point is to preempt potential threats in the present moment (Amoore 2013). While a post-9/11 landscape contributes to such an approach to risk, the rise in school shootings similarly contributes to this approach, especially for domestic terrorists and a kind of backyard security theater, to invoke Browne (2015). Therefore, the point of saying something is to prevent something from happening, namely a school shooting (or suicide, as the program addresses both). The mechanisms to say something—a mobile app, a website, and a telephone hotline—allow for anonymity and thus encourage the form of "lateral surveillance" that is the cornerstone of the If You See Something, Say Something campaign (Reeves 2012).

While the prevention of school shootings is of paramount importance, undeniably so, and Sandy Hook Promise does claim that this is a "proven, life-saving program," I want to draw attention to the continued securitization of education and the school, a notion I revisit in chapter 5. Here, however, my point is that educating students to know the warning signs, to be vigilant by "seeing something" and then being *responsible* by "saying something," security has woven into the daily lives of children in rather unexpected—though seemingly unavoidable—ways. I am left with a question, informed explicitly by my earlier research (Gitzen 2023) and Toby Beauchamp's important book *Going Stealth* (2019) about the intertwining of US security and surveillance practices and transgender politics: what actually counts as a potential threat, and might nonnormative individuals—or individuals behaving contrary to what one deems normative behavior—be reportable? Beauchamp (2019) recalls a 2008 American Express advertising campaign that somewhat preempted the If You See Something, Say Something campaign. In the advertisement, a man with a credit card covered in kittens is seen as suspicious and thus security is called over to deal with the man, while another man with a plain American Express Gold Card is treated as a preferred customer. The latter man's gender normativity renders him acceptable while the seeming gender nonnormativity of the former marks him as a threat. Beauchamp's point, and the root of my question, lies in that nonnormativity as reportable—for while, according to Masco (2014, 28), "social structures of abandonment" are not reportable or addressed by national security with this campaign, the campaign clearly reifies normative gender and sexuality.

Who, then, gets anonymously reported when they are less of a threat and rather fall outside the confines of normative gender and sexuality? With regard to the deluge of Don't Say Gay laws sweeping the country, how might the very mention of gender identity and sexual orientation be read as a threat? Are these laws thus similar to the Say Something program that encourages reporting? And who suffers, who gets labeled as a threat, in response? I contend that, as demonstrated throughout this chapter, it will be gender and sexual nonnormative individuals, including queer students.

Securitizing Sex

Moving from DADT to no homo promo laws to Don't Say Gay laws is meant to draw genealogical connections between different queer discriminatory laws that hinge on the speech acts of saying gay. While I discuss in more detail J. L. Austin's (1975) distinction between illocutionary and perlocutionary speech acts in chapter 3—the former being a speech act that speaks into immediate existence the object said, and the latter producing an effect that follows from the speech act—I want to briefly dwell further on the idea that saying gay is a speech act in need of regulation. Saying gay, invoking Irvine (2002), would speak into existence nonnormative sexualities and behaviors. This may work as either an illocutionary or perlocutionary act, for by saying gay the possibility of gay now exists, though the effect of that speech act may not come fully to fruition until the future. It is the fact that saying gay in the present may have future effects that engenders panic, for we supposedly do not know the full effects of what the speech act as perlocutionary act has in store, particularly for children.

Regulating the speech act thus compares to the If You See Something, Say Something campaign that hinges on the expression of the speech act as, again, both illocutionary and perlocutionary speech act. On the one hand, as illocutionary speech act, saying something manifests the risk of the object or observed act into existence in the moment of utterance. Yet on the other hand, the effects of that utterance may not be immediate; what happens to the object or the suspicious person one observed and reported?

The laws examined above, including the lateral movement into the If You See Something, Say Something campaign, all work to securitize sex and sexuality. While securitization theory may focus primarily on things said—on the interplay between discourse and practice in a social field—regulating what is said through laws and policies is itself a securitization practice. Not saying gay because of laws, being limited to what one can talk about, is also a way one participates in security and demonstrates how one lives a securitized life. Again, these laws aim to reduce corruptibility of the child and, by extension, the family and nation—both central concerns for national security—and so partaking in such regulations, not saying gay, is regulating speech acts and manifesting security in the moment the speech act is *not* said.

Whether schools and school boards are banning books or banning words, restricting what is said and read—what one has exposure to—is a decidedly securitized practice. It is not enough to say that the goals of these regulations—the protection of children, and, by extension, the family and nation—are what make such practices security practices. Rather, it is the amalgamation of goals, mechanisms, and temporalities that render sex panics like Florida's Don't Say Gay law or nationwide book banning security panics. The expressed goal may be the protection of the child's innocence, but it is done by regulating speech, by regulating access; by imagining futures where uncertainty reigns supreme and preparing for that uncertainty in the present, we are working to preempt that potential catastrophe. In short, considering sex panics as discourses and practices of security, as security panics, enables us to gleam the interwoven mechanisms and ideologies that inform both, to see how sex continues to be a concern for security, and evaluate just how violent the fears on which sex panics rely are when threaded with security.

That both parents' rights and opposition to Don't Say Gay laws invoke the family—that families will suffer, one way or another, if either these laws are passed *or not*—mark family as the quintessential institution in need of protection. For proponents of these laws, the family is saved and protected by limiting children's access to information and potential speech acts. But for opponents of these laws, the family is protected from attacks on free speech and individual sexual freedom of both parents and children by doing away with such regulations and methods of control. Securitization works in both instances, both in the promulgation of sex panics and in its opposition because the terms of the debate—family and nation—are representative of fundamental security concerns and thus it may be nearly impossible to have a public debate without it pointing us toward broader security concerns of the family and the nation.

Chapter Two

Radical Presentism

> Welcome to the present. Say Goodbye to the past. The future is dead.
>
> —*Teenage Kiss: The Future Is Dead*

Youth temporally fluctuate, a look back for adults remembering their own childhood. Caught between a past and a future, the child is foreclosed a present, their experiences interpreted within the preset ontological pathways of maturation, growing up, coming-of-age, and becoming an adult (and, thus, a full-fledged person). The child or youth's sexuality, too, is a continuous look back at a moment that matured in the future. The motto of the Brazilian HBO Max show discussed in the preface, *Teenage Kiss* (2023), and shared in this chapter's epigraph, highlights this tension in temporality, both the fluctuation and a youth-centered approach that favors the present over both the past and the future. For the queer youth of *Teenage Kiss*, the future holds their inevitable fate and transformation into adults—a future they would rather not face—and thus they find meaning, intimacy, and relationality in the lateral movements they take in the here and now.

The *Teenage Kiss* motto also acts as a bridge between the sex panics and future orientation discussed in the previous chapter and the lateral movements queer youth take in the immediate present in this and subsequent chapters. If the future is where security lies, but comes at the cost of adulthood and monochromatism, then living and moving in the present becomes queer youth's best option. And as I shall illustrate in this chapter, bucking against security's futurity enables a radical way of living and relating in the present.

Take the now oft criticized "It Gets Better" liberal campaign and coming-of-age narrative that featured a range of celebrities and contributors on video explaining to queer youth contemplating suicide or self-harm that while things may be difficult now, as many of those in the videos can attest, things get better later. The mere invocation of getting better is fraught with not only class privilege but white (male) privilege, started by US author and LGBTQ+ activist Dan Savage and his partner. As Jasbir Puar (2017, 10) opines, It Gets Better "reflects a desire for the reinstatement of (white) racial privilege that was lost by being gay, one that is achievable through equality rights agendas like gay marriage and participation in neoliberal consumer culture. In other words, [It Gets Better] is based on an expectation that it was supposed to be better."[1] As I explore in chapter 5, the emphasis placed on homophobia and bullying in the wake of queer teen suicide and the It Gets Better campaign ignores the structural and institutional conditions that enable bullying, homophobia, and suicide. The focus on the individual bully relegates the suicide as neoliberally individual rather than part of a much larger problem of whiteness or white supremacy and gender and sexuality-based discrimination.

But the It Gets Better campaign also displaces the present experience for promises that may not ever materialize—things may, in fact, get worse. These videos feature adults talking about their own experiences of when they were young and how things got better, how their then insecure presents led to safe and secure futures. The youth watching bear witness to the adults' past suffering and insecurity and are to embody that past self, midcrisis and suffering, on their teleological journey of becoming better-off, more secure adults. It is a coming-of-age tale that, like all coming-of-age narratives, not only looks back on youth from the perspective of the adult, but assumes a linear temporality of growing *up,* getting *older,* and becoming *secure.*

Part of the way things get better, or so we are told in this coming-of-age narrative, is by finding one's community of queers that are like-minded and of similar propensity whereby one feels at "home" with those around them. Here, too, is a look to the future without consideration of the present. On the one hand, the queer community one finds is often imagined existing post-youth. For instance, in the 2020 Hulu coming-of-age show *Love, Victor*—a follow-up to the 2018 film *Love, Simon*—Simon, the protagonist from the film and current college student in New York

City, tells Victor, a high school student in Atlanta's suburbs, that he will be able to find his people after high school. Simon explains that once he graduated from high school and moved to New York City, he found a community of people that accepted him, people that are queer, trans, and nonbinary. Simon is instructing Victor to wait, to endure until later when he can get himself to a metropole like New York City (Weston 1995; Gray 2009), because only later are the gates to the queer community opened. As Puar (2017, 7) writes of Savage's It Gets Better video, "[H]is message translates to: come out, move to a city, travel to Paris, adopt a kid, pay your taxes, demand representation; save yourself; that's how it's done."

On the other hand, the insistence of seeking queer communities and connections becomes a moralizing proclamation for youth, as if the connections they have already formed are somehow not good enough or not queer enough to shepherd the youngling into their decidedly queer future. Waiting also implies spatialized deferment, where not only the now but the here is seemingly insufficient for forming *true* queer subjectivity; one must wait to find one's people elsewhere, in the metropole. Puar (2017, 7) continues: "The focus on the future normalizes the present tense of teen bullying and evacuates the politics of the now from culpability, letting contemporary conditions, along with any politics attempting to redress it, off the hook."[2] I would add, as I explore in this chapter, that the focus on the future displaces the possibility of what can happen in the here and now—future communities hide the importance of present relationalities.

It is not my intention to upend the importance and meaning of queer communities, the historical necessity of communities that enabled survival, endurance, and change. I also recognize that many queer youths do not have supportive friends or networks in high school and are thus in search of their "people," but this also happens in the present. Rather, following Kadji Amin (2017), I note the utopic vision of queerness, queer culture, and queer communities—what Amin names as *idealization*—to refocus attention onto the present experiences and connections of queer youth without invoking a pastness or deferring to a future. *Radical presentism* is from the perspective of the child or youth themselves. It does not capitulate to the future, nor is it a nihilistic undertaking that washes away meaningfulness. Instead, radical presentism enables a durational perspective of one's life and sociality, as the connections one makes now (in high school, primarily) are meaningful in the here and now for navigating the ever-precarious present of the contemporary moment. José Esteban Muñoz's (2009, 20) conception of queerness as a condition of the not yet future, a disposition that orients one toward "what could be, what should be," deftly leads us to the importance of relationality. Yet where Muñoz contends that "queerness is not quite here" (2009, 21), I suggest a heterotopic narrative in which queer youth are firmly concerned with the queerness of the here and now rather than the utopic placelessness of the coming-of-age narrative and its antecedents like the It Gets Better campaign. *Teenage Kiss* nicely encapsulates this notion of radical presentism, for the teens in the show are wholly concerned not with their impending future and the illness that befalls all adults when they turn eighteen but with the intimacy and relationality experienced in the present. The kisses they continuously share throughout the show embody this radical presentism and the importance of relationality in the here and now.

I examine the heterotopia of radical presentism by exploring a narrative of youth and queer sexuality stitched together in the Norwegian teen web drama *Skam* (translated as "Shame," produced by public television channel NRK P3 and broadcast from 2015 to 2017) and its now seven international adaptations that began airing since 2018. Each iteration takes place at a high school and features a cast of relatively unknown actors as they navigate daily life, with each season spotlighting a different character and their "shame." I focus specifically on the story of Isak Valtersen, the central character of season three of *Skam*, and his counterparts in *Skam France, Skam Italia,* and *wtFOCK* (the Belgian adaptation; see table 1 for a detailed breakdown of characters, counterparts, seasons, and dates of broadcasting). For most of the season, Isak (and his counterparts) struggles with his sexuality, intensified by his attraction to and budding relationship with Even, a transfer student who we learn near the end of the season is bipolar. Rather than narrate queer youth intelligibility through risk, danger, or the "well-adjusted, out, and proud gay youth" (Talburt 2004, 18), *Skam* and its iterations stay with the awkwardness and unease, the incompleteness or unfinishedness and continuous confusion emergent in the nexus of youth sexuality, friendship, mental health, and love. There is no insistence for Isak to "find his people" or socialize into a queer community or culture; Isak's openly gay roommate, Eskild, never makes such a suggestion even after Isak admits to Eskild that he and Even have "a thing." Instead, Isak comes to understand and even accept his sexuality through his interactions with his existing friends, as Even also does not provide Isak the space to discuss his general feelings or attractions toward boys. He and his friends engage in what anthropologist Mary Gray (2009, 21) calls "queer-identity work . . . the collective labor of crafting, articulating, and pushing the boundaries of identities . . . labor carried out among and through people, places, media texts, and a host of other circuitous routes." In short, the solution for Isak's sexual insecurity is not a queer community but the queering of community, or rather, a queering of Isak's consideration of community, his friend group, and sociality as he learns that his friends are nothing but supportive of him. Some of the other iterations of the show interject added drama into this important realization, as I discuss below, but the point is not an idealization of Isak's existing sociality as much as it is a recognition that Isak's shame is a piece of a much larger mosaic of teen shame and precarity that only teens themselves can navigate and resolve.

Skam is groundbreaking in not only its format, as discussed below, but its intentional focus on teenage shame (Krüger and Rustad 2019). Sara Ahmed (2004, 103) insists that shame is an embodied response that one feels, an "exposure—another sees what I have done that is bad and hence shameful—but it also involves an attempt to hide, a hiding that requires the subject turn away from the other and towards itself." It is this inward turn, this intense introspection to hide one's shame, that also renders one's actions as "simultaneously a turning away from [oneself]" (Ahmed 2004, 104). Sally Munt (2007, 2) makes an analogous claim as to the embodied characteristic of shame, writing that "shame can become embedded in the self like a succubus" whereby "the fleshy intransigence of shame means that it can take an unusual grasp of a person's whole organism, in their body, soul and mind, sometimes in eccentric ways." The totalizing emotion of shame "sticks" to us in ways that make it seem unremovable, irreplaceable, and thus render us as perhaps unrecognizable. All these effects manifest in *Skam*, particularly in season three with Isak, and thus my use of *Skam* is meant to tap into the actual shame that queer youth experience.

Table 1. *Skam* Character Chart.

	Skam	Skam France	Skam Italia	wtFROCK
Run dates	2015–2017	2018–2023	2018–present	2018–2023
Protagonist	Isak	Lucas	Martino (Marti)	Robbe
Love interest	Even	Elliott	Niccolo (Nicco)	Sander
Gay friend	Eskild	Mika	Filippo	Milan

Source: Created by the author.

In the realm of shame and the child or teen, the child's realization of their sexuality (and nudity) brings with it shame for the child and the shame of the child (Angelides 2019). In response to photographer Bill Henson's 2008 exhibit that featured photos of a nude child, Steven Angelides (2019, 9) writes that this photo is read as a portrayal of shame: "[I]t is that [Henson] has captured an image that so resoundingly resonates with cultural narratives about the oft-referred loss or shattering of childhood innocence [. . .] it is an image of self-awareness intricately entangled with the knowledge of one's nakedness, the social strictures around the presentation of nude bodies, and an internalized understanding of privacy with regard to one's genitals." According to Angelides (2019, 11), shame becomes a way to regulate sexuality, "the appropriate norms of sexual expression and interaction."

Particularly salient are the material realities that *Skam* demonstrates with regard to the shame of queer folks, in general, and queer teens in particular. David J. Allen and Terry Oleson's (1999) landmark study demonstrates the correlation between shame and internalized homophobia in gay men, and illustrates the inverse relation between internalized homophobia and self-esteem. For queer youth, shame is prevalent in their daily lives, including their interactions with (social) media. As Sander De Ridder and Sofie Van Bauwel (2015) illustrate, shame about one's sexuality may often limit how one interacts online, the profiles one produces, and the subsequent feelings one has of oneself. One of their interlocutors notes that "most gay people are ashamed of being gay; therefore, I think they will not put this on their profiles very clearly" (De Ridder and Van Bauwel 2015, 784). Shame also frames how queer youth may interact with their families, for as Lynne Hiller and Lyn Harrison (2004, 86) report of Australian queer youth, "Some young people were concerned that disclosing their sexual preferences would bring shame upon their families and that this in turn would bring shame upon them." It is also important to consider race and religion, as I discuss in subsequent chapters, in the production of shame for queer youth (and adults) for these intersectional forms of shame-based oppression might manifest differently in these queer youth (e.g., Javaid 2020). However, some queer youth find ways to counteract or avoid their shame through strategies of minimizing homophobia, focusing on individual responsibilities, and substituting shame with pride (McDermott, Rohen, and Scourfield 2008; De Ridder and Van Bauwell 2015).[3]

Each season of *Skam* also provides a similar rejoinder to the central character's shame, namely that while shame may be individuated to the person and confronted by the central character, the broader precarity that gives rise to the character's shame is best mitigated through relationality. Yet the third season nuances this equation with temporality, derived not necessarily from Isak's sexuality but from Even's bipolar condition. After Isak learns that Even is bipolar and the two talk following one of Even's depressive episodes, Even laments that he does not think the two of them will work because "I'm just going to hurt you and then you'll hate me" (episode 10). Isak objects: "You don't know shit about how this is going to end. I mean, we might get a nuclear bomb dropped on our heads tomorrow and, and then discussing this is just a waste of time. So I suggest you just screw talking about the future and then the two of us will just take this thing completely chill." Isak then offers up a game for the two of them to play titled "Isak and Even: Minute by Minute," whereby they only consider what they will do in the next minute. Isak's minute-by-minute philosophy, as a response to Even's counterparts insisting that they will just hurt Isak's counterparts because of their condition, slows down time while deepening relationality. The focus is not on moving through the present into the future but rather on feeling the present, experiencing it, and maneuvering laterally. Lateral movements at once draw attention to the way "time binds" within future-oriented capitalist societies, to invoke queer theorist Elizabeth Freeman (2010, 3), and how such binding engenders "chrononormativity, or the use of time to organize individual human bodies towards maximum productivity." The very coming-of-age narrative forecloses the ability for children and youth to dillydally, to be present, as it relies on the chrononormativity of capitalist production implicit to adulthood: things will get better, surely, when one has stable employment and is a productive member of society.[4] "In Western cultures, we chart the emergence of the adult from the dangerous and unruly period of adolescence as a desired process of maturation; and we create longevity as the most desirable future, applaud the pursuit of long life . . . and pathologize modes of living that show little or no concern for longevity" (Halberstam 2005, 17).

Lateral maneuvers thus inject a necessary queerness into temporality, coalescing "points of resistance to this temporal order that, in turn, propose other possibilities for living in relation to indeterminately past, present, and future others: that is, of living historically" (Freeman 2010, xxii). Judith (Jack) Halberstam (2005, 14) makes an analogous observation regarding the notion of queer time, for in addition to being about "annihilation" in the wake of the AIDS crisis, "it is also about the potentiality of a life *unscripted* by the conventions of family, inheritance, and child rearing" (emphasis added). *Skam* offers a way for the characters to move laterally, to unshackle themselves from the demarcations of an adult-created and curated narrative of growing up and coming-of-age (Stockton 2009; Bruhm and Hurley 2004)—to unscript their present—and to embrace and reside in the messiness of being queer (Freeman 2010, xxi).

This is what I am calling *radical presentism*, for in refashioning the relationship in terms of duration—worried only about how they will move through and experience each minute—Isak divests from a future too far distant, a promise of things getting better as well as any underlying suggestions that he will more fully understand himself and his sexuality once he finds "his people." Isak's philosophy, though, exceeds the season and his own immediate experiences; it reverberates through the entire show, each character, and even into the very format of the series. As I discuss in the next section, *Skam* (and its adaptations) traded conventional television format for a segmented and transmedia format, uploading short clips (between one to five minutes) throughout the week in real time to the series' website, including as well relevant social media posts that the characters made. The clips were then stitched together to form an "episode" and aired Friday nights on NRK3.

Minute by minute thus braids the ideological, textual, and mechanical foundations of the series and each of its adaptations, but it also weaves through a narrative of queer youth that emerges in the series. In short, such radical presentism is a youth-oriented temporality, a temporality that allows—even facilitates—lateral movements that explode the chrononormativity of the coming-of-age narrative. My goal is to demonstrate how the show projects alternative ways that youth, especially queer youth, navigate through and engage with relationality in the now, representing a nascent basis for a heterotopic articulation of queer youth identity and possibilities for thriving. The show and its adaptations stitch together a narrative that challenges the teleology of coming-of-age narratives like "It Gets Better," staying with the messiness and unfinishedness of youth, and thus queers community by embracing one's immediate community rather than deferring it for later. As a narrative of radical presentism, minute by minute provides new language for a queer politics that embraces youth on their own, "unfinished" terms instead of the deferred adulthood and queer metropolitan utopia implicit in coming-of-age narratives such as the "it gets better" narrative. But rather than solely a polemic critiquing these narratives, minute by minute takes the precariousness of both the present and the future as given and offers a method of durational maneuverability and endurance.

On Epistemology and Worlding

The transmedia format and subsequent multimodal reading of *Skam* begins with the show's conception and purpose. One clear motivation for the show was to reverse the mass exodus of Norwegian teenage television viewers since the 1990s to other platforms (Krüger and Rustad 2019), and so *Skam* was the latest in NRK's online teenage dramas that first emerged in 2007 (Sundet 2020). Telling, however, is *Skam* writer and director Julie Andem's admission that "the public service broadcaster's responsibility is the spine of the show—we do not produce *Skam* to make money!" (Andem in Krüger and Rustad 2019, 76).[5] I am less concerned with the validity of Andem's declaration than her invocation of NRK's responsibility as a public broadcaster, as her implication is that *Skam* emerges from a responsibility to serve the public's welfare as a common good: "*Skam*'s public service mission is to show its teenage audiences how to live well while transitioning through the challenges of their formative years in a media-saturated culture full of risks, pitfalls, and temptations but also of joyful possibilities" (Krüger and Rustad 2019, 76). The material reality of shame in the lives of youth (including queer youth) thus supposedly forms the bedrock of *Skam*, representing not only the shame teens experience and feel but also potential paths forward in the youth's precarious present. The challenge NRK and *Skam* creators faced was to fulfill this responsibility by narrating teenage transition without moralizing the teenager from the perspective of the adult, to make youth intelligible to themselves rather than to adults (Talburt 2004).[6] Andem and social media manager Mari Magnus thus utilized the needs, approach, benefits, and competition model NRK employed with past shows to obtain "in-depth information on Norwegian teens, in order to portray them in a relevant and realistic way, but also identify and uncover how the new online drama concept could serve the needs of this particular audience" (Sundet 2020, 74).[7] The research began with an admission that their target audience would be sixteen-year-old girls, and so they underwent four months of preproduction research, conducting around fifty in-depth three-hour interviews along with "speed interviews" with two hundred school classes (Redvall 2018, 151). Magnus noted that these in-depth interviews in particular helped creators avoid moralizing practices, "forcing the [*Skam*] team to hear about the world from the perspective of the young girls rather than having preconceived, and maybe moralising, ideas form an adult perspective" (Redvall 2018, 152). Moreover, the *Skam* team also relied heavily on input from the teenage actors themselves during production, along with audience comments on the online materials in developing storylines (Krüger and Rustad 2019, 77).[8] The effect of the research, unknown actors, and constant input—coupled with the format as described below—was a show that featured characters and storylines "so close to reality that it could be true" (Nyborg in Sundet 2020, 74). An added benefit that NRK and the *Skam* team soon realized was the advantage such a deep-dive into the Norwegian teen had when compared to the big-budget US drama series, and the ways such closeness to the source (the Norwegian teen) would resonate globally (Sundet 2020, 75).[9]

Past NRK online teen dramas, such as *MIA* (2010–12) and *Jenter/Girls* (2013–17), instituted what became the key novelty and innovation of *Skam*, namely a "character-driven" series that was "revealed" in real time with video clips, pictures, and chat messages uploaded to the *Skam* website (Sundet 2020).[10] Each clip is time-stamped at the start in yellow block lettering and uploaded at that time on that particular day. Pictures and chat messages are derived from the relevant video clip uploaded, also in real time. For instance, the text exchange between Isak and Even after their first kiss (episode 5) was uploaded to the *Skam* website at the same time Isak and Even texted each other (Sunday at 17:32). Most of the characters also had Instagram accounts, operated by Magnus and her team, that would post throughout the series, considered "in world" and canonical to the actual series. This transmedia distribution facilitated the multimodal viewing, as creators recognized that most of the audience would likely be watching on their smartphones at different junctures throughout the day, and so this strategy "embedded *Skam* as deeply as possible into the mediatized lives of its main audiences" (Krüger and Rustad 2019, 77).[11] The irregularity of the real-time distribution model meant that audiences would need to constantly check the *Skam* website (Sundet 2020, 78), particularly given that a key feature of *Skam* was the utter lack of advertisement of the series, as it was meant to be found and shared by teens themselves.

The disinterest in advertising, akin to Andem's insistence that *Skam* was not made to accumulate money, enables a temporality not predicated on capitalist production. It engenders what Halberstam (2005) calls "queer time," as the emphasis is placed on the experiences of young people rather than the inscription of adults' desires and beliefs—intelligibility—onto the bodies of adolescents. The wandering of teens to find and share the show mirrors the wandering made possible in queer time in lateral movement as the very notion of wandering, of being without focus and simply exploring the here and now, shrugs off attention to potential futures and growing up, and it resides radically in the present.

Approaching *Skam* and its adaptations through television studies enables consideration for different temporalities. In contrast to novels and films that have definitive ends, television shows are often more opaque about endings, in part because the end of one episode heralds the continuation of the show into the next episode. This is particularly true of serial dramas (rather than sitcoms, for instance, which may share story plots across episodes but are in and of themselves wholly contained within each episode). The time *between* television episodes as well allows for potential lateral movements, especially among fans as they discuss and comment on the show or engage in the production of fan fiction (Lindtner and Dahl 2020). This, in part, invokes Vilde Schanke Sundet's (2021b, 146) notion of "youthification" that "represents a central reference point for addressing current changes within the television industry and, more precisely, within online youth drama productions."[12]

Skam must also be interpreted, though, through the production deluge of streaming television, which interrupts the linearity of time and consumption (Sundet 2021a), on the one hand, and intensifies the experience of the present, on the other hand. Such a mode of "real-time" storytelling outlined above "thus adds immediacy and intimacy to the experience, allowing the users to live with the characters in a way that the regular television schedule of episodes or even binge watching does not allow" (Rustad 2018, 507). Here we witness the radical presentism of the series manifest in form and distribution, where the series exists durationally across the week in short transmedia form rather than wholly contained in a thirty-minute television time slot. In Isak's words, the show quite literally takes things "minute by minute." The fragmentation of distribution equally contributed to greater audience involvement and commenting, not just a commentary of the media itself but an interaction with the media and other audience members, including the production of fan fiction (Lindtner and Dahl 2020; Sundet 2020, 2021a, 2021b; Krüger and Rustad 2019; Bengtsson, Källquist, and Sveningsson 2018). Synnøve Skarsbø Lindtner and Johh Magnus Dahl (2019, 55) argue that such commentary and fan interaction also signal a type of "civic talk and discussions connecting people to public discourse," whereby *Skam* may ultimately be "conceptualised as a resource for citizenship."[13] Each adaptation followed almost the same format, from fragmented and irregular distribution to embedding the series into the lives of its audiences through social media: there was a continuous blurring of the world of *Skam* and the "real" world (the world of the audience encapsulated in social networking sites like Facebook and Instagram).

In addition to television studies, however, I argue that an anthropological approach to *Skam* proffers a useful set of considerations in comparing adaptations and highlighting the temporality of queer youth sexuality. The more common anthropological approach to media involves audience studies. *Skam* and its adaptations created a mediated world that attempted to intertwine the world and characters of the series with its audiences, whereby the characters were perceived as not wholly separate from the audience watching but as one of their friends, an acquaintance, someone with shared sociality. To the anthropologist, this mediated world is ethnographically and theoretically rich, bridging earlier anthropological studies into television and media (e.g., Ginsburg, Abu-Lughod, Larkin 2002; Lukacs 2010; Mankekar 1999; Abu-Lughod 2005) with more recent digital anthropological studies (e.g., Boellstorff 2008; Boellstorff et al. 2012; Nardi 2010). However, if the show's distribution model encourages a radical presentism in its audience—where the audience experiences watching clips, waiting for text replies, and interacting in real time, what Sundet (2020, 78) calls a "double liveliness"[14] (see also Fuller 2019)—then while these mediated worlds can certainly reverberate throughout an individual's life, that experience is attainable only in those moments. In other words, the show encourages one to experience its unfolding in real time, as that experience is quintessential to the series and mediated world. We could refer to this as media ideologies, "a set of beliefs about communicative technologies with which users and designers explain perceived media structures . . . what people think about the media they use will shape the way they use media" (Gershon 2010, 3).[15] What then for those, like me, who watched the collected weekly clips as an "episode" rather than the fragmented distribution throughout the week? How are we to both experience the series and, for the anthropologist, interpret and decode its radical presentism?

Therefore, I offer a different mode of anthropological inquiry that moves through the show and its various adaptations, not only to compare "casts, linguistic practices, and performances, as well as production style and aesthetics to illuminate concepts of the self and sociality, the visual and visuality," but more fundamentally, to trace "epistemological difference . . . as an entry point for a textual reading" (Gershon 2019, 176). Some anthropologists have done this by analyzing reality television, be it the examination of classic anthropological concepts like primitivism and kinship in similar shows (Ball and Nozawa 2016), explication of social organization and capitalist critique in adaptations of the same reality television program (Gershon 2019), or even cross-cultural translations and interpretations of a program like *Iron Chef* (Lukacs 2010). *Skam* presents a unique anthropological opportunity to query the interstitial space of form, epistemology, and text, especially given the empirical and experiential research that continued to inform the show's development and the atypical format of the show as *not just* a television show. Complicating further this inquiry is that the adaptations of *Skam* utilized both its form and its storylines, so each iteration of Isak must come to terms with his sexuality via his attraction to Even's counterparts who we learn near the end is bipolar (or, in the Italian version, has borderline personality disorder). These are storylines driven by research into Norwegian teenagers, and yet they still powerfully resonate with their intended audiences. This was part of the strength that producers and creators found in *Skam*, that it was able to tell a fundamentally localized story and yet speak to global audiences and even desires (Sundet 2020, 75).

As such, my goal is to chart a hybrid course—weaving television studies and anthropology together—attending to the interplay of epistemology and text while taking seriously the worlding of *Skam* (Gitzen and Gershon 2024), not only as a Norwegian series and mediated world but also as interconnected to its adaptations. Here I borrow again from Isak, who explains to Even—while the two smoke, kiss, cuddle, and talk in Isak's bed—that he believes in parallel universes: "Everything that can happen, will happen" (season 3, episode 5). Isak provides the example of the curtains, where the two of them may be lying in the exact same place but the curtains in a parallel universe are yellow. Both Robbe and Lucas offer Sander and Elliott the same theory at this juncture in the series, all lying on a bed while contemplating the possibility of parallel worlds. If we suspend the scientific implications or accuracies of Isak's claim and instead consider the epistemological and textual mattering, Isak's multiverse theory connects the adaptations together in a constellational narrative: the local worlding of each individual version of *Skam* momentarily matters less than the assemblage of stories that produce a broader narrative, what anthropologist Susan Lepselter (2016) would call "narrative resonance."[16] Apropos, when I speak of a narrative of queer youth or youth sexuality, this is a narrative formed in this constellation, in these worldings that expand beyond Norway, France, Belgium, and Italy. In the remainder of this chapter, I attend to the epistemological and textual differences found in the narrative of queer youth, not to call into question the validity of the narrative but to illustrate how the pieces still resonate together to form a narrative that is in fact not over determined, totalizing, or wholly generalizable. I begin with the way sexuality is "thingified" by Isak and his counterparts as a way to keep a fluidity to his sexuality and subjectivity.

The "Thing" of Sexuality

Isak and his counterparts have an aversion toward labels. When Marti tells his friends about Nicco and him, his friends ask him if he is gay, to which Marti replies, "I'm not gay. I don't know actually. I'm not into all boys" (season 2, episode 7). Each also focuses primarily on the relationship with Even and his counterparts, for when each talks to the outwardly gay Eskild and his companions, they focus almost wholly on the relationship rather than their individual sexuality. By this point, Isak and company have each contemplated their sexualities and feelings for Even. This includes searching the Internet for "gay quizzes" and even signing up for the queer app Grindr, before quickly turning it off when inundated with messages. Prioritizing the relationship over individual sexuality is not necessarily a deflection of self-acceptance, though Isak and company all do struggle with internalized "homophobia" and issues of masculinity. Shame, for queer youth, as discussed above, is quite palpable and indicative of a broader historical trend regarding gay men, shame, and internalized homophobia (Allen and Oleson 1999). There is a shared moment for Isak and his friends watching a group of female dancers and their male instructor, to which Isak comments on the instructor's gayness. His friends retort by asking why that matters and why Isak is being critical of the instructor's perceived sexuality. Except for Lucas, each are not brought over to the side of "out and proud homosexual" once they accept their attraction and feelings for Even but rather are content with that acceptance. We witness Isak admitting that he has a "thing" with Even. Generative to a narrative of queer youth sexuality is the use of "thing" to talk about sexuality.

In *Skam*, "thing" becomes the way that not only Isak but others around him talk about his relationship with Even and even his burgeoning sexuality. Vilde, a rather nosy classmate, randomly texts Isak while he is in class, asking if he is gay. Isak, taken aback, asks where she heard that, to which Vilde replies that "someone said that you and that guy Even had a thing" (season 3, episode 7). In the final episode of the season, the same group of dancing girls featured earlier in the season randomly approach Isak to invite him to a party, noting that they hear that he "has a thing with Even, that guy in third year" (season 3, episode 10).

Associating "thing" with a particular sexuality is often averted. In one instance, Isak is talking to his friends and tells them that he and Even "had a thing." His friend Magnus asks if he is gay, but Isak replies that he is not gay: "Okay, maybe I'm a little bit gay then, but . . . it's not like . . . I'm not into you guys, for example. It's not like I'm attracted to every single guy I see" (season 3, episode 8). While Isak's response may in part be read as a defense of his sexuality, I read it as carving out the borders of his sexuality. Robbe, for instance, tells Milan that "because I have something with Sander" does not mean that Robbe is gay or is like Milan (season 3, episode 5). For Lucas, sexuality becomes even more of a thing when he talks to Mika, stating, "I can never be fully into the gay thing, you know?" Mika replies, upset, "Lucas, I'm not 'fully into the gay thing.' I'm just myself" (season 3, episode 5). Yet as Gray (2009, 168) argues of queer youth and the politics of visibility in rural United States,

> [I]n our media-saturated world, they [rural queer youth] are not isolated from narratives about queer difference. When they scan mass media and the Internet for materials to incorporate into their queer sense of self, a politics of LGBT visibility comes up on the screen. These representations organize recognition of queer difference through a grammar of narrowly defined LGBT identities, a "visible minority," underwritten by capital of urban counterpublics that have no equivalents in rural areas . . . the politics of LGBT visibility are literally built into the counterpublic landmarks that demarcate gay and lesbian urban community spaces.

While the rural/urban divide may not carry over to the world of *Skam*—the show took place in the capital of Oslo—I suggest that a similar politics of visibility permeates the show, namely that what Isak sees does not resonate with who he thinks he is or wants to be. Those are "counterpublics," to use Gray's language, "that have no equivalents" in Isak's life, despite being in a metropole.[17]

In linguistic anthropology, Isak's use of "thing" to explain both his relationship with Even and his sexuality may be termed an "avoidance register" (Mitchell 2018) or "mother-in-law register" (Fleming 2014), where "thing" is used to avoid specificity. "Thing" is both a general word that sidesteps specific identification (i.e., gay, boyfriend, lover) while also specifying one particular and contextual relationship with Even and his counterparts. It is both vague and pointed. Roman Jakobson (1971, 131) refers to this as a shifter, a word that "cannot be defined without reference to the message." As Julia Kursell (2010, 219) explains, "[T]he message guarantees that the temporal, spatial and personal meaning of words such as 'I,' 'now' and 'here' can be understood; the same applies to those verbal categories which Jakobson defines as 'shifters.'"[18] In *Skam*, "thing" is meaningful or definable once placed in relation to a "message," namely a relationship between Isak and Even. "We had/have a thing" implicates both the speaker (Isak) and the other (Even) in the plurality "we," whereby having the "thing" acts as referent to the undefinable characteristic of their relationship. This undefinable characteristic is partly due to Even's behaviour, which we later learn is part of his bipolar condition. "Thing" might thus be specified vis-à-vis the message or reference, but that message is also intentionally vague or nonspecific because Isak is both unsure of his relationship with Even and not committed to the concretization or labeling of his sexuality. As Robbe notes, despite the "something" he has with Sander, he is not necessarily a specific sexuality (i.e., gay).

The "coming out" experience of all iterations of Isak is that it is piecemeal, messy, and often not resolved with the declaration "I'm gay." Being gay is not where Isak's experience lies; it emerges from his interaction with and mutual attraction to Even, and so that experience is definitive of his "coming out." It happens in stages, and happens with friends who ultimately are just as messy and as much of a novice as Isak himself. We see in these instances Isak oriented toward already existing friends groups instead of looking past them to a queer community that has yet to come. Isak is queering his own community, imbricating his friends in his queerness through relationality. His friends and community are familiar, to again invoke Gray (2009, 38), "a semblance of sameness . . . [that] purchases something valued . . . [and contributes to] the sense of familiarity and belonging so central to structures of rural life." Despite each adaptation taking place in a city, Gray's attention to familiarity for queer youth resonates with Isak and his counterparts, not only because his own family is fractured—his mother is neurodiverse, and this creates friction with his father, whom Isak blames, which is why Isak, Robbe, and Lucas do not live at home but with friends—and his friendships represent a familiarity and support system he cannot get from his family. However, because all youth are so intimately woven into a tapestry of youth familiarity, forsaking the familiar for a queer community not yet realized or present seems fanciful. And as such, Isak and his friends are all engaging in Isak's "queer-identity work" to counteract the visible counterpublics of the out and proud queer, as all identity work—but particularly that of queer youth relying on familiarity and expanded notions of family (Weston 1991)—labors through relationality. Ultimately, thingifying sexuality in this way not only places importance on Isak's relationship with Even and his friends, but, as I explore in the next section, it makes sexuality radically present.

Minute by Minute

Isak's thingification of his sexuality and his orientation toward an already existing community displaces the assumed "happy object" (Ahmed 2010) explicit in the coming-of-age "it gets better" narrative and out and proud queer, namely a promise of the good life in the future once the individual sheds the chrysalis of youth and finds their people. Sara Ahmed's (2010, 32) explication of what she calls the happy object depends on both the orientation of the body toward objects circulated in an affective economy and "the promise that the lines we follow will get us there, where the 'there' acquires its value by not being 'here.'" The materiality of Isak's thingness of sexuality indexes an alternative orientation that points Isak away from future promises. Yet Isak experiences a disconnect, between how he thinks he ought to feel and how he actually feels, calling forth the disappointment and rage Ahmed (2010, 42) recognizes as implicit in this disconnect: "The experience of a gap between the promise of happiness and how you are affected by objects that promise happiness does not always lead to corrections that close this gap [. . .] rage might be directed against the object that fails to deliver its promise." The radical presentism I explore below upends not only already circulating happy objects predicated on future enjoyment and happiness but also the very promise that happiness is somehow deferred to the future. Ahmed's recognition that "the there acquires its value by not being here" must also be read alongside its temporal companion, that the future *then* acquires its value by not being *now*. Yet in Isak's thingness of sexuality and his insistence on a durational approach to his relationship with Even and his own sexuality, here and now carry with them immense affective value.

We learn that Even is bipolar (or that Nicco has borderline personality disorder) after Isak has mostly accepted his sexual attraction to Even. While some behaviour is due to his diagnosis—such as, for instance, disappearing from school for a couple days—those related to Isak result from Isak's initial frustration with mental illness given his mother's depression and delusions (season 3, episode 5). For instance, Isak explains how his mother once said that she was related to Donald Trump. Isak mentions to Even that he would do better without mentally ill people in his life, not knowing that Even is bipolar. Even ends the budding relationship as a result, unbeknownst to Isak. However, Even continues to send Isak notes and cartoons, but never replies to Isak's next messages following the breakup. Such actions thus result from both Even's diagnosis and Isak's verbalized frustration with mental illness.

Isak initially believes Even's attraction to him is a result of his bipolar condition. But Isak is later educated by one of his friends (Magnus) given that his friend's mother is bipolar and thus teaches Isak that Even's attraction and feelings for Isak are genuine and not a result of his diagnosis. When Isak eventually accepts this (season 3, episode 9; season 3, episode 10 in wtFROCK), he searches for Even following a troubling text:

> Dear Isak. I'm sitting now where we met each other for the first time and I'm thinking about you. It's soon 21:21. I want to say a thousand things to you. I'm sorry for scaring you. I'm sorry for hurting you. I'm sorry for not telling you that I'm bipolar. I was afraid of losing you. I had forgotten that it's not possible to lose someone, that all people are alone anyway. In another place in the universe we're together forever, remember that. Love you. Even

Isak, Robbe, and Marti find Even, Sander, and Nicco at school, and Lucas finds Elliott under a bridge that Elliott had previously showed Lucas and where they shared their first kiss. In each instance, Even and his counterparts are mid–depressive episode and Isak and company take them back to his room to watch over him until the depressive episode ends. When Even tries to object to their relationship after the depressive episode, Isak responds with the declaration from the start of this chapter, that they cannot be certain what will happen.

Skam France provides an interesting take on this interaction. In lieu of a rather simple cut of Isak watching Even sleep after finding Even at the school, *Skam France* provides a montage of Elliott sleeping and Lucas buying flowers, cooking dinner (his plate empty and Elliott's plate full), reading in bed next to Elliott, and chatting with his friends as Elliott gets up to go to the bathroom before returning to bed. Elliott sleeps all weekend, and when Lucas watches Elliott sleep before school on Monday, Elliott objects and states that he does not need Lucas to watch him sleep. When Lucas returns home, Elliott is finally awake and playing games with the housemates. Elliott apologizes to Lucas for earlier but is quick to note that it will happen again. While Lucas feels he is capable of dealing with Elliott's condition, Elliott will not let him brush over the nitty-gritty of his diagnosis: "I'm gonna put you through hell, see?" The conversation is crucial in the deromanticization—or, in Amin's (2017) words, "deidealization"—of mental illness, as Elliott's words juxtapose with Lucas, for instance, buying flowers to put in the apartment. Yet if considered alongside Even's belief mid-depressive episode that he is meant to be alone, then Elliott is also trying to foreclose a potential relationship with Lucas and, by extension, happiness through relationality. Both Isak and Lucas can see through Even and Elliott's ploy and, essentially, call bullshit. Isak says that Even "doesn't know shit" about what will happen between the two of them, a sentiment Lucas repeats. But Lucas adds that regardless of how hard it might be, "I'd rather have you annoy me, than not have you at all" (season 3, episode 10).

Once this is established, Isak and counterparts introduce the core philosophy of their relationship and, I argue, of the series as a whole: minute by minute. In each adaptation, Even is concerned about the what-if of the future, the possibility that things will change, and, as Elliott states, he does not want things to change.[19] Rather than a concern for the future and either its potential unfoldings or its seemingly certain revelations, minute by minute advocates for a slowing of the relationship and experience, and of time to an even more fundamental unit. The minute is recognizable, it is understandable and manageable: surviving a minute is easy, especially when juxtaposed to hours, days, or weeks. Taking things minute by minute still allows, or expects, time to flow from one minute to the next, but it locates the experience and the relationship within each individual minute.

Dividing time and the relationship into a series of minutes draws attention to the duration of time, the "thing" of Isak's sexuality, and the concurrent "thing" of Isak and Even's relationship. Relationality is predicated on the movement of time, where even if we were to halt the clock and take a cross-section of a relationship, it can be meaningful only in relation to what came before and what comes after. Relationships and bonds are forged and managed over time. Similarly, Isak and Even's relationship is a movement through time, whereby minute by minute makes duration divisible into segmented minutes. But as a movement through time, it is not fixated on the future but each minute as it passes—this is what makes the present radical, for each minute is both connected to that minute that came before and that which will follow, but it is also inextricably its own minute as well.

Here, a lateral movement into arrows may prove useful. In explaining one of Zeno's four paradoxes, the "arrow in flight that is always at rest, in eternal freeze-frame, never reaching its target," anthropologist Eduardo Viveiros de Castro (2011, 141) notes that "at each instant (indivisible, by definition), Zeno's arrow occupies a portion of space equal to itself; if it were to move during the instant, it would have to occupy a space larger than itself, for otherwise it would have no room to move."[20] Granted, Viveiros de Castro is speaking of instants and moments, much like Henri Bergson (2004, 248) argues in relation also to duration and Zeno's arrow: "These points have no reality except in a line drawn, that is to say motionless."[21] While the minute is itself comprised of an indeterminable number of moments, it still acts as that slice of the longer durational unit, the "thing" or the relationship. At the end of the third season finale (episode 10), Elliott surprises Lucas by showing up to a party at the lake, explaining that he has 1,573 minutes to make up for since they last saw each other, roughly one day and a couple hours. Time passed even when the two were not together, but the hyperbole of making up 1,573 minutes imagines that each minute, like the arrow moving through both space and time, can be fully experienced. Each minute "occupies a portion of space equal to itself" (Viveiros De Castro 2011, 141), and can be experienced in that individuating capacity. Lucas is not concerned yet with stringing those minutes together, connecting the moments of the arrow into a line of trajectory.

Yet the experiential paradox of Isak's philosophy is that as the movement from minute to minute slows time and experience to the present, forgoing deference to the future and its uncertainty, it simultaneously speeds up both. Elliott's reference to 1,573 minutes is a useful tether, as he quantifies this paradox with the number of minutes. Slowing down to each individual minute attempts to transform each minute into an individuated experience, as Marti gives Nicco the option of either eating breakfast in this next minute or kissing; Nicco chooses kissing (season 2, episode 10). Yet as with Elliott's counting of minutes, each minute represents an experience following a choice, that when juxtaposed to something as all-encompassing as Elliott sleeping for days at a time, duration is far more radical, presentist, and quicker than it may initially seem. Each minute is to count, sometimes quite literally, but it mirrors Even's manic state, for when we witness each adaptation's version of mania, Even and his counterparts all speak more quickly, have a harder train of thought to follow, jump around in the conversation, are incredibly energetic, and eventually leave the room and roam the streets of the city naked.[22] My own bipolar condition and manic experiences similarly find me more excitable and hyperfocused, compared to the typical multitasking disposition and set of practices with which I would otherwise engage. In practice, much like the thingification of sexuality, the future is invoked in the present as plans are made. Even, for instance, invites Isak to his house to meet his mother the following day (season 3, episode 10).

 The coming of age "it gets better" narrative of queer identity is inversed in *Skam* and partially embedded in the minute-by-minute approach: things may actually get worse given Even's struggles with mental health. Yet as a philosophy for experiencing and understanding queer youth sexuality, minute by minute expands the possibility of sexuality beyond identity or categories and refocuses it on the minutia of relationality. Not only is the promise of finding one's people made almost irrelevant with attention to the radical present, but it does not capture the actual experience of living minute by minute with those already entangled in the youth's relationality. In many ways, Isak's insistence that he and Even approach this "thing," their relationship, by taking it minute by minute is equally a reflection on his own orientation toward his sexuality, given that he had to piece together an understanding of his sexuality, his own "thing," with his friends. Minute by minute is not predicated on isolation. When Isak tries to understand his sexuality alone or online, he is visibly frustrated and made even more agitated to the extent that his friends remark on his attitude. Here we again witness the rage Ahmed (2010, 42) details. Yet when he finally opens up to his friends, even his mannerisms—from avoiding eye contact to looking at someone straight in the face—shift to indicate that he is more at ease, less frustrated, and not easily agitated. Each of his friends offers advice on his feelings for Even, validating Isak's sexuality in the moment/minute. Without fully realizing, Isak queers his community by inculcating them in both his "queer-identity labor" (Gray 2009) and his relationship with Even. The concern is not with Isak's identification but with the "thing" he has with Even, an ever-evolving relationship that Isak is taking minute by minute. I explore the importance of relationality, coming out, and sexuality further in the next chapter.

Antidote for Shame

Sexuality for Isak is person-driven, whereby he must come to terms with his sexuality by considering not only his feelings for Even but also his experiences and interactions with Even and Even's bipolarism. While Isak may have been recognizing his same-sex attraction before Even, it is Even that enables him to confront his attractions and emotions, to understand them and give them a name or materiality. As with the universe of *Skam*, the focus is on how the central character confronts their own shame vis-à-vis friends, to learn how to turn sociality into the antidote for shame and the way to face the ever-encroaching precarity of teenage relationality. As such, Isak's insistence on a durational approach to his relationship with Even—minute by minute—is a recognition of shame's ever-present value tied to the seeming spiraling precarity of difference. Isak recognizes the cliché of his own aphorism, that living is about the here and now (season 3, episode 10), but it is clichéd because it had been an empty notion until he had to navigate the difficulty of imagining too far into the future. What began with Even's bipolar condition seeps through his continued sexual and emotional navigation, thus becoming a mode of understanding social life more broadly. And it begins (but never ends) with his peers and friends, as he recognizes that living is about the here and now as it is done with others. The durational approach, the radical presentism Isak embodies, thus not only represents his relationship with Even and his sexuality, but it queers his already-existing relations and community, tying them too to the arrow.

If we take Ahmed's (2006, 68) queering of sexual orientation and introduction of queer phenomenology as "an approach to sexual orientation by rethinking how bodily direction 'toward' objects shape the surfaces of bodily and social space," then Isak's attraction toward Even orients his body toward a gendered and sexual object to the extent that his own phenomenological experience and existence are affected. This is evidenced by Isak's own "thingification" of sexuality and his relationship with Even, as the object, or thing, is actually an orientation toward the thing and object. And given Even's bipolar condition, the phenomenological effect on Isak's orientation manifests in the durational approach of minute by minute as a strategy of care and self-realization. Taking their relationship minute by minute eschews the stress and anxiety about an uncertain future while also reinforcing their attraction and feelings for one another and relationality more broadly. Adding the formatting layer of the series and its adaptations, minute by minute presents as a phenomenological philosophy for viewers, as they also must orient their sense of time, expectations, and experiences toward the gradual and durational unfolding of the series over, quite literally, a series of minutes at a time.

This minute-by-minute approach to sexuality and relationality—and radical presentism more broadly—is ultimately a way to unscript the present, to dislodge the focus of future uncertainty and preemptive actions and instill an emphasis on each individual minute. That the producers and creators crafted a show that must be experienced durationally may create expectancy or even hope for what will happen next, but that is different from anticipation or preemtpiveness. Hope affectively connects people together, it works to stitch together minutes, to tether the past and future to the present. Rather than anticipation for an event or state far flung into the future—it will get better after graduation, after moving—the hope and expectancy felt in the unscripting of the present is as manageable as the minute that preceded it. And this is the point, that the present is made to be maneuvered through, manageable and discernable, rather than clouded in the haze of a potential future. Radical presentism concretizes the relationship, makes it less of a flight of fancy and more of an actionable and encounterable *thing*.

As demonstrated in this chapter, both a television studies and anthropological approach to the series of *Skam* adaptations takes seriously the epistemological and textual format of the series with the worlding of *Skam*. Rather than a comparison between adaptations, this chapter coalesces the adaptations into an overarching narrative of youth and youth sexuality that symbolizes a queer politics burgeoning in this media. These shows resonate together and with audiences—to the extent that *Skam* was adapted, form and all, in Italy, France, and Belgium, in addition to the Netherlands, Germany, and a short-lived version in the United States. This narrative resonance, to invoke Lepselter (2016), renders the stories and characters as tethered to the present as the minutes that comprise it.

Eliding sexual identities and categories, Isak and his counterparts focus instead on a more present and relational understanding of sexuality, thingifying it while also taking his sexuality minute by minute. Each minute might yield something different, but that is part of the hope of living, I would argue. That the promise of something else, something more, in the future is ignored throughout the season, queer youth sexuality orients toward the present relationships and experiences of individuals without being reducible to individuals. In other words, sexuality, as I explore in the next chapter, can be relational and experiential for individuals without being individuated. The focus is on the youth themselves, the characters as youth navigating a precarious present in the contemporary moment. Stated alternatively, why focus on the uncertainty of the future when the present is precarious enough?

Following Amin (2017, 6), this chapter sought to "inhabit unease"—a notion and feeling I extrapolate further in chapter 5. I avoid idealization or even utopic imaginings of queer sexuality or youth sexuality and instead imagine queer youth sexuality as an issue or *thing* of the present and existing relations, moving laterally or parallel to a queer insistence of forging "relations outside of tired old blueprints." What if, this chapter asked, the already-existing relations forged by youth in their ever-unfolding development are enough, sufficiently queer to shepherd the young queerling into a future that they themselves make queer? It is therefore not a matter of queer not yet being here, as Muñoz (2009) claims, but queer as always in the making by those in the present. Such a question and approach to queer youth sexuality highlights the nascent queer politics embedded in this media while also gesturing toward new language that takes youth on their own terms, in the unfinished and unscripted present of here and now.

Chapter Three

Relationality and the Contractual Self

In the popular 2018 film *Love, Simon*, the titular character, Simon, sits down with his mother after having come out as gay to his family on Christmas Day. He has been isolated from his friends and facing backlash at school, as he had been outed by a fellow student. In the emotional conversation between Simon and his mother, his mother admits that she hates the fact that Simon must figure out his sexuality alone. The story up until that point supports that very point, for Simon relies only on email correspondence with the unknown student "Blue" to share thoughts on his sexuality. Simon's narration at the start of the film indicates that he already knows he is gay, but Blue is the first "person" he tells. This narrative of individuality proffers that queer sexuality is something that autonomous young people must grapple with alone, for even if there are resources and other individuals with whom one can converse, queer sexuality is a truth only the individual can ascertain.

    The neoliberal rendering of the self as an autonomous individual with individual capacity and marketable traits is a hallmark of American society (Gershon 2019). To understand the connection between neoliberalism and American society, we must first define neoliberalism. I am partial to queer studies scholars John Elia and Gust Yep's (2012, 880) definition as they use it to discuss LGBTQ+ acceptance and inclusion:

> Central features of neoliberalism are a) lifting the government oversight of free enterprise and trade, thereby not providing checks and balances to prevent or mitigate social damage that might occur as a result of the policy of "no governmental

interference:" b) eliminating public funding of social services; c) deregulating governmental involvement in anything that could cut into the profits of private enterprise; d) privatizing such enterprises as schools, hospitals, community-based organizations, and other entities traditionally held in the public trust; and e) eradicating the concept of "the public good" or "community" in favor of "individual responsibility."

This last point about "individual responsibility" is what I wish to dwell on below. For "neoliberal perspectives have incorporated as a central belief the knowledge that all that is social could be otherwise" (Gershon 2011, 538). This otherwise existence relies on the boundedness of the self, comprised of moving parts in service to the self as marketable and responsible.

In her theoretically rich article, anthropologist Ilana Gershon (2011, 539) explicates the rise of "neoliberal agency," a "concept of agency [that] requires a reflexive stance in which people are subjects for themselves—a collection of processes to be managed." The key for Gershon is that people become "a bundle of skills," to invoke anthropologist Bonnie Urciuoli (2008), a fragmented self "that is composed of usable traits . . . [that] the neoliberal agent brings to relationships" (Gershon 2011, 539). Elsewhere Gershon (2016, 2017) ethnographically explores how such neoliberal agency renders potential job seekers into individual brands or businesses, including college students that approach higher education as preparation for crafting skills and traits that are marketable in our neoliberal society.

Neoliberal agency, however, requires one to never be "in the moment," as one is instead "always faced with one's self as a project that must be consciously steered through various possible alliances and obstacles" (Gershon 2011, 349). This is a telling distinction, for as I continue to argue, security temporality displaces the present for attention to the future, attention to "one's self as a project" that interprets queer youth, in particular, as a waypoint for a future self when one is well-adjusted, out, and in control of one's "brand."

In some ways, Simon's individuated experience of his sexuality and coming out is not surprising given that individual responsibility weaves through American society in ways that credit identity to the individual, despite, as Mary Gray (2009) contends and as discussed in the previous chapter, the notion that "queer identity labor" relies on the relational construction of queer identity.[1] Regardless of how queer identity or sexuality is actually formed and managed, the belief that one's sexuality is an inner truth to be discovered (Foucault 1990)—an individual experience to be made legible for others—still circulates in American society.

Compared to this neoliberal narrative of individuality found in several US popular television shows and films is a narrative found outside of the United States (namely, Europe) that focuses on relationality and the ways queer sexuality involves young people negotiating the contours of their queer sexualities with friends and lovers alongside the (re)evaluations of their friendships altogether. This is not to say that neoliberalism does not weave through European society, but rather that a strong emphasis on individuality features less in some popular European films and television shows that feature queer characters. In the first season of the Italian show *Prisma* (2022–present) on Amazon Prime, identical twins Marco and Andrea navigate friendships, love, sex/uality, and relationships in Latina. In the series, Marco's friend, Daniele, is talking to Andrea dressed as and pretending to be a girl using a fake profile on social media. They begin to develop feelings for one another (explored more fully in season 2). Daniele confides in his friends about his feelings and considers what to do—he eventually admits to his friends at the end of the first season that he does not care if the person on social media is a boy or girl, he wants to meet them. Andrea similarly confides in some of his friends over social media about his feelings for Daniele. Andrea is shown to enjoy dressing in women's clothing, wearing makeup, and talking with Daniele, Andrea's friend Nina going with him to Rome to hear a transgender poet speak. Talking with Nina enables Andrea to become more confident in his sexuality and gender identity. These representations, I contend, narrate queer youth sexuality through an in-place or emerging relationality of friendships and peer relations; queer youth sexuality is a collective journey.

The number of popular media artifacts that include central young queer characters and storylines has rapidly increased in recent years due in part to a normalizing effect of queer youth representation in television and film, given that "at the same time that more queers are making it to television [and film], television [and film are] . . . being remade, some might say, as more queer" (Joyrich 2014,135).[2] Furthermore, there is a move away from presenting queer characters, especially queer male characters, as sick or dying, including representations in literature (Browne 2020). The inevitable death of the queer character indexes "the assumption that to be queer is to hurtle toward a miserable fate" (Ahmed 2017). Newer media that focus on queer youth, however, work to unscript this fatalistic narrative in favor of narratives that recognize fragility (Ahmed 2016) but also offer positivity and even iterations of "educated hope" for a better life in the present (Muñoz 2009).[3] Queer youth storylines have become more prominent as both coming out and same-sex affection (or more) have woven into multiple genres and television channels (Sarkissian 2014; Jenner 2014), while homosociality and queer relationships (not always predicated on same-sex desire) become more common in mainstream cinema (Hughes 2014). I complicate this seeming queer inclusive narrative in chapter 5 as I discuss both the simultaneous violence still committed against queer youth, especially queer youth of color.

Yet what particularly contributes to this significant uptick in queer youth media is the advent of streaming services like Netflix and Hulu, alongside multimodal distribution and consumption channels that invite audience participation (Fuller 2019).[4] Such streaming services not only provide access to lesser-known titles that feature young queer characters and storylines, but they produce far more content that appeals to more niche audiences. And while cancellations of shows happen, there are still numerous single-season shows that explore queer storylines (e.g., *Teenage Bounty Hunters*; *Generation*; *The Bastard Son & The Devil Himself*).[5] Such streaming content mirrors the plethora of online media artifacts created and/or consumed by queer youth, such as coming-out videos on YouTube (Wuest 2014; Alexander and Losh 2010), the "It Gets Better" campaign (Pullen 2014; Berliner 2018), and social media engagement (de Ridder and van Bauwel 2015; Hanckel et al. 2019).

If queer youth media are becoming more prominent, then the narratives of queer youth sexuality found in these media artifacts both make queer youth sexuality ordinary while also affecting how queer youth understand themselves (Gray 2009; Sarkissian 2014; Robertson 2018). The narratives of individuality and relationality mentioned above are meaningful, I argue, because through acts of coming out and navigating queer sexuality these narratives proffer theories of selfhood. In other words, these narratives of queer youth sexuality are constructed through coming out practices and queer characters figuring out their sexualities—whether they are done individually or relationally—and in turn, those narratives offer up different understandings of the self. It is important to note that these are not wholly separate narratives; they may, in fact, be dialogical rather than strictly dichotomous. Yet I heuristically disentangle them to interrogate the media texts discussed and comment on theories of selfhood that these artifacts propose through their queer youth representation.

I suggest that one potential reason for these two different narratives lies in perspective. The narrative of individuality renders queer sexuality as something to be made intelligible to adults (Talburt 2004) rather than experienced by young people themselves. Narratives of coming out thus become a fixed point in time to look back on, rather than a durational process contingent on interactions and relationships, as discussed in the previous chapter. As such, queer youth sexuality is made individualistic as a product of adult intelligibility, for even if it is queer adults narrating/writing the story, the story becomes a way to either comprehend sexual difference as exceptional (read as outside the heteronormative present) or a version of the past self that teleologically matures into the presently well-adjusted queer adult. To take young people on their own terms instead of a perpetual look back or quest for intelligibility reorients the narrative of queer youth sexuality away from individualism and toward relationality and friendships. It favors the here and now, a temporality that slows to the interactional practices of young people and draws attention to how they make sense of their sexualities. And such an approach highlights the cultures of care that emerge in the interactions between peers and friends that are necessary for navigating daily life (Byron 2021).

Another reason for such a difference is the emphasis American society places on individualism, an individualism that permeates both popular culture narratives and lived experience, underpinned, as Gershon (2024) argues, by contracts: US Americans are in contractional relations—in the workplace, in families, in society—whereby each party is considered an individual. While Gershon is primarily concerned with contracts that put individuals into certain kinds of work relations and obligations, the contract—much like social contract theory (i.e., Hobbes and Locke)—marks a kind of US individuality that not only sees the United States as exceptional but also relies on the individuality of the self.[6] Anthropologist Julienne Obadia (2022, 515) refers to this as "the contract complex," an expansion of neoliberal market rationality into the home and relationships in ways that sees, for Obadia, polyamorous partners in the United States forming contracts with one another over their relationships. Inspired by anthropologist Marilyn Strathern, Obadia (2022, 516) argues that "the terms of the contract manage the relationship, *not the relata*. They allow for the elaboration of potentially long networks of relationships, but . . . they simultaneously cut such networks through individualized and individualizing logics of self-ownership that prohibit any form of mutual inhabitation or the extension of debts, responsibilities, or agency beyond the individual relata."

Such contractual relations, imbued with a form of neoliberal agency, engenders what I call the *contractual self*, a notion of selfhood that renders individual relationality between seemingly autonomous people contractual, a set of obligations and expectations that model relationships after business contracts (see also Stout 2014, chapter 3). There is an important distinction between the social contract of Hobbes and Locke and the contractual self I am discussing, namely that while Hobbes sees the social contract as one between the individual and the state, and Locke discerns it as a relation of property,[7] I suggest that the contractual self works between individuals rather than just between individuals and institutions. This follows the idea that persons are now seen as businesses (Gershon 2011; Obadia 2022), and so if people are now businesses, then the neoliberal contractual relations individuals create with their jobs and in the workplace act as models for how individuals interpret daily life in relation to one another.

The contractual self also differs from the forms of relationality discussed in the previous chapter and that I explore in this chapter as well. The forms of relationality discussed in the previous chapter sees the self's management of sexuality as a relational endeavor, whereby friends and lovers assist in the discovery and understanding of one's same-sex feelings. Talking, as I discuss in this chapter, is quintessential to how the self comes to understand sexuality, though silences are equally as important. The contractual self relies on the gumption of the individual, the belief that sexuality is a truth that only the individual can uncover and realize, despite that not always being the case. For instance, a common narrative that permeates coming-out stories is that when individuals come out to their friends or family, the friends or family members will tell the individual that they already knew, whereby the individual may retort, "Then why didn't you tell me?" The assumption in this exchange is that the individual had to figure out their sexuality for themselves—despite friends and family "knowing" that the individual has a particular sexuality, it is not their *job* or their *obligation* to tell the individual. This is the contractual self, for the individual is believed to be responsible for their own sexual awakening, realization, and journey, even if others are aware of or important to the person's journey. The journey is still individuated.

Narratives of coming out thus fit within a contractual relation the (queer) individual has with others and with society, for one is expected to be intelligible by adults and society writ large (Talburt 2004) in exchange for corresponding treatment (including both rights and stigmas). Coming out must be an act of interpellating the queer individual as an individual, otherwise how can they exist within a contractual relation with others? Yet the fact that European media texts (re)orient queer youth sexuality away from individualism and toward relationality and friendships illustrates that relationality means something different in Europe than it does in the United States. Such narratives of relationality favor the here and now, a temporality that slows to the interactional practices of young people and draws attention to how they make sense of their sexualities (see chapter 2).

In this chapter, I draw out both narratives stitched into popular media representations of queer youth sexuality, the US-based narrative focused on individualizing queer sexuality and the European narrative that allows for interpersonal negotiation. These narratives hinge not only on specific understandings of queer youth sexuality but also on the ways coming out contribute to the construction of the self. I therefore bookend my discussion of these specific narratives of queer youth sexuality in my selected media texts with the theoretical framework of coming out and self making and a more pointed discussion of the coming-out narratives in these media artifacts.

I primarily pull from six media texts: the US films *Love, Simon* and *Alex Strangelove*; the US streaming show *Love, Victor*; the UK streaming show *Heartstopper*; the Norwegian show *Skam*; and the French film *Being 17*. These artifacts were chosen for several reasons: the protagonists are all queer male high school students, all feature at least one coming-out scene, and all attempt to capture the daily life of its characters. All six represent a material reality for queer youth, both in the United States and in Europe, namely how coming out and comprehending one's sexuality is either meant to be a form of individual responsibility or a collective and shared construction and journey. They throw into stark contrast the difference in locations and culture—the neoliberal and contractual self colliding with the relationally defined self—but they also act as a potential mirror for queer youth watching to recognize their own journeys represented in the media while also acting as a touchstone for comparison if, say, US queer youth watch *Heartstopper* or *Being 17*.

Furthermore, I focus specifically on artifacts in the United States and Europe for comparison to try and unpack a so-called Western perspective on queer youth sexuality and coming out. This is certainly an imperfect heuristic, but one that is often invoked and therefore part of my goal is to show the conflicting and overlapping contours of such a "Western" perspective. This has limitations, especially in my selection of media artifacts and inclusion of what counts as Europe. It is also important to again emphasize that while I present a seemingly steadfast separation between the United States and Europe—between individuality and relationality—these are not always mutually exclusive. In fact, as I argue below, there may very well be a difference between the narrative promulgated (namely, of individuality) and actual experiences. I discursively analyze and follow queer youth agency in these representations, as it is queer youths' acts that ultimately construct the narratives of queer youth sexuality and coming out at hand. I focus specifically on the protagonist's interactions (or lack thereof) with others in their navigation of their sexualities—who, if anyone, helps the protagonist comprehend his queer sexuality? Who does he come out to? What language does he specifically use? How do others aid in his construction of queer sexuality and self? And how does the language of coming out also aid in such construction?

Conduits of Coming Out

The narratives of individuality and relationality that emerge in the queer media artifacts I discuss below intertwine with different coming-out narratives. These narratives also contribute to queer youth's self-making process, whereby act(s) of coming out and the stories told of how one comes out craft queer selves; the *doing* of coming out and the *telling* of coming out are where my foci lie. As Jen Bacon (1998, 249) writes, "[F]urther evidence suggests that the necessity to share that identity with others through narrative has both political and personal repercussions for the storyteller, and . . . repercussions for our understanding of rhetorical practice as well." While there have been countless studies of coming out from multiple disciplines employing varying methods, the theoretical discussion herein derives from the media artifacts themselves.

The different narratives of queer youth sexuality found in the United States and Europe are enmeshed in the narratives and processes of coming out for each set of characters. On the one hand, the narratives of individualism found in the US media artifacts feature the queer character revealing their inner "truth" (Foucault 1990)—their sexuality—to another character. This takes the form of a declarative statement: I am gay. There may be questions that follow, but the statement speaks to something essential of the queer character that mirrors their secluded journey to discover their sexuality.[8]

On the other hand, the narratives of relationality found in the European media artifacts feature the queer character not coming out as a sexuality but as being in some sort of relationship with another character.

As discussed in the previous chapter and elaborated below, Isak in the Norwegian show *Skam* talks about his sexuality as a "thing"—he has a "thing" with Even—rather than declaring that he is gay. If a queer character does eventually make such a declaration of a sexuality, it is done only after they have established their relationship with another character, indicating that the relationship is quintessential to understanding their sexuality. Furthermore, the narrative of relationality includes multiple "coming out" moments at different stages, illustrating the continued *work* of coming out.

Coming out involves a speech act, whether that is a declarative statement or an explanation of a relationship, but it also involves shifting perspectives. I take my cue from J. L. Austin (1975), who distinguishes between illocutionary and perlocutionary speech acts: "[T]he former are speech acts that, in saying do what they say, and do it in the moment of that saying; the latter are speech acts that produce certain effects as their consequence; by saying something, a certain effect follows" (Butler 1997, 3).[9] I suggest that coming out is both illocutionary and perlocutionary, insofar as there is the immediate effect of becoming queer (or however one comes out) in the moment of the utterance. "I am gay" thus transforms the unmarked speaker into a marked speaker, from not gay to gay. Yet as a perlocutionary speech act, the effects may not be known or instantiated until later, until certain conditions are met.[10] While one might contend that all those futures and unknown effects become the potential of the illocutionary speech act in the present, my point is that the speech act of coming out is not a static act nor does it index a static identity. Sexual identity, as with all identities, are fluid. As queer feminist poet and scholar Gloria Anzaldúa (2009, 166) beautifully writes,

> Identity is a river—a process. Contained within the river is its identity, and its need to flow, to change to stay a river—if it stopped it would be a contained body of water such as a lake or a pond. The changes in the river are external (changes in environment—river bed, weather, animal life) and internal (within the waters). A river's contents flow within its boundaries. Changes in identity likewise are external (how others perceive one and how one perceives others and the world) and internal (how one perceives oneself, self-image). People in different regions name the parts of the river/person which they see.

Furthermore, as I continue to argue in this book, the preemption of the future's uncertainty in the present is characteristic of a security temporality that seeks to displace present experience in preparation for an inevitable future. Therefore, allowing for the perlocutionary speech act to follow from the illocutionary speech act enables a different sort of temporality, whereby immediate effects transpire, and future effects are left for the future. The present allows for maneuverability, allows for a feeling and experience of those immediate effects. I follow Anzaldúa (2009) in thinking of identity as fluid, while also recognizing, as Gray (2009) and anthropologist Margot Weiss (2011) do, that identity and sexuality are constructed and managed through social relations. Even though coming out presents—and is commonly understood, at least in the United States—as an individuated speech act of conveying one's truth to the hearer, it is far more complex and messier.

Let me explain. According to Bacon (1998, 251), coming out "is a shift from the private sphere to the public, and also a shift from silence into speech."[11] Stories of coming out (particularly self-narratives) are important because "to tell such stories is to speak one's way into existence in an almost tangible way" (Bacon 1998, 252).[12] Here we see the importance of coming out as an illocutionary speech act, where the immediate effect of declaring "I am gay" is that the speaker *becomes gay* to the hearer. For Bacon, "one's way" is indicative of one's sexual identity and self, the two inextricably linked in the coming-out story. However, both one's sexuality and one's self exist only when spoken, when the coming-out story is told. Michel Foucault (1990) makes this very point, for when science co-opts Christianity's confessional model of truth-telling, the telling of a truth about sex becomes an object to uncover, to interrogate, and to proclaim as a sexuality that "embod[ies] the truth of sex and its pleasures" (68).[13] Truth is some*thing* innate to the individual that must be confessed and analyzed: "[W]e demand that sex speak the truth (but, since it is the secret and is oblivious to its own nature, we reserve for ourselves the function of telling the truth of its truth, revealed and deciphered at last), and we demand that it tell us our truth, or rather, the deeply buried truth of that truth about ourselves which we think we possess in our immediate consciousness" (Foucault 1990, 69).[14] But more specifically linked to the act of coming out is the pleasure Foucault contends that arises in knowing the truth, so that one is compelled to come out to not only know one's truth but also because there is pleasure (or release) in that act of coming out (Foucault 1990, 71).[15]

The metaphor of a conduit proves useful in interpreting coming out. In linguist Michael Reddy's (1979) assessment of "the conduit metaphor"—a metaphor for how Standard American English speakers discuss the nature of language as the conveying of information and meaning from a sender/speaker to a receiver/listener in a unidirectional manner—meaning is something the sender/speaker has inside them. Meaning is thought to exist irrespective of others, much like sexuality, and conveyed along a conduit to the receiver/listener: "[C]ommunication achieves the physical transfer of thoughts and feelings" (Reddy 1979, 286). Reddy (1979, 286) provides a few linguistic examples, including "Try to get your thoughts across better" and "You still haven't given me any idea of what you mean." In these examples, the "dead metaphor," according to Reddy, demonstrates how meaning is conveyed from a speaker to a hearer. The metaphor is one of container: "If language transfers thought to others, then the logical container, or conveyer, for this is words, or word-groupings like phrases, sentences, paragraphs, and so on" (Reddy 1979, 287). To "get your thoughts across" implies, then, a conduit that allows the thoughts to transfer from speaker to hearer, effortlessly, so it is implied.

Here, too, we can see contractual relations at work, for the speaker and listener engage in a contract of linguistic expectation whereby the speaker must uphold their end of the contract for the listener to uphold their end. Furthermore, both the speaker and hearer are considered autonomous individuals, whereby the speaker contains all the information and is thus responsible for conveying that meaning to the hearer. The responsibilities of the speaker and hearer may be different, but they are already existing expectations, thus contributing to the contractual self. The statement "I am gay" is that internalized meaning to be conveyed to the listener, the Foucaultian truth that must be said out loud, not only marking an essential quality of the self—I *am*—but the feelings and attractions queer characters have for their respective love interests become that conduit whereby one can make such essentialized statements about their selves.

Reddy's (1979) broader argument, however, is that the conduit metaphor does not accurately capture how language actually works, as language and meaning are interactional, collaborative, and contingent on the relationship between the speaker and hearer.[16] Such interaction takes enormous effort, Reddy (1979, 295) argues, for "human communication will almost always go astray unless real energy is extended." Mikhail Bakhtin (1981) makes an analogous point about truth, for truth emerges from the dialogic interaction between people. Mobilizing Bakhtin, Bacon

(1998, 257) notes that "language is not used in isolation, but does its *work* when people communicate *with* each other. So knowledge is necessarily social and necessarily requires *a negotiation* of meaning."[17] Language and meaning take work precisely because they are interactional and not contained within any one individual, otherwise communication would be even messier than it already is (Reddy 1979, 295).[18]

Sexuality and coming-out narratives operate the same way, for sexuality is that knowledge, or truth, that "requires a negotiation of meaning." For Bacon, the work of coming-out narratives "describe[s] a process of identity negotiation while simultaneously enacting that identity construction with their very performance" (1998, 257). Negotiation here indexes that interactional quality of language and meaning—if we extend meaning to an understanding of the self—and so the self is both made and enacted relationally. Yet what I am arguing is that the iterative process of coming out—invoking Judith Butler's (1993) discussion of lesbian identity as a repeated performance—is not only a dialogic process, but coming out as a relational process contributes to the relational construction of the self. Therefore, sexuality is not only iterative, it is also relational.

Invoking both Reddy (1979) and Foucault (1990), the story we tell ourselves about queer sexuality and coming out locates meaning and the truth of one's sexuality wholly within the individual. This is necessary for one to be in contractual relation with others and with society, to be intelligible to the other *as* a sexual individual with an individual sexuality. Different expectations exist for the individual coming out and the individual(s) who "receive" the coming-out declaration. Therefore, in the narratives I outline below, we bear witness to these competing stories of queer youth sexuality and coming out. The effect is that narratives not only theorize the self differently, but they potentially offer queer youth who are watching insight into how they ought to understand and navigate their queer sexualities.

Narratives of Queer Individualism

Alex, high school senior and protagonist of the 2018 Netflix film *Alex Strangelove*, is awkward around his girlfriend whenever they talk about sex. Despite verbalizing that he wants to have sex with her, it is clear he is uncomfortable with the very idea of any sexual interactions with her. The film explores Alex's struggle and his realization that he may not be heterosexual. Not until he meets high school graduate Elliott, who has already come out as gay, does Alex begin questioning his sexuality. He eventually admits to himself that he is gay and tells his girlfriend.

In many ways, the film *Alex Strangelove* contains several of the quintessential tropes found in queer high school films, television, and novels in the United States and throughout Europe: Alex is consciously unaware of his queer sexuality, he dates a girl, he meets a boy that awakens him, he realizes he is gay, and he ends up with the boy. I am less concerned with these major tropes and plot elements than I am with how his queerness manifests and how it is represented on screen.

Perhaps most noticeable is the way Alex's queer sexuality is tied to his anxiety, obsessive compulsion, and aversion to sex. On the surface, these associations are not all that surprising, and in fact are supported by studies that correlate queer youth sexuality to anxiety (e.g., Borgogna et al. 2019; Wozolek, Wootton, and Demlow 2017; Mason 2021). In part, denying his queer sexuality is what causes his anxiety and obsessive compulsion. Holding in a secret no doubt creates stress and anxiety, especially when one is (socially) contractually obligated to come out if one is not straight (the assumed sexuality of all people). But for Alex, it is not the secret that manifests the embodied experience but an unconscious, presocial sexuality, one he does not know he has until later, that yields the corporeal responses. In short, queerness is pathological, an individually cultivated and realized identity that exists within him and must be pulled out and proclaimed as the antidote to (some of) his anxiety and obsessive compulsion.

Such a pathology of queerness is further supported by Alex's climactic realization and proclamation that he is, in fact, gay. After his failed attempt to have sex with his girlfriend, he joins his friends at a college party, gets drunk, and attempts to have sex with a random girl at the party as if to prove that he is, indeed, heterosexual. Yet after this failed attempt, Alex flees the party and falls into a random swimming pool, whereby he begins to have visions of his childhood. As revealed in a flashback, Alex was humiliated at summer camp while showering with other boys because he had an erection. There were no indications prior to this third-act revelation that such an episode had happened, thus indicating that Alex suppressed this incident—and his queerness—to avoid further humiliation. The embodied responses of anxiety and obsessive compulsion thus become diagnostic of his suppressed sexuality, one he only remembers once intoxicated and underwater. He emerges from the pool, which symbolizes his unconscious, and says aloud to his girlfriend, now checking to make sure he is okay, that "I am gay." This secret sexuality is a truth about an essential part of the self that is ascertained only through confession (Foucault 1990); in this film, confessing the truth is the act of coming out both of the pool and as a sexuality.

The internalization of Alex's queer sexuality ties the narrative of pathology to one of individualism, whereby Alex's queer sexuality is something he must figure out, navigate, and embrace alone. In fact, when Alex confides in his friend Dell that he thinks he may be bisexual, Dell immediately dismisses this admission by exposing his penis to Alex and asking if Alex "wants this," gesturing to his penis. Alex is horrified as Dell talks Alex out of thinking that he is bisexual. Thus, even when Alex does seek support and advice from friends, those friends brush off the possibility that Alex is anything but straight.

Given that Alex must navigate his queerness alone, his anxiety and obsessive compulsion not only increase but also manifest as defensiveness against his friends, his girlfriend, and Elliott. After spending an evening at a concert, dinner, and talking with Elliott, Alex arrives home to see his girlfriend waiting in front his house, after midnight, wanting to talk with Alex. In response, Alex gets mad and defensive with her, causing her to storm off. In a different scene, Alex and Elliott are hanging out in Elliott's room when Alex kisses Elliott, causing Alex to pull away, panicked, and get defensive around Elliott, saying that he was only giving Elliott "what he wanted." While Alex's awkwardness and anxiety around sex carry throughout the film, his anger and defensiveness emerge only after meeting Elliott and after he begins to navigate potential deviations in his sexuality alone.

It is this individual navigation of one's queer sexuality that forms the bedrock of this queer youth narrative. In many ways, such individualization maps onto a form of American exceptionalism that treats everyone as exceptionally different and standalone—what Jasbir Puar (2007) might call US sexual exceptionalism—whereby the experiences one faces, though likely shared by others, are interpreted and narrated as individual and unique. Gershon (2019, 183), in her comparison of the US and UK versions of the reality television show *Undercover Boss*, notes that the US version's "way of managing social relationships fits in more with contemporary capitalism's emphasis on the unique individual." Elsewhere Gershon (2011, 539) notes that "a neoliberal perspective presumes that people own their skills and traits" whereby "these skills, traits, or marketable capacities are what the neoliberal agent brings to relationships." Even when burgeoning queer youth have friends, their sexualities are described as one's own problem, one's own responsibility, whereby queerness becomes representative of American exceptionalism.

Take the Hulu show *Love, Victor* (2020–22), set at the same high school as *Love, Simon*, that focuses on Latinx high schooler Victor as he moves from Texas to Atlanta. The series begins with Victor thinking that he is gay and reaching out to Simon, the protagonist of *Love, Simon*, to vent and ask for advice. Texting with Simon becomes the only way for Victor to share his anxieties around his sexuality despite making friends at school. The first season carries on in this fashion, where Victor acclimates to a new school, begins dating a girl, pines over the openly gay boy with whom he works, and navigates an anxious homelife.

Victor's journey shifts dramatically after he kisses Benji (season 1, episode 7), the gay student with whom he works, and flees to New York City to meet Simon for advice only to find Simon absent and Simon's boyfriend and friends present to handle the situation (season 1, episode 8). While at a drag show, Simon's friends reveal that they know about Victor's situation with Benji, much to Victor's embarrassment, and as a result, Victor confronts Simon when he arrives. Simon admits that he needed advice from his friends to help Victor navigate his own situation, and the two eventually reconcile. Only after this trip does Victor admit to himself that he is gay, and he comes out to his best friend, Felix, the next day (season 1, episode 9).

On the surface, this interaction seems to encourage queer youth to talk to friends about the challenges they face with their sexualities. Victor is consistently asking Simon for advice, almost exclusively via text, while Simon seeks advice from his friends for how to advise Victor. Yet the advice Simon provides is often sporadic and comes only after a decision or action has taken place. For instance, in the fourth episode of the second season, Victor asks Simon about having sex with Benji, now his boyfriend, but Simon's advice—which is essentially that sex is something to be discussed with one's boyfriend—comes (via text message) while Victor and Benji are having sex, a point I revisit in the next chapter. The fact that Simon must ask his friends' advice about Victor's situation is also telling, as Simon is not asking about his own sexuality but Victor's.

More importantly, these are queer and trans friends Simon makes in New York City *after* graduating high school, drawing a rather distinct line between the types of friends one has in high school versus those after high school, as discussed in the previous chapter. Only after Victor goes to New York City and experiences queer spaces and other queer folks can he finally admit that he is gay, thus implying that his surroundings and friends are insufficient for his queer sexual journey. This first season episode, while some may find it liberating and important, reinforces a common trope among queer youth narratives, that young folks will find their "people" after high school. This is not to diminish the importance of queer spaces or community; both are quintessential to queerness and queer identity, especially for young people. However, as discussed in chapter 2, the present is deferred to a future where things are supposed to "get better," when one grows up, becomes an adult, and is a productive member of the neoliberal society. None of Simon's original high school friends, for instance, are even mentioned in this episode despite being a quintessential part of his life in high school. The here and now matter less than the future, where one must grow up and mature to appreciate the importance of friendships.

Love, Simon provides one potential explanation for the absence of Simon's high school friends in *Love, Victor* and further evidence for the narrative of queer individuality. One of Simon's fellow classmates finds his emails with Blue and blackmails Simon into setting him up with one of Simon's female friends, Abby, despite his other male friend liking her. Eventually his classmate outs Simon to the school around the same time his friends discover that Simon had been lying to keep his two friends apart. Despite Simon's explanation that he was being blackmailed, his friends blame Simon and leave Simon to handle the fallout of his public outing alone.

Some may interpret this interaction as a "deidealization" of Simon's queerness, to invoke Kajin Amin (2017), insofar as despite Simon being gay, he can still make mistakes and take advantage of his friends. This is certainly part of my interpretation, but even this can be explained by the overarching narrative that Simon was to handle his sexuality and take responsibility alone. Individuals are assumed to be responsible for their own actions, fallouts, and journeys. Like Victor, the most Simon had in terms of advice were text-based interactions with Blue.

Yet the more significant problem with this scene is that Simon's situation—one that is horrific and traumatizing—plays second fiddle to the heterosexual love triangle of his friends. His friends show little sympathy for Simon's painful and emotionally harmful predicament, not only prioritizing the primacy of heterosexuality but normalizing queer trauma and violence. Even after Simon is publicly ridiculed by two students in the school cafeteria, with his friends witnessing the entire event, none reach out to Simon for support. Simon's lying and orchestrating a half-baked heterosexual romance between his classmate and friend, thus denying the true heterosexual romance between his friends, are more problematic for his friends than Simon's safety and emotional well-being. It is Simon that must apologize and make amends with his friends, placing the responsibility for not only his queer sexuality but also the heterosexual relationship at Simon's feet (Edelman 2004). This film—and the interactions between Simon and his friends—demonstrate that Simon's contractual self, as the closeted homosexual, is not only expected to navigate his sexual journey alone and come out once that sexuality is settled, but the contractual self is also obligated to uphold the primacy of heterosexuality.

Therefore, every step along the way, from admitting to one's queerness to navigating such queerness and even to the heterosexuality of friends, is to be wholly experienced and handled individually by the burgeoning queer youth. At a time when anxiety runs rampant, as Alex demonstrates, for queer youth friends are not the outlet and resource that we may think them to be. In the case of *Love, Simon*, they are part of the problem queer youth must face and manage, while in *Love, Victor* the answer is to find new friends only after coming out and to move to a queer metropole like New York City. In the narrative of queer individualism and the contractual self, stitched together from these three texts, high school friends are inadequate at helping the young queer protagonist as he grapples with his sexuality.

A Different Sort of Narrative

If *Love, Victor* favors a deference to future friendships and post–coming-of-age relations for queer youth, then the Norwegian multimodal show *Skam* (2015–17) advocates for the importance of already existing friendships in the journey of queer youth navigating their sexualities. Initially, Isak attempts to navigate both his feelings for Even and his broader attraction to men alone, resulting in several incidents of anger, defensiveness, and insomnia. For instance, after Even puts an end to their initial relationship despite giving Isak mixed signals, Isak spots Even and his ex-girlfriend kissing at a party (season 3, episode 5). Isak becomes angry, getting into a fight with one of his friends, storming off, and kicking a trashcan on the sidewalk. The next day at school, Isak apologizes to his best friend,

Jonas, to which Jonas says, "No one is mad at you . . . we're just worried. We don't get what's up with you . . . you've been behaving weird lately" (season 3, episode 6).

Isak eventually sees the school nurse about his insomnia, asking for sleeping pills, but the nurse notes that his problem is likely psychological and that he needs to "talk to someone who will help you sort out your thoughts" (season 3, episode 6). The nurse explains that every person is an island and the only way to connect with bridges to other islands is with words. The nurse follows up with "You can't keep isolating yourself. Everything is harder on your own . . . don't you have someone you can talk to?"

At this point, Isak approaches Jonas and asks if they can talk. While sitting on a bench eating kebabs, Isak begins, "You know that thing about me being weird lately? It's because of a person that I like." Isak admits that who he likes is not a girl and Jonas guesses that it is Even. The two talk about the way Even is a "back and forth kind of guy," alluding to the mixed signals he receives from Even. Jonas's advice is that Even needs to break up with his girlfriend. The next episode features Isak soliciting advice about Even from his openly gay roommate (Eskild) and his other friends, his friends urging Isak to give Even an ultimatum, which results in Even showing up at Isak's house and the two reconciling (season 3, episode 7).

Isak's journey begins akin to Alex's own journey, insofar as both internalize their struggles and attractions to the point of stress, anxiety, and defensiveness. Yet where Alex mostly resolves his struggles alone before admitting that he is gay—separate from his feelings toward Elliott—Isak's sexuality is tied to the "thing" he has/had with Even, and so talking about that and resolving that "thing" is part and parcel of coming to terms with his sexuality. To do this, however, Isak relies on conversations with his friends and roommate, their advice directly affecting Isak's actions and mood. There is no collective negotiation that takes place in *Alex Strangelove*, whereas Isak's friends openly discuss with Isak how to craft his text message ultimatum to Even (season 3, episode 7). Queer sexuality, like communication, is thus a collaborative and interactional effort in *Skam*.

The importance of friendship, both with regard to navigating one's attractions and queer sexuality and in general, is a central theme in the UK Netflix show *Heartstopper* (2022–present). Such an importance also indexes actual chains of friendship that span online and offline spaces, saturating daily life with cultures of care (Byron 2021). The show focuses on the friendship and then relationship of out gay high schooler Charlie and the closeted bisexual Nick. For most of the first season, Nick is seen coming to terms with his sexuality and attraction for Charlie as the two grow closer to one another, culminating not in their relationship—they kiss at the end of the third episode and are a couple at the start of the fourth episode (out of eight episodes)—but in Nick's coming out as bisexual to his mother (season 1, episode 8). The majority of the second season sees Nick struggling with coming out to others until he posts on Instagram not only that he and Charlie are boyfriends but that he is bisexual (season 2, episode 8). Bisexuality comes *after* boyfriends.

Throughout the first season, Nick not only spends time watching videos of what it means to be bisexual, but he speaks with an old friend, Tara, and her girlfriend Darcy about his relationship with Charlie and his attraction toward guys (season 1, episode 6). Tara and Darcy do not pressure Nick into coming out—and neither does Charlie, who talks to Nick about how Charlie knew he himself was gay—but they offer Nick a space to talk about his sexuality. Important here is that Tara and Darcy are Nick's peers, Tara only recently coming out as a lesbian (season 1, episode 6), compared to Victor seeking advice from Simon, who had been out for some time while living an out life in New York City. Tara asks Nick how he feels having told someone about his relationship with Charlie, to which Nick admits that it feels good to have told them.

In a similar vein, Charlie grapples with his burgeoning feelings for Nick by asking advice from his three best friends: Tao, Elle, and Isaac. They never brush him off, unlike Dell when Alex confesses that he may be bisexual, but that does not mean friends always provide sage advice. Tao, for instance, continues to be wary of Charlie's friendship with Nick and he attempts to dissuade Charlie of his feelings, not only because Tao assumes Nick is straight but also because Nick is part of the rugby team. Some members of the rugby team were responsible for Charlie's bullying the year prior, and thus Tao is doubtful that rugby players could actually be Charlie's friend. The point is not the content of the advice but that advice *is given*, that Charlie feels safe and comfortable enough to talk with his friends about his feelings for Nick. When Tao accuses Charlie of being a bad friend and keeping his relationship with Nick a secret from him (season 1, episode 7), unlike Simon, who must shoulder all responsibility, both Charlie and Tao apologize for not being a good enough friend before sharing a reconciliation hug (season 1, episode 8).

Interestingly, as Nick opens up to others about his relationship with Charlie and his sexuality, Charlie begins hiding his relationship and problems from Tao in particular. Charlie turns inward—partly a result from the bullying he experienced prior to the start of the series, as explored more fully in the second season—not talking to anyone about his insecurities and fears, culminating in an admission to his older sister Tori that he thinks everyone would be better off without him (season 1, episode 8). When Charlie internalizes his anxieties over Nick and his friends, Charlie falls deeper into despair and insecurity. When he verbalizes his anxiety to his friends and Nick, the interaction gives Charlie added confidence and lightens his mood. Charlie is noticeably less anxious, for instance, after he and Tao reconcile and is seen cheering his friends on during the school's sports day event (season 1, episode 8).

If the importance of Charlie's friends is quintessential to the story of *Heartstopper*, then Nick's reevaluation of his friends is equally important. This begins after Charlie spends the day at Nick's house, Nick's mother commenting that Nick seems "more like [himself]" around Charlie (season 1, episode 2). In the following episode, Nick admonishes his friend Harry for being homophobic toward Charlie, admitting that he does not like Harry before walking away. Nick begins to admit to Charlie that he does not really like his friends, particularly after spending time with Charlie and his friends during Charlie's birthday party (season 1, episode 5). Nick's aversion to his friends culminates in a physical altercation between Nick and Harry after Harry begins picking on Charlie for being gay. Nick's reevaluation of his friends is partly based on his feelings for and relationship with Charlie and that Nick likes who he is (and has become) when around Charlie and his friends. Season two then sees Nick as well-integrated into Charlie's friend group, now considered Nick's friend group as well.

While both Simon and Alex are equally presented with problematic friends for different reasons, neither uses that to reassess their friendships. Instead, both become even more isolated and individually responsible for resolving their feelings, problems, and sexualities without the aid of others. Simon eventually does make friends that are accepting and a positive influence on him, as depicted in *Love, Victor*, but the point of their inclusion is to prove to Victor that things will get better *after* high school. What if Simon, like Nick, had called out his friends for their ill-treatment of his situation, admitting that yes, mistakes may have been made, but their heterosexual relationship cannot be compared to the humiliation and violence that eventually befalls him after he is forcibly outed? Doing so, however, would admit that the problems Simon faces, the problems associated with his queer sexuality, are not his alone, that others are imbricated in how he navigates and cultivates his sexuality.

That Nick is able to talk to Charlie about his confusions and insecurities around his sexuality illustrates that partners, in addition to friends, are coconstructing one's sexuality. Sometimes, however, coproducing sexuality is not entirely verbalized and happens through mutual silences. In the 2016 French film *Being 17*, protagonist Damien is navigating his attraction to fellow high school student and bully Thomas, particularly when Thomas comes to live with Damien and his mother because it takes Thomas over an hour to get to school each day. In this enemy-to-lover teenage drama, Damien channels both his frustrations with and budding feelings for Thomas into learning how to box from a family friend. Boxing couples with the mutual silences and looks that both Damien and Thomas exchange throughout the film, as if both are attempting to figure out why they fight and what they may feel. That silence between them—a nonverbal agreement to hold inside a seemingly mutual desire—is not meant to counteract verbally confronting their feelings, but rather it coconstitutes their feelings and their relationship. That which is *not* said can be just as important as that which *is* said, as discussed in chapter 1.

While seemingly demonstrative of that individual struggle for the truth of sexuality in the construction of the contractual self, the silence *shared* between Damien and Thomas is itself a relationship between the two boys. Linguistic anthropologist Keith Basso (1970, 225) details the use and placement of silence in Western Apache language and culture, arguing that "keeping silence in Western Apache culture is associated with social situations in which participants perceive their relationships *vis-à-vis* one another to be ambiguous and/or unpredictable." While Basso illustrates what the relationship may be among Western Apache, I take from Basso the fact that silence, what Basso (1970, 215) calls "extra-linguistic factors," is part and parcel of social situations and relationality. Linguist Tiina Vainiomäki (2004, 347) turns the dialectical key further, arguing that silence sits at "the core of shaping meanings in human culture," and as such Vainiomäki refers to silence as a "cultural sign."[19] Building on both Basso and Vainiomäki, I contend that silences work to coconstitute social situations and relationality between people, for not only must we know when to keep silent, when "silence is golden"—that silence is valuable—and when to speak up, but *sharing silences* renders those silences meaningful in how we come to know and understand each other, our relationship to one another and, ultimately, culture. That silences *speak* volumes, as the familiar idiom proclaims, implies that silence does something, it does work and is quintessential to the interactional meaning-making process of language: "[S]ocial interaction inseminates our silences with meaning, impregnating our pauses" (Bilmes 1994, 74). The absence of a speech act is still the presence of a silence, and following anthropologist Jack Bilmes (1994, 74), "somehow we have made nothing, an absence, a void, mean something."[20]

For Damien and Thomas, it is Damien who first breaks this unspoken, mutual understanding that silence must be kept between them. One night, after Damien admits to Thomas that "I don't know if I'm into guys or just you" as the two are driving back from Damien's failed hookup, the two are studying Damien's notes on Plato. Damien recites a passage that juxtaposes the need for male-female sexual intercourse and the desire and mutual satisfaction of male-male sexual intercourse. Thomas responds with "you are heavy-handed," his way to chastise Damien for breaking their silent bond, for their relationship and feelings—still building and Damien unsure if they are mutual—is predicated on the silence they keep, the silence they share. It is a mutual understanding, one that is no doubt confusing for Damien and Thomas, that they ought not verbalize their feelings, otherwise they must confront the potential present reality that they have feelings for a guy, for each other. Eventually, Damien verbalizes his feelings to Thomas, confessing that he loves Thomas, to which Thomas responds, "What a pain. You talk too much. You couldn't even see I was scared." Thomas then kisses Damien and the two have sex. That Damien "talks too much" not only indexes the mutual silence they are to share, but by talking too much, Damien is unable to *see* that Thomas feared what he felt for Damien. In other words, silence is meant to heighten the other senses, sight especially. By staying quiet, by paying attention to not only body language but also the absence of the speech act, the boys are meant to perceive the mutual difficulty and fear they share, all embedded in the silence. Silence works to interlace both Damien's and Thomas's sexualities, whereby to understand one's sexuality and one's self is to understand the other—the mutuality of the silence contributes to the coconstitutive nature of their sexualities

Silence must thus be paired with both listening and witnessing. When Damien eventually tells his mother why Damien and Thomas had fought at school—that Damien tried to kiss Thomas and Thomas became upset—he asks his mother, "Nothing to say?" His mother pauses before responding, "No, I'm listening. And what's to say?" His mother's insistence that she is listening pairs with Thomas's annoyance that Damien "talks too much" because what Thomas wants from Damien is to be witnessed, for his fear to be seen and understood. Damien is quick to talk, quick to break a silence, and thus he forgets that silence represents one's listening practices and one's witnessing practices. Silence may be the lack of speech acts and talk, but that does not make it meaningless. Indeed, that silence can be *felt*, that it is palpable to those engaged in its practices, imbues silence with incredible meaning-making power in ways that speech acts are sometimes unable to capture.

Silence is affective. Cultural theorist Teresa Brennan (2004, 1) famously asked readers if they had ever walked into a room and "felt the atmosphere." For Brennan, this shared feeling embodies the notion of affect, particularly its ability to be transmitted without speaking. Silence is also wordlessly felt: how many times have we thought about the heaviness of a silence or that a silence is deafening? Silence is not just an absent of a speech act; it is the presence of an affective force that ties those present together in invisible, though profoundly felt, knots. Silence is thus an ordinary affect that punctuates daily life: "a surging, a rubbing, a connection of some kind that has an impact" (Stewart 2007, 128). As anthropologist Kathleen Stewart (2007, 2) writes of ordinary affects, they are "the stuff that seemingly intimate lives are made of." Ordinary affects entangle one another, entwines bodies together insofar as our relationality is rooted in who we are *in the present*. They are not promises for tomorrow but a listening and a witnessing of the here and now. Silence as an ordinary affect is not meant to universalize the reason for silence; Basso (1970) reminds us that silences are contextual, and their meanings situated. Rather, silences work to entwine and entangle in ways that *seem* ordinary but are not. The silences between Damien and Thomas do not give rise to a named sexuality—Damien never says or wonders if he is gay, only if he is "into guys or just [Thomas]." Naming the feeling matters less than feeling it in the present, allowing the silence of their mutual attraction to entangle Damien and Thomas even further. Breaking that silence has consequences, but it also allows for Damien and Thomas's relationality to grow or move, for confusion to be pushed aside for the other ordinary affects quintessential to queer relationality: intimacy and sex.

Coming Out: A Comparison

The different narratives of queer youth sexuality in the above media artifacts manifest also in moments when sexuality is made public: coming out. The way characters come out to friends and family fall along this narrative divide, where US media representation of coming out centers on the naming of the sexuality—gay and bisexual—while European media representation focuses on the relationship with other characters. And as with the narratives discussed above, the ways one comes out intertwines with perceptions of self.

In *Love, Simon*, Simon first tells his friend Abby while driving home from the Waffle House. He stops his car and tells her that he is gay. Similarly, when he comes out to his family on Christmas Day, he again repeats the same words: "I'm gay." In *Love, Victor*, Victor calls his best friend Felix to meet him in front of their building, Felix facing away from Victor as Victor admits that "I like guys" (season 1, episode 9). The first season ends (and second season begins) with Victor coming out to his family, stating, "I'm gay." Likewise, in *Alex Strangelove*, when Alex lays drenched on the poolside, his ex-girlfriend standing above him, he quickly admits, "I'm gay."

In each instance, despite the protagonists having an attraction to a particular guy, naming the sexuality—engaging in the illocutionary speech act—supersedes attraction and feelings, as the character must be individually intelligible in their contractual relation with others and society. They have always been gay, but it was either awakened or made undeniable after meeting their individual love interest. It is their expectation and obligation to realize their sexualities and then share them, via coming out, with interested parties (i.e., friends and family). The love interests become a catalyst for the protagonists' making public their sexualities, but their sexualities are not reducible to a single interaction. Rather, these queer sexualities are quintessential to the identities and selves of each individual character, internal parts that exist irrespective of others, and thus they can engage with others as intelligible and contractual individuals. The very notion of the self becomes a fully contained bastion of information and truth that one must speak and convey for the truth to be known (Foucault 1990). A catalyst is not a piece of the self but a conduit that enables the deliverance of internal information to external receivers of information (Reddy 1979).

Skam, *Heartstopper*, and *Being 17*, however, offer a different coming-out experience. Recall above that when Isak "comes out" to Jonas, he does so by admitting that he has a "thing" with Even, nearly identical to the way he tells his roommate (Eskild) and his other friends. Isak's "thing" with Even becomes the cornerstone to how he not only understands his queer sexuality but also of how he verbalizes it to others. His illocutionary speech act does not imbricate Isak into a sexuality or community but into a relationship or "thing" with Even. Similarly, when Nick comes out to Tara, he does so by saying that he and Charlie are together; Nick has yet to settle on his bisexuality, though he does discuss it with Charlie (episode 6). Likewise, when Nick comes out to his mother, he begins by saying that Charlie is his boyfriend, then follows by explaining that he likes both guys and girls *before* saying that he is bisexual. Damien's "coming out" is perhaps even more tenuous than Isak and Nick's because he tells his mom, after she had asked him why he and Thomas were fighting, "I tried to kiss [Thomas]." No sexuality is named—just like when Damien tells Thomas for the first time that he's not sure if he is into all guys or just Thomas—and his relationship with Thomas is still predicated on silence, despite Damien wishing for things to be actually said.

The primacy of the relationship is key to Nick's coming out and admission of his queer sexuality, not because his sexuality is reducible to a single person but because his sexuality is produced and practiced interactionally. More than catalysts, Charlie and Even are partners in how sexuality is experienced and defined, indicating a collaborative narrative and, ultimately, a collaborative model of queer youth sexuality. Damien's and Thomas's mutual confusion with their feelings and subsequent intimacy are both reliant on one another because silence itself relies on listening and witnessing by the other; mutual silence followed by their mutual feelings and intimacy also works to coconstitute their queer sexualities. For these characters, sexuality cannot exist in a vacuum and separate from others. The self in this narrative is interactional and relational, not reducible to any one relation or interaction. I again take my cue from both Gray (2009) and Weiss (2011), who similarly contend that social relations are the bedrock of queer identities and sexualities. However, my goal is to highlight the interactional quality of these social relations—it is not just the existence of others and the relationalities that exist but the doing, practicing, and *interacting* (often through talk and silences) that work to produce sexualities and queer identities.

Such an interactional model returns us to both Reddy (1979) and Bakhtin (1981), for the work of the interaction is to produce meaning, to produce the self. Here, *Skam*, *Heartstopper*, and *Being 17* bear witness to the ways sexuality, like language and silences, is collaborative and interactional, between not only Isak and Even; Nick and Charlie; or Damien and Thomas but also Isak and Jonas, Eskild, and his friends; Nick and

Tara, Darcy, and his mother; and Damien and his mother. Admitting that they are in relationships or have (implied) feelings for one another as the declaration of their sexualities, as the illocutionary speech acts, pivots on the relationality between individuals rather than on the internalization of sexuality. If sexuality is the meaning to be conveyed, it must be conveyed as a relationship to others, not an internal truth essential to the self. And equally important, then, are the ways friendships come to matter for how sexuality is understood, and the meaning produced therein; sexuality is interactional and pivots on cultures of care that enable Isak, Nick, Damien, and even Thomas to navigate their burgeoning queer sexuality (Byron 2021).

Interesting in Reddy's (1979) assessment of language is that despite language actually operating interactionally and collaboratively, what he calls "the toolmaker's paradigm" to language, the conduit metaphor still persists. The same, I contend, is true of (queer) sexuality. If we follow Foucault (1990), all sexuality is produced at the moment of confession, therapy, and expert analysis, modes of coercion operationalized to produce categories of knowledge and "truth" (e.g., the homosexual). Compared to narratives of queer youth sexuality, US-based representations of queer youth sexuality still seem to narrativize queer sexuality as a meaning internal to the self, a meaning that the *individual* must discover alone to be intelligible in their contractual relation. There may be catalysts to that discovery, but they simply act as conduits to convey the internal truth of queer sexuality. US-based representations and the narratives they construct limit how audiences, including queer youth, might think, feel, experience, and come to know queer sexuality.

Other Matters

My task in this chapter was not to explain how queer sexuality actually operates in the United States and Europe. I invited such comparisons given Reddy's (1979) and Foucault's (1990) assessments about language and sexuality, respectively, to draw attention to the fact that narratives constructed from representations may not align with the actual experiences of individuals. Therefore, when I draw a distinction between US and European narratives of queer youth sexuality, I do so not to essentialize how sexuality is practiced in the United States and Europe but instead to center how media representations narrate how queer youth sexuality operates.

It is perhaps clichéd to say that representation matters, even if we are to parse through the kinds of representation presented in different media.

What I suggest matters more than the representation of identity is the representation of relationality. Representations of queer young people on screen no doubt influence how queer young people perceive themselves, their sexualities, and their surroundings (e.g., Craig et al. 2015; Pullen 2014; McInroy and Craig 2015). But more than representations of individuals with sexualities, representations of individuals negotiating sexualities, interacting, collaborating, and producing sexualities through interactions offer queer young people a glimpse into how sexuality may operate.

As argued above, the different narratives of queer youth sexuality align not only with different understandings and interpretations of queer sexuality but also with different ideologies of the self. For US-based representations, the self exists separate from all others, an individual that contractually interacts with others, and is ultimately fully responsible for their own actions. This contractual self creates a set of expectations and obligations around one's individual sexuality—how one comes to know one's own sexuality, how one is to share that sexuality, and what is expected from those to whom one comes out. Those expectations are individually defined, whereby the individual comes to know their own sexuality on their own with little to no interaction with others. The hearer of the coming-out admission is thus expected only to receive the message, as if along a conduit. For European-based representations, in contrast, the self must exist in relation to others, in part because the person is always inadequate to exist separately from all others; relations form the bedrock of not only identity but the self as well. Sexuality thus becomes a way to understand broader implications of the self in society.

Representations of queer youth sexuality may very well, then, contribute to the crafting of queer youth selves. As Gray (2009, 168) observes, "[W]hen [queer youth] scan mass media and the Internet for materials to incorporate into their queer sense of self, a politics of LGBT visibility comes up on the screen. These representations organize recognition of queer difference through a grammar of narrowly defined LGBT identities, a 'visible minority.'" Certainly, queer youth are not alone in media-related self-crafting, but Gray's point is that the lack of representational variety makes that which is represented much more meaningful and impactful (see also Robertson 2018, chapter 4).

However, such differences in representations and narratives may also be the result of the influence of the adult. In the US-based representations discussed in this article, we can take each story and main character as a look back from the eyes of a fully maturated adult version of the main character. For a fully maturated adult, queer sexuality may be something understood and integral to their identity, it may very well be a truth hidden in the past, in their teenage years. The story of maturation exists linearly—growing up from child to adult—and sexuality thus evolves or unfolds in a similar fashion: there was a point when I would not admit I was gay, but now, I *am* gay (and always have been). Yet *Skam*, *Heartstopper*, and *Being 17* dramatically shift the perspective and experience to the young people themselves. These are stories that take place in the moment, maneuvering laterally, not a look back at one's younger years. These are tales of "growing sideways" (Stockton 2009), not growing up, and therefore sexuality is not something one needs to fully understand or *know*, but instead it is something that enables experiences, practices, and interactions between people. Coming out is thus not about coming out as a sexuality but coming out as having a relationship that may, one day (who knows?) contribute to a sexuality.

The differences in these narratives and explanations therefore align when we consider that not only are conceptions and ideologies of the self perhaps different across cultures, but that conceptions and ideologies of the self may be different between adults and youth. Yet my point is not to then fit such a difference into a coming-of-age narrative of growing up and maturation, that the youth perception of the self will become the adult perception of the self. Rather, I want to dwell, like *Skam*, *Heartstopper*, and *Being 17* do, on the perception of self of these particular young people and their lateral movements into coming out. Here my point about representation comes to matter even more, for if the representation of a self contingent on relationality instead of individuality is presented to young people, might that perception of the self not only reflect one's life but perhaps even be adopted by young people? And more importantly, need there be any consideration of the future if the relations in the here and now provide satisfaction and happiness in the moment? These types of questions work to unscript the present, to unshackle the contractual expectations one has to the future and find meaning and relationality in the here and now.

Chapter Four

The Ascendancy of Queer Pleasure

> Sex is finding kids, targeting them, but they don't seem to desire our protection.
>
> —Kathryn Bond Stockton, "The Queer Child Now and Its Paradoxical Global Effects"

In the last episode of the seventh season of the popular German web-based show *Druck* (2018–present),[1] genderqueer protagonist Isi and his/their best friend turned lover Sascha are cuddling in Isi's room, talking about their feelings for one another as their fingers roam along each other's bodies.[2] The scene ends with the two intensifying their touching and kissing as their fingers begin undoing the others' pants. Part of what the two talk about is Isi's neglect of Sascha and their friendship in previous episodes, Isi having found new friends at the start of the season. Isi asks Sascha if he/they had hurt him, to which Sascha replies that he was hurt, but that things eventually worked out. They both express concern that things may be moving too fast, but neither offers a resolution as the scene shifts to the two beginning to undress the other.

In their book *Sex, or the Unbearable*, Lauren Berlant and Lee Edelman (2014) write about a form of "sex without optimism," a type of sex and sexuality that sits uncomfortably between the "causes of or repairs for the precarity of life" (7). Sex without optimism enables a consideration of sex that sidesteps or elides hidden futurity that may reside in sex, that sex exists beyond the here and now. The scene of Isi and Sascha's talk and subsequent implied sex is a type of sex without optimism because their conversation contrasts with the sex that they then have, as if there is no resolution to either Isi's actions toward Sascha nor their anxiety about the potentially ruined friendship. Sex may be a way to solidify their relationship and their romance, but it is also an act that does not wash away the anxiety, only momentarily sidesteps it in favor of an embodied experience that enjoins the two together. It may be about pleasure and relationality, but it may also just be sex, full stop.

The broader theoretical point that Berlant and Edelman (2014, 4) wish to make is that "sex undoes the subject," whereby sex manifests a series of seemingly unbearable situations and contradictions that we still manage to find ways of enduring. Part of that unbearability resides in the relationality engendered by sex, the interstitial space formed when bodies collide and coalesce in libidinal fashion. As Berlant (2022, 40) opines elsewhere, "Even the simplest sexual pleasure involves a collaboration of tangles."[3] One reading of Berlant and Edelman returns us to neoliberal agency, US exceptionalism, and the contractual self, for if sex—a relationality—undoes the subject, then the implication is that the subject is an individuated being that in moments of sex, one gives oneself over to another in ways that undo or disaggregate the tightly wound self. Sex pulls at the thread to unravel the individuated subject, but read in this way, sex is *not* contractual, for if it can undo the subject, then sex exists without obligation as it does without optimism.

A second reading, however, lies in the tension and seeming contradiction relayed in the previous chapter, that while the contractual self may present as the embodied experience of US individualism, sexuality is actually relationality constructed and managed. If this is the case, then sex, a type of relationality, can lay bare our intimate relationalities and call into stark questioning our seeming reliance on autonomy and individuality. In other words, sex reveals our interdependence, in a splendid and libidinal manner, and this reveal—this tension—is, in Berlant and Edelman's words, unbearable. Following Judith Butler (2004, 23), sex may be akin to grief, for "what grief displays . . . is the thrall in which our relations with others hold us, in ways we cannot always recount or explain, in ways that often interrupt the self-conscious account of ourselves we might try to provide, in ways that challenge the very notion of ourselves as autonomous and in control." Indeed, as Butler eloquently writes, "Let's face it. We're undone by each other. And if we're not, we're missing something." We believe we are autonomous and in control, only to be shown our deeply embedded relationalities that make and unmake us over and over again.

For Isi and Sascha, their romance relies on their friendship, but both are laid bare when they have sex: their relationality is exposed, without any actual resolution, when they have sex. But as I demonstrated in chapter 1, queer youth sex is viewed as dangerous, a cause for panic in such extreme fashion that laws regulating youth's access to materials must be passed and mandated or else the future will rot with corruptibility. Considering Berlant, Edelman, and Butler, we could interpret such panicked rhetoric around sex as an exposure of relationality, interdependence, and the lack of autonomy. If we consider childhood sexuality, more broadly, as the problem, the fear lies not only in the loss of innocence and corruptibility of the family and nation but also in the implication of innocence itself. Our dirty little secret as adults may not be the pleasure of sex but the exposure it contrives, the relationality it requires when we spend too much time fixated on our individuated capacity to live autonomous lives, exceptionally so. Sex unmasks the truth, spills the tea in such spectacular fashion that it is almost impossible to deny the lies we tell ourselves and our children.[4] However, this does not stop us from trying.

For queer youth sex, this is doubly problematic. Not only does queer youth sex reveal our interdependence and ability to be unmade, but it is saturated in nonnormative relationality. We may be undone by one another, but queer youth sex undoes us in queer ways, ways that buttress the "reproductive futurism" of the child (Edelman 2004), the narrative of growing up (Stockton 2009), and the assumed heterosexuality of the child. These are dangerous relations, threatening even, and when made manifest through queer youth sex, they leave participants as exposed as others. Yet as Kathryn Bond Stockton (2016, 508) writes in the epigraph to this chapter, "Sex is finding kids, targeting them, but they don't seem to desire our protection."[5] Queer youth are having sex and do not need our protection from it because sex is perhaps not something to fear but something to have and embrace. It makes and unmakes us, and perhaps that is precisely the point of not just sex but the human experience more broadly.

I am reminded of Butler's (2004, 23) rejoinder, that even though we are undone by one another, "if we're not, we're missing something." Sex without optimism may leave us exposed, and it may do little to rectify contradictions—sex may, in fact, proliferate such contradictions—but that is not to say sex is inherently negative. I am not arguing that sex is inherently positive—sex is, as I explore below, a negotiation with others but also with the self. Not all sex involves another, but it does, first and foremost, involve the self.

This chapter explores US and European streaming shows that feature a protagonist in scenes of queer youth sex. I am writing from a US-centered position, querying the importance of queer youth sex representations in television by looking toward both US representations and European representations. Sex panics manifest differently in different places, and the US context no doubt frames queer youth sex representation as itself fraught with panic. Mobilizing European representations, then, allows for an expanded narrative of queer youth sex(uality) while also recognizing the possibility of cross-pollination and influence. By bringing different shows into conversation with one another, as I have done throughout this book, I contend that queer pleasure *supplants* the panic featured in each show—and panic around sex more generally—by framing the scenes of queer youth sex as destigmatized, legitimate, and even mundane. This is the broader representational narrative of queer youth sex(uality) that such framing constitutes, for while each show's scenes of queer youth sex are not identical, they do contribute to a broader narrative of queer pleasure's *ascendancy*.

Such ascendancy of pleasure supplants panic in the public discourse of queer youth sex(uality), the narrative of ascendancy recognizing and acknowledging fear and panic and offering not regulation but exploration. In other words, queer youth sex challenges security's panicked hold on sex more broadly, unscripting expectations of heterosexuality and innocence in impromptu moments and times when (sex) plans go awry. Susan Driver (2008, 3) notes that "as queer youth enter the purview of popular and academic texts, the discourses used to describe and interpret this group of minority youth often ends up foreclosing the ambiguous, desiring, relational, and ephemeral dimensions of their experiences." This in part is due to circulating narratives of queer youth as victims, intelligible only as a population in need of protection by the liberal state. This victimhood also becomes a touchstone for coming-out experiences and identity formation narrated in the present, as discussed in the previous chapter, thus relegating queer youth to either a past experience to overcome/understand or a present population in need of protection.[6] Such a victimization trope, then, leaves "little space within which to listen for alternative youth voices that might express complex strengths, pleasures, and curiosities" (Driver 2008, 4).

What if queer youth pleasure were an end in and of itself, not a mechanism for adult intelligibility (Driver 2008; Talburt 2004, 2018),[7] but a meaningful experience for its own sake? What if we consider queer youth sex without optimism, without a future orientation and instead as a way to expose our interdependence on one another? We would then be looking at a different sort of queer theory, one concerned with what I described in chapter 2 as a radical presentism of queer youth sexuality. Radical presentism is an insistence that queer youth sexuality is better understood through a focus on the present rather than either a look back at the past (from the perspective of adults) or an aspirational narrative of a future where things will "get better." Driver (2008, 8) calls for a reconfiguration of theory, as "queer youth have the potential of invigorating theory through their culturally expressive assertions of desire in a culture that scorns the queer perversions of young love and lust." This means that we must attend to the "complex desiring selves" of queer youth (Driver 2008, 10), which in turn works to unscript not only the assumed heterosexuality of the child but also the foreclosure of queer youth desire.[8] The complexity of desiring selves again invokes Berlant and Edelman's argument that "sex is a site at which we encounter the incoherence of self and identity; it is not a way to know (oneself or another) as coherent, bounded, objects of mastery, but a field of rupture, disorganization, or misrecognition" (Weiss 2020, 1358).

Taken together, the ascendancy of queer pleasure elides a categorization that would label some sex as dangerous and panic-inducing and instead favors attention to the fact that queer youth *can* and *do* experience pleasure in the present—it is not something they hope for in the future but something they experience in the here and now. Such attention is a method of unscripting present expectations of youth, and queer youth in particular, as sexless protopeople on their path of maturation, whereby the future of the soon-to-be-adult is governed in the present through sieving scripts that regulate and manage sexuality. However, such a method that focuses on queer youth sex is no doubt messy and may seem as though it can potentially "rupture" the self—to invoke Margot Weiss's (2020, 1358) explication of Berlant and Edelman—but is the "self and identity" ever coherent to begin with? The US neoliberal belief in the individual does proffer, to an extent, a coherent, individuated self (Gershon 2011, 2016), yet as I explored in the previous chapter and discussed above, this may be a story we tell ourselves to retain some semblance of control over our autonomy.

Sex may thus be the site where the belief in a coherent, individuated self breaks down, where the incoherence is more palpable given the fact that sex with others is reliant on the presence of an other (though pleasure is certainly not reliant on such a presence). I argue, then, that the panic that saturates the scenes described in this chapter—akin to the scene between Isi and Sascha—is also tied to a realization of the incoherent self, that pleasure is contingent, not always on another but on an always already fractured self, and as such one panics when one realizes that one's self and identity have never been bounded or coherent. We panic when we realize we do not have absolute control over ourselves. Here, too, is what a comparative study affords us: a more explicit recognition of the unbounded nature of the self, despite a belief in its boundedness and coherence.

A comparison of popular culture artifacts that feature queer protagonists, as examined throughout the chapters of this book, relies on an increased visibility of queer characters in mainstream media. Teen television shows are on the rise, especially with the advent of streaming services like Netflix and Hulu. Historically, teen television was not taken seriously by scholars (Davis and Dickinson 2000), though that has certainly changed over the past two decades given the rise in studies that have explored the relevance of teen television to teen identity and sexuality (Ross and Stein 2008; Greene 2012). Multiple studies demonstrate how the sexual scripts that permeate teen shows are not only predominately heterosexual but work to frame romantic and sexual expectations in rather narrow ways (e.g., Dajches and Aubrey 2020; Aubrey et al. 2020; Dajches et al. 2021). Much of teen television that features queer characters, like *Glee*, rely on normative expectations and representations of queerness that fit within a broader heteronormative context (Dhaenens 2012; Sarkissian 2014). The US and UK teenage shows *Skins* offer an interesting example of the ways casual sex is not represented as a problem to overcome "but as everyday facts of teenage life" (Berridge 2013, 786). It is this banality of sex that I wish to dwell on, for queer youth representations are changing to account for the nonnormative sex they have.

The expansion of streaming services and multimodal distribution, as discussed in the previous chapter, has likely contributed to the increased presence and diversity of shows featuring queer youth representations (e.g., Cummings 2022; Christian 2020; Macintosh 2022). These streaming services and distribution platforms (such as YouTube) also generate their own content and can thus create shows that appeal to a variety of populations—many of the newer queer shows are created by streaming and multimodal platforms. Moreover, as these platforms generate their own content, they can tap into a multitude of international production and consumption populations that US television simply cannot handle.

Audiences are thus exposed to a greater variety of international shows featuring diverse characters, storylines, and scenes (Goddard and Hogg 2019; Asmar, Raats, and Audenhove 2023). One result, I suggest, is a broader representational narrative of queer youth sex(uality).[9]

Streaming platforms provide cross-pollination and an expanded repertoire for building mediated worlds. The popularity of the Netflix UK show *Sex Education*, first released in 2019, ought to be read alongside subsequent streaming shows that focus on teen sexuality, such as HBO Max's *Generation*, and alongside older shows with transnational appeal and even adaptations, like *Skins*. Even within Europe, queer representations can and do shape shows transnationally (Grandio and Bonaut 2012; Heim 2020), for as I explored in chapter 2, the popular Norwegian show *Skam* spurred multiple European adaptations, including the Belgian show *wtFOCK* and the German show *Druck*.

This chapter thus charts the pleasure amid the panic. It specifically features scenes of impromptu and spontaneous sex and conversations, moments that are unplanned, and thus they unscript those moments to lay bare the collision of pleasure and panic. It takes a textualist approach to the contemporary popular teen series discussed below. This means that I read and deconstruct renderings of queer youth sex(uality) to paint a broader queer youth narrative that speaks particularly to a panicked US context. I value such a textualist approach as it enables broader theorization of queer youth sex and sexuality instead of arguing within TV cultures, productions, and contexts. My goal is to work toward a queer theory of queer youth sex(uality) through textual depictions of queer sex that take seriously the ascendancy of queer pleasure in the wake of sex panics and render queer sex as legitimate practice for queer youth.

To take such a textualist approach means close and careful readings of a specific number of US and European texts. This no doubt limits the diversity of texts, especially when considering European texts, but I contend that those selected, though not representational of all potential texts, do enable a broad reading on queer youth sex(uality). The texts discussed span streaming platforms and genres, some, like *Shadow and Bone*, are teen fantasy shows not necessarily focused on the development of queer sexuality, while others, like *Love, Victor* and *wtFOCK*, focus explicitly on how the queer protagonist explores their queer sexualities. The different texts examined herein fit within a larger genre of teen shows, including those that feature explicit sex scenes (such as Netflix's Spanish show *Elite*) and those that do not (such as Netflix's UK show *Heartstopper*).

Normalizing Queerness, Exceptionalizing Sex

A discussion of queer sex scenes, particularly among youth, must first recognize not only the difference between various platforms, but also that there has been, historically, a desexualization of sexual diversity in the United States (Beirne 2006; Ng 2021; Maris 2016). As Eve Ng (2023, 11) writes, "The gay characters on these broadcast series tended to be desexualized and serve as narrative fodder for the heterosexual characters." Precursors to diverse representations of queer youth on streaming services include both paid cable channels, like Showtime and HBO, that can "counter the safe and obedient image of major television networks" (Dhaenens 2012, 221; see also Becker 2006 and Gross 2001), along with gay-themed paid networks like Here! (Owens 2019). Shows like *Queer as Folk* and *The L Word* allowed for more explicit queer sexual content and diverse representations given that they are on paid cable channels (Beirne 2006; Peeren 2006; Manuel 2009).

Yet such sexualization in the United States is limited. Ron Becker's (2006) classic study of the rise of gay TV not only highlights how gay representation connects to industrial logic but also how gay TV sits against a backdrop of heteronormativity. The NBC show *Will & Grace*, for instance, "works to enforce hegemonic social relations of inequality" as representative of "new homophobia on TV" given that such representations of sexuality are deemed "separate from social constructs of race, sex, and class" (D. Mitchell 2005, 1052). Frederik Dhaenens (2012) proffers a theory of queer resistance within gay male domesticity and gay homemaking in shows like *Six Feet Under* and *Brothers & Sisters* that see gay characters reconfiguring the confines of the home and domesticity to fit their desires and lifestyles. Shows like *Queer Eye for the Straight Guy* and *Glee* render queer sexuality normative within a heteronormative context (Papacharissi and Fernback 2009; Dhaenens 2012; Sarkissian 2014). Even queer representations outside of the United States provide normative and homogenous portrayals of queer characters, limiting the diversity of representation (van Wichelen and Dhoest 2023; Heim 2020).

Recognizing such normalization of queer representation, particularly in the United States, frames the panic that arises around queer youth sex(uality) and makes panic much more palpable. Andre Cavalcante (2015, 456) notes how "the normalization of LGBTQ characters operates within a much wider field of signification and generates a symbolic remainder" that Cavalcante calls "anxious displacement." Cavalcante (2015, 455) defines this as "the *over*loading of negatively codified social differences and symbolic excess onto figures and relationships that surround LGBT . . . characters." In shows like *Modern Family* and *The New Normal*, "anxious displacement contributes to the legitimization of gay parenting, the subversion of homophobia, and the affirmation of gay masculinity" (Cavalcante 2015, 456). Lynne Joyrich (2014, 138) likewise comments on these two shows, noting how they both offer normative representations of queerness, and "it's exactly that supreme—even extreme—normality, that obsession with normalness, that I find intriguing." I also find such normality interesting, but I am more interested in the process of becoming ordinary, and how scenes of queer youth sex come to consider the sex queer youth have as ordinary and even mundane. Ordinariness is not the same thing as normative or normal; queerness can be ordinary but still be nonnormative.

Sex scenes in film and television have evolved over the years, both in front of the camera and behind it. The use of intimacy coordinators is now the standard, but as Jane Ward (2023, 372) insightfully demonstrates, there is commensurability between the work of actors (used as a gender-neutral term) and sex work, insofar as "the line between acting in sex scenes and being a sex worker is more about stigma management and boundary work, with actors avoiding shame and stigma by delineating between simulated sex and real sex, artful storytelling and porn." The bifurcation between simulated and real also collides with television shows like *Girls* and *Sex Lives of College Girls* that intentionally highlight the ordinary, the imperfect, and the "real" through representations both of female bodies and of the sex they have (Perkins 2014). Such attention to realness also emerges in queer cinema and television, such as John Cameron Mitchell's 2006 film *Shortbus* that features explicit scenes of sex meant to simulate "real" queer sex, and Nick Davis (2008) illustrating how Michael Warner's (2002) "counterpublic" easily captures both the messages and scenes explicit in the film (see also Malakaj 2023). Warner's counterpublics is also a useful framing for watershed queer shows like (the twice-made) *Queer as Folk* (Fraser 2006), while the explicit queer sex scenes in the US version in particular—including an early episode in which high school student Justin gives fellow high school student and future bully a hand job—likewise attempts to tell a story that does not necessarily sugarcoat queer sex, but also shows that queer sex may be sudden and impromptu.

Scenes of queer youth sex are thus quintessential because they buttress, for instance, empirical data that details how parents of queer boys are often at a loss about—at times willfully ignorant of—queer sex, giving the impression that it "doesn't exist" (Flores et al. 2019). Popular culture more generally, especially television shows, can potentially rupture heteronormative expectations and narratives laden in society, and thus prove useful for the classroom as itself a queer pedagogy (Quinlivan 2012). Even queer young adult novels, like Shaun David Hutchinson's *We Are the Ants*, offer encouraging messages of love and connection in their scenes of romance and sex that attempt to counteract internalized homophobia (Clark and Blackburn 2016).

As such, queer narratives found in shows like Netflix's *Sex Education*, as I explore below, draw much needed attention to the role of queer youth in the production and consumption of sex itself. This, too, contributes to the ascendancy of queer pleasure, as we no longer ought to consider youth in general as a population to protect against sex—they are having it and talking about it regardless—but as active producers and consumers in their own (queer) sex and sexualities. This means, then, taking queer youth pleasure seriously, despite our own potential panic or awkwardness as we navigate these media artifacts and scenes.

Sexual Projects

To take seriously the sex between queer youth is to challenge fundamental assumptions about the sexuality of the youth—that they have sexuality, to begin with, but also that they have the potential to have a queer sexuality. It is to displace the panic that surrounds the child and their potential sexuality and supplant it with the possibility of pleasure, queer pleasure at that. As noted above, there is typically little consideration taken for sex between queer youth, be it theoretical, discursive, or even empirical consideration. Entertaining the possibility of youth pleasure—especially high school youth pleasure—seems even more taboo than youth having any sexuality whatsoever. Pleasure may be part of sexuality, but simply claiming that youth have sexuality does not immediately index their pleasure; this is often a separate conversation to be had, one that is as awkward as the talk about sex itself. In other words, talk about sexual pleasure is of a different order than talk about sex in general—both are awkward, but perhaps the former is more so (see Hirsch and Khan 2020; Wade 2017).

Returning to Gayle Rubin's (2011) classic piece "Thinking Sex" proves useful in interrogating sex between queer youth. As Rubin (2011, 145) boldly states, "[A] radical theory of sex must identify, describe, explain, and denounce erotic injustice and sexual oppression." She proposes such a theory by delineating six axioms or "ideological formations" that inform Western notions of sex and sexuality. The first is sexual essentialism, which posits that "sex is a natural force that exists prior to social life and shapes institutions" (146). Such essentialism disavows society's and history's roles in the formation of sex and sexuality, whereas Rubin argues that sexuality is a "human product."[10] As discussed in chapter 1, Rubin then posits that sex negativity is the most important of the ideologies given that it shapes a general attitude toward sex, particularly emerging out of a Christian tradition that interprets sex as sinful. Pleasure and "erotic behavior," Rubin (2011, 148) notes, "is considered bad unless a specific reason to exempt it has been established." The next ideology is the fallacy of misplaced scale, a "corollary of sex negativity," whereby "sexual acts are burdened with an excess of significance (Rubin 2011, 149). Sex laws carry some of the harshest punishments, and given Christianity's influence, sex becomes a zero-sum game of sin. This leads to the fourth ideology, the hierarchical system of sexual value that sees sexual behavior categorized into degrees of good and bad sex, where good sex is considered both morally sound (normal) and in the best interest of the family, kinship, and religion (procreative/productive). Part of Rubin's point is that there is a continued necessity to distinguish between good and bad sex, for while the wall separating the two may be ever moving, there will always be a wall, a separation between the two. This distinction, Rubin (2011, 151) argues, assumes a domino theory of sexual peril insofar as "the line appears to stand between sexual order and chaos . . . if anything is permitted to cross this erotic demilitarized zone, the barrier against scary sex will crumble and something unspeakable will skitter across." Taken together, the ideology necessary for "a pluralistic sexual ethics" is "a concept of benign sexual variation" (Rubin 2011, 154). While variation is a foregone conclusion, a fact of all forms of life, "sexuality is supposed to conform to a single standard" (Rubin 2011, 154). Rubin's (2011, 177) broader point with these six ideologies is that they come to shape normative sexual practice: "[T]hey operate to coerce everyone toward normality."[11] Understanding the construction of normativity helps to disentangle sex panics from sexual practice, particularly queer sexual practices. Not only does queer youth sexuality challenge the assumptions that children have no sexuality, that they are replete with an innocence that stands in stark contrast to sexuality (an adult possession), but that any sexuality that they may have in the present or will have in the future is heterosexual.[12] The same holds true for sex between queer youth, for if they lack sexuality then they invariably lack sexual behavior. Yet the moments discussed below of sexual encounters between queer characters proves not only that this is clearly not the case but also that their sexual behavior stands in contrast to the panic about specifically their queerness.

By focusing on these queer sexual encounters, I work to destigmatize queer sex itself by following these unscripted moments of sexual activity that move laterally to the expectations of youth and queer youth in particular. While these impromptu moments work to supplant panic with pleasure, they also draw much needed attention to the sexual agency of queer youth themselves. To highlight the sexual agency of queer youth, I borrow Jennifer Hirsch and Shamus Khan's (2020, xiv) notion of "sexual projects," or "the reasons why anyone might seek a particular sexual interaction or experience." While "pleasure is an obvious project," there are several other reasons someone may have a sexual encounter: to build relationality, to build reputation, to foster comfort. The decision *not* to have sex is also a sexual project (Hirsch and Khan 2020, xiv). In their research into college sex and sexual assault, Hirsch and Khan (2020, xv) write that "the young people in whose world we were immersed were frequently figuring out their sexual projects through trial and error, to no small degree because no one had spent much time talking to them about what a sexual project might be." Crucial in this admission, and in their study, is that little education exists for youth regarding sexual projects—there is little effort by educators, as discussed in chapter 1, to talk with youth about *why* we have sex, why youth might have sex. Without such conversations and space to talk about sex, to invoke Carole Vance (1992a), youth are left to fill in the blank themselves. Queer youth are even far more disadvantaged, for any consideration of queer pleasure is beyond an afterthought; it is sometimes illegal (see chapter 1).

A crucial difference between the sexual projects in Hirsch and Khan's (2020) study and those of the queer characters discussed below is that for Hirsch and Khan (2020, 92), "many approach sex as a skill rather than as a form of interpersonal interaction" given that "many see casual sex as a fundamental part of the college experience—a core way to 'be college'" (see also Wade 2017).[13] While I mention an instance of hooking up below, pleasure seems to be the dominant sexual project for these queer characters. Such pleasure is often mixed with other projects, namely building relationality between characters, especially boyfriends, while one instance also involves an act of rebellion against one's mother as part and parcel of both his sexual project and his pleasure.

I foreground pleasure given that queer pleasure is often erased because it is considered dangerous, threatening, or even illegal. It is essential to consider the sexual agency of queer youth, to unpack their sexual projects, as they are often ignored. The lateral movements these queer youth take throughout this chapter hinge on their sexual agency and the importance of their sexual projects as they motivate the scenes and work to destigmatize and even demystify queer sex. By destigmatizing and demystifying queer sex, these scenes and my exploration illustrate the ways pleasure's ascendancy supplants the sex panics that continue to script the present and youth expectations, even for a moment. Attention to pleasure's ascendancy is thus a way to unscript the present and queer expectations: what is expected of (queer) youth and how do queer youth quite literally fuck with those expectations? These may be mere moments, but as I argued in chapter 2, minutes and moments are profound intervals of time that enable a different way of being, a different way to fashion the self and build relationality. And this is a necessary point, that the fashioning of selves and the building of relationality that takes place in these moments are tied to the sexual projects of the queer characters. This then becomes another crucial reason for attending to the sexual agency of queer youth: their pleasure comes to matter in who they are, how they interact with one another, and how they navigate an insolvent future not made or destined for them.

Let's Talk about Sex

Given that the queer representations on television have become normalized (Joyrich 2014)—while some have proffered a (hetero)normative representation (Chambers 2009; Dhaenens 2012; Sarkissian 2014)—the growing number of television shows and even films that feature scenes of queer youth does, in part, contribute to the making of queer youth sex as mundane. This is again different from claiming that queer youth sex is normative, for despite the growing representation of queer youth sex and presentation of such sex as ordinary—queer youth have sex, so what?—this does not automatically make such sex normative. In an episode of season one of Netflix's teenage fantasy show *Shadow and Bone* (2021–23), Jesper

Fahey, the seventeen-year-old sharpshooter member of the group of thieves known as the Crows, is seen flirting with a stable boy in one scene, making out with him in a second scene, and then collapsing (presumably naked) into a pile of hay with the stable hand in a third scene (season 1, episode 5). The sex that these two have is never mentioned by the others, though some of Jesper's fellow Crows do remark in general about Jesper's flirting. Jesper's queer sex is thus as mundane as scenes of heterosexual romance and sex despite being nonnormative, stitched into the episode not as a significant reveal or even plot point but as a moment of sheer pleasure at an otherwise stressful time, namely the attempted kidnapping of protagonist Alina Starkov. Even Jesper's romance and sex with fellow Crow Wylan Hendricks in season two is treated nonchalantly, discussed casually between the two characters at various moments throughout the show until it culminates in sex and a relationship. In fact, when Jesper finally recognizes Wylan, it is revealed that the two had previously had sex prior to Wylan's membership in the Crows, but that Wylan left before Jesper awoke because he thought Jesper would do the same (season 2, episode 4). There is nothing sensational about the sex they had or the sex they later have; queer sex is simply part of the tapestry of the show, the inner workings of how characters form relationality with one another.

However, if sex among queer youth is becoming unremarkable—or, rather, remarkable for being unremarkable—talking about queer sex is still a marked practice that calls attention to itself. There are two potential reasons for this markedness. The first is that talk about sex, especially queer sex, is taboo and awkward, particularly given the panicked world in which we live (e.g., Rubinsky and Hosek 2020; McDavitt and Mutchler 2014). Moreover, as discussed in chapter 1, such talk about sex, especially queer sex, is seen as dangerous and mitigated by adults for fear that just the mere mention of sex would lead youth down a path of corruptibility. The second reason is that even if such talk is awkward, it can be necessary and so calling attention to the practice of talking about queer sex attempts to destigmatize not just talking about but having queer sex. Here, too, we see the connection between the speech act and what the speech act does, for if talk about sex works to destigmatize the speech act then the perlocutionary effect is a desensitizing of queer sex itself.[14] Below I explore both reasons through the shows *Sex Education* and *Love, Victor*.

Perhaps the very impetus behind Netflix's popular show *Sex Education* (2019–23), set in the United Kingdom, is to both point to how talk about sex is awkward and to destigmatize sex and sex talk. The show focuses on the sex lives of the students at Moordale Secondary School and the "sex clinic" that Otis, son of sex therapist Jean, and his business partner Maeve run to provide advice to students about sex. In the very first episode of the series, we are presented with the awkwardness of sex talk as Adam, the headmaster's son, reluctantly talks to Otis about his inability to achieve an orgasm with his girlfriend. The conversation was pure happenstance, as Otis and Maeve stumble upon Adam and his priapism hiding out in an abandoned bathroom. Adam had previously embarrassed Otis as a "sex freak" given his mother's profession, itself a stigmatized profession as it hinges on individuals talking about their sex lives and receiving advice and affirmation from the therapist, Jean. By talking to Otis about his sexual dilemma, however, Adam is finally able to achieve an orgasm with his girlfriend. Talking about sex thus becomes the pathway to having more pleasurable sex.

Talk of queer sex, however, is even more awkward and taboo. We again visit one of Adam's sexual problems in the second episode of season three as he now identifies (albeit secretly) as bisexual and is dating Otis's best friend Eric. Each time Adam and Eric move toward having sex, Adam stops Eric because, as we find out, he wants to bottom. Eric initially assumes that Adam simply does not want to have sex with him partly because Adam cannot accept himself as a man desiring another man, but also because Adam cannot bring himself to tell Eric what he wants. He again has another reluctant conversation with Otis, the latter coaching Adam as to how to openly converse with Eric about his sexual desires. The point of their conversation is to encourage Adam to have a conversation with Eric, that he has to openly express what he wants, express his sexual project and expectations with Eric. Adam eventually visits Eric's house, sneaking into his bedroom in order to explain to Eric what he wants. However, Adam cannot face Eric, and he therefore turns around so that he is not face-to-face with Eric, as Adam tells Eric that he wants to bottom. Eric is pleasantly surprised by the revelation as the two have sex and spend the night together. In this scene, queer sex talk is still awkward but made more bearable and thus a pathway to queer pleasure by not being literally faced with the problem—Adam turns around before telling Eric what he wants. Adam's embarrassment at having to verbally convey to Eric his sexual desires initially stands in their way, as both a couple and a couple wanting sex. Yet the multiple conversations Adam has—first with Otis and then with Eric—are the necessary practices to facilitate resolution and pleasure. Even if Adam cannot face Eric in their conversation, an indication that the queer sex talk is still awkward, the talking is the more effective and affective mode of conveying desire.

The awkwardness that Adam feels with regard to queer sex talk also points us toward a broader panic captured by the taboo and even danger of queer sex talk. If *Sex Education* is attempting to legitimize sex and sex talk more broadly, and queer sex (talk) in particular instances and scenes, then it begins with the supposition that (queer) sex talk is itself stigmatized and potentially threatening (to heterosexuality). The series makes this exact point in the first episode with Adam and Otis's "sex freak" status thanks to his mother's sex therapy practice. Similar to *Shadow and Bone*, though, the treatment of queer sex in *Sex Education* creates an equivalency between queer sex and heterosexual sex. Otis can, on multiple occasions, provide advice to queer students (Adam included) regarding their sex problems. While recognizing the awkwardness inherent in sex talk, especially queer sex talk that is indicative of a broader panic around queer sex, *Sex Education* works to destigmatize and make mundane queer sex itself in the present; there is no deferment to later. Adam must talk to Eric now in order to save the relationship.

As *Sex Education* demonstrates, despite the awkwardness of sex talk, it can lead to more fulfilling sex and queer pleasure. This is also well-captured in Hulu's show *Love, Victor* (2020–22). At the start of the second season, Victor and Benji are a couple navigating Victor's recent coming out. The fourth episode of season two, titled "The Sex Cabin," features a nervous Victor wanting to lose his virginity but knowing nothing about gay sex. This is part of a broader set of sexual projects that he and his friend Felix share, to have sex with their partners while they have absconded to Benji's family's cabin. Victor tries to contact Simon (from the film) for advice but is unable to reach him. Simon later explains to Victor that he cannot give Victor advice because sex is a personal matter that can truly be talked about only with one's partner. The advice comes only after Victor has had sex with Benji, the two having discussed Victor's apprehension before Victor suddenly and spontaneously initiates the sex.[15]

Both *Love, Victor* and *Sex Education* follow a similar blueprint insofar as both Victor and Adam seek advice from a third party—Simon and Otis—only to have both explain that they must have this conversation with their partner. Once they do this, both Victor and Adam are able to have sex and experience queer pleasure. Queer/gay sex becomes something that must be talked about in part because it is not the standard form of sex that either one has been taught or has experienced through representational narratives (i.e., popular culture). Queer/gay sex is always marked because it is nonnormative, and, as explored in chapter 1, even mentioning or talking about queer sex or queer sexuality in schools is illegal in some states, cast as a dangerous and corrupting topic of conversation. While talk about sex will likely facilitate pleasure in general, talk about queer/gay sex is necessary in order to destigmatize the sex and to make it a mundane (though pleasurable) part of one's life.

If the panic in *Sex Education* lies in the taboo of queer sex talk, such panic is far more palpable in *Love, Victor*. The panic focuses specifically on Victor's relationship with his family, which prevents Victor from fully grasping his sexuality in the first season and strains his relationship with Benji in the second season. His mother in particular is a devout Catholic and finds it difficult to square her faith with Victor's sexuality. Victor's racial identity as Latinx also contributes to the difficulty he experiences, especially with his relationship with Benji, as Victor laments that Benji cannot fully understand his experience and position because Benji is white. Victor thus bonds with his sister's friend Rahim, who similarly comes from a religious Iranian Muslim family that Rahim finds difficult to navigate given his own queer sexuality. While Victor is momentarily torn between Benji and Rahim, and ultimately chooses Benji, Victor's hesitation is rooted in panic infused with family, religion, and race, for Victor shares this panic and experience with Rahim, a panic and experience that Benji can never fully comprehend. Indeed, the arguments between Victor and Benji often center on family and race—which are intimately intertwined for Victor—for while Benji tries to be sympathetic, he finds it difficult to parse Victor's hesitation over the contours of his sexuality amid Victor's continued invocation of family, and, to a lesser extent, race. That Rahim becomes a lightning rod in Victor and Benji's relationship underscores the importance of being a queer student of color from a religious household for Victor, one Benji can only superficially grasp.

The panic boils over in season two when at the end of episode seven and start of episode eight, Victor's mother walks in on Victor and Benji having sex, certainly an unscripted moment when queer plans go awry. In the scene, elongated at the start of episode eight, we see Benji and Victor kissing and removing each other's clothes before Benji climbs on top of Victor. We catch a glimpse of Victor's bare legs arched upward; this coupled with Benji's rocking motions is meant to imply the two are engaged in anal sex. It is then that Victor's mother opens Victor's bedroom door, shocked at the scene before her. The explicitness of the scene, of the sex, matters, as it is to compare with Victor's mother's subsequent outrage and the panic that both Victor and his mother in turn feel. There is no hesitation in what she witnesses given that the scene had already established Victor and Benji's nakedness and actions. The outrage and panic must be as visceral as the pleasure itself to act as foil or challenge to overcome.

While the end of the season narratively wraps up the outrage and panic, pleasure is not seen to overcome the panic until season three, when, after Victor and Benji break up, Victor begins hooking up with Nick, a student from another school. This not only mirrors the everydayness of casual sex found in the shows like *Skins* (Berridge 2013), *Girls* (Perkins 2014), and *Sex Education* but also indexes the social reality of casual sex among youth in the United States (Wade 2017; Hirsch and Khan 2020). If the second season presented Victor's sexual hesitancy amid his panic, the third season sees his panic replaced with pleasure. Hooking up with Nick (whom he is not dating), a sexual project he may have never imagined engaging in the previous season, becomes a common practice for Victor. And it is in those acts of hooking up—having experienced pleasure, panic, and now pleasure again—where queer pleasure is destigmatized and made mundane. There is no concern for what Nick and Victor might become, only an emphasis on the queer pleasure they experience in the here and now.

Sexual Banality

An even more sensational panic lies at the heart of Netflix's Swedish teen drama *Young Royals* (2021–24), which tells the story of Swedish prince Wilhelm as he navigates boarding school and his budding feelings and sexual awakening for fellow student Simon. The panic may be familial, not unlike Victor's panic, but it is also national, for as heir to the throne, Wilhelm must produce offspring for the sake of the monarchy. Yet interestingly, if both *Love, Victor* and *Sex Education* locate the panic in the queer sex or sex talk, *Young Royals* locates panic in the implications of the sex, or Wilhelm's sexuality more broadly. Wilhelm and Simon's sex is treated as the reward for the hurdles they must navigate, for pleasure is not the opposite of panic but rather it supplants—if only momentarily—panic. The two first have sex in the first season after Wilhelm accepts his feelings for Simon and tells Simon what he feels (season 1, episode 4). Their sex is treated as the point not only when Wilhelm fully accepts his feelings for Simon but when the struggle he had been facing transforms into a need for the other, both libidinal and emotional. Like Isi and Sascha, sex caps the struggle and opens them up to a relationship, the sexual project for both being one of pleasure and relationality.

When the two have sex in the fifth episode of the second season, it is treated again as another cap to their season-long struggle of trying to get over the other, to no avail, and thus opens both up to a new stage in their relationality. The two have sex as a form of reconciliation, at a point when Simon is no longer in denial regarding his feelings for Wilhelm, inverting the reason from the first season. The sexual project mirrors that of the first time they have sex. Pleasure may be momentary, but that is also the point: it is a way to supplant panic in the present moment, unconcerned with what comes next.[16]

It is this queer pleasure of the present that threads through this chapter and a queer theory of/for queer youth. By not calling attention to the nonnormativity of Wilhelm and Simon's sex—only, perhaps, the implications of the sex (i.e., that Wilhelm may not provide an heir to the monarchy)—*Young Royals*, akin to *Shadow and Bone*, works to make queer sex unremarkable. The remarkability lies not in the queerness of the sex but in the queerness of the romance between a male prince and a male student. In what follows, I explore further the unremarkableness of queer sex and pleasure through the shows *Generation* and *wtFOCK*, demonstrating how making sex even more explicit, and downright sensational, both popular culture artifacts legitimize queer pleasure through sexual banality.

The one-season show *Generation* (2021) created by HBO Max features a group of high school students navigating their conservative California community alongside their sexualities, including queer and nonqueer relationships and interactions alike. The show fits within a larger repertoire of high school–themed shows with explicit sexual content on HBO Max, including *Euphoria* and *Gossip Girl*. Yet *Generation* offers a unique premise as a show about the exploration of sexuality and the pleasures, connections, and disconnections that typically follow. Stated alternatively, the show is an exploration into the sexual projects of southern California high schoolers. One of the central characters is the openly gay Chester, who is often caught with a dress code violation given his choice of clothing (or lack thereof).[17] Chester contrasts with the closeted bisexual student Nathan, a twin who comes from an incredibly conservative household with an overly controlling mother. Throughout the show we watch as Chester and Nathan become closer, Nathan becoming more comfortable with his bisexuality given the time spent with Chester.

This development matters because Nathan's demeanor is sufficiently panicked at the start of the show, even when he is having sex. We learn in the first episode that Nathan is hooking up with his twin sister's boyfriend, Jake, as the latter sends Nathan a picture of his penis before Nathan's sister discovers the picture. Later in the episode Nathan and Jake then meet at a party to hook up. The two begin by kissing, Nathan expressing his worry as to what they are doing given that Jake is his sister's boyfriend: "I feel shitty. Do you feel shitty?" Jake asks Nathan if he wants to, implying that Jake wants Nathan to give him a blowjob, at which point Nathan suddenly gets on his knees, as if an impromptu action, and begins pulling down Jake's pants. The camera captures the scene behind Jake, including Jake's butt, as Nathan looks at Jake's penis and attempts to touch it. Yet as he tries to, Jake orgasms all over Nathan's face, much to Nathan's surprise and dismay, promptly ending their encounter.

This is not the first time in the episode we witness Nathan covered in semen. The first scene from Nathan's perspective features him sprawled out on his bed naked, his laptop covering his genitalia as he masturbates. Eventually Nathan finishes, his semen ending up on his upper torso and chest, Nathan smiling and reaching for a sock to clean himself. As he is cleaning himself, Nathan tastes his own semen, his face contorting only slightly before the scene cuts to him having a bowl of cereal in the kitchen. This contrast in visible orgasms and its end product (semen) invites multiple interpretations. The first regards whose semen ends up on Nathan, for if it is his own then, as we witness with the smile on Nathan's face, Nathan is satisfied in his pleasure. Given that Nathan is sprawled naked on his bed while masturbating insinuates that Nathan finds pleasure in his nakedness coupled with his masturbation, rather than, say, quickly masturbating fully clothed. Yet if it is Jake's semen, Nathan gets angry and upset, rushing out of the room. This could be read as shame and guilt for both hooking up with his sister's boyfriend—the physical remnant of that is semen in his eye—and for desiring men in general. Another person's semen on his body, especially his face, makes the encounter irrevocably tied to his closeted bisexuality, a physical manifestation of deriving pleasure from hooking up with men. The fact that Jake's semen ends up on Nathan's face signifies a greater sexual shame, often tied to a form of humiliation and even domination. These three emotions—shame, guilt, and humiliation—thus physically instantiate Nathan's panic about both his bisexuality and his hooking up with his sister's boyfriend.

An interesting pendulum swings between pleasure and panic. On one hand, Nathan's initial pleasure alone in his bedroom momentarily supplants any panic he may feel, which we do not fully understand until we follow Nathan to the party where he and Jake spontaneously hook up. We witness glimpses of this panic as Nathan sits in his older sister's wedding rehearsal, Jake messaging him first a shirtless picture and Nathan admitting he feels bad about the situation. Then Jake sends a picture of his penis, which Nathan's sister sees and records to use as blackmail later. This contributes further to Nathan's panic, and he denies to his twin that he is anything but straight. When we then see Jake and Nathan hook up, a mixture of pleasure and panic saturates the scene. Each time Nathan pulls away or verbalizes his "shitty" feeling, the panic washes over him and we bear witness to his hesitancy and guilt. Yet the desire for sex, his sexual project aimed at queer pleasure, is stronger than his panic, for despite Nathan's outwardly spoken feelings of guilt, he continues down the rabbit hole of pleasure. Nathan may very well be experiencing pleasure, but it is actually Jake's pleasure that comes to ultimate fruition, for his orgasm and semen are the true supplantation for Nathan's panic. Yet Nathan's panic immediately returns when Jake ejaculates onto Nathan's face. Pleasure thus literally collides with Nathan's panic, his surprise-stricken face covered in semen symbolizing both stark contrast between pleasure and panic and a manifestation of Nathan's contradictory feelings. The physical manifestation of the pleasure—ejaculation and visible semen—are thus necessary tools to play foil to Nathan's panic, accentuating both the panic and the pleasure through the explicitness of the scenes.

We witness another scene later in the series, less explicit, in which pleasure not only supplants panic but collides head-on with it. In episode nine, we watch as Nathan and Chester begin making out in public, surprising all their friends. Yet it is Nathan's mother, watching from a car, that represents the existential panic Nathan had been feeling up until then. In episode three, Nathan comes out to his entire family (and the wedding party) as bisexual, thus angering his mother and his older sister who is to be married. While we might read Nathan's make-out session with Chester as a form of resistance or even refusal (Prasse-Freeman 2022), I read this scene more as an embracement of pleasure over panic, with Nathan feeling comfortable enough to make out with Chester—not just kiss, but a full-blown make-out session—in front of friends and family. Nathan is supplanting his panic, consciously, with pleasure in a way that makes unmistakable his sexuality, feelings, and desires. We are left with only pleasure, and, of course, Nathan's mother's own panicked feelings. Such queer pleasure does not supplant Nathan's mother's panic but buttresses it. This mirrors the end of the first episode of the Brazilian HBO Max show *Teenage Kiss* (2023), discussed in the preface, that features the TK teenagers in the hallway kissing as panicked teachers pull the fire alarm to shower them in water from the sprinklers. The panic of the teachers collides with the pleasure and intimacy of the students kissing, the water from the sprinklers symbolizing the physical manifestation of panic that gets supplanted by the teens' kissing.

An equally explicit scene takes place in episode eight of the third season of the Belgian show *wtFOCK* (2018–23).[18] Season three features Robbe, a student coming to terms with his attraction toward men. He initially panics that he is attracted to art student Sander, for after the two kiss in episode four, Robbe rejects Sander in the following episode, claiming that Sander tricked him into the kiss. Robbe eventually comes to terms with his feelings for Sander and the two reconcile. In episode eight we see Robbe and Sander stay the night in a hotel room, eating food, cuddling and chatting on the bed, and engaging in anal sex in the shower.[19] Viewers know the kind of sex in which the two are engaging given not only the partial nudity featured in the scene but also the fact that Sander stands behind Robbe thrusting at/into the other. This scene is foreshadowed in the previous episode when we witness the two beginning to have sex in Robbe's room, Robbe lying on his back and wrapping his legs around Sander's torso.

These scenes of queer pleasure supplant multiple moments of panic. These range from Robbe's internalized "homophobia"—though I am hesitant to fully embrace the term given that Robbe never really comes out as gay or as any sexuality in the season, as discussed in chapter 2—to a violent confrontation that Robbe and Sander have with men at a bar, the two boys being beat up for their public display of affection. Queer pleasure thus contrasts with these two visceral instances of panic—the violence an embodied instantiation of "homophobia." Robbe's panic is actualized in this moment of violence, but the sex he has with Sander, following this violence, becomes a way to clap back at homophobic violence. Queer pleasure is not necessarily an antidote to violence and panic as much as it is a reorientation of the entire situation: fucking supplants bashing. Such

The Ascendancy of Queer Pleasure | 133

sexual projects are thus as much about pleasure and relationality as they are about Robbe and Sander finding their voices, taking back the power that the men robbed them of when they attacked Robbe and Sander.

Yet another form of panic forms immediately following Robbe and Sander's eighth-episode sex scene. While Robbe is trying to sleep, Sander continuously wanders around the room, talking fast and making little sense to Robbe. Sander then leaves the room naked in search of food, awakening Robbe to dress and go after him. A panic-stricken Robbe roams the city in search of Sander, only to find him being loaded into an ambulance, and Robbe being confronted by Sander's ex-girlfriend, who informs Robbe that Sander is bipolar and was experiencing a manic episode. While Robbe is initially distant from Sander in the aftermath—confused as to what bipolar disorder actually is and mistakenly thinking that Sander's attraction and affection for Robbe is only a result of his condition—he eventually searches for Sander after the latter checks himself out of the psychiatric clinic and disappears. Though Robbe is panicked, he becomes even more so after he receives a message from Sander and imagines that Sander will attempt to hurt himself. When Robbe eventually finds Sander, Robbe expresses how scared he was, implying that he thought Sander would hurt himself (season 3, episode 10).

Sander's bipolar disorder presents a different sort of panic for Robbe, one captured not by sexual panic but by mental health panic. We cannot necessarily compare these different kinds of panic—homophobia/violence and mental health—both are equally embodied and affective in their presentation/representation and resolution. Queer pleasure may not necessarily supplant the panic of mental health (e.g., Stangl and Earnshaw 2019), though queerness in general does reorient the moment away from panic and toward a messy and turbulent but equally meaningful and pleasurable relationship. Queerness is meant not to sweep this kind of panic under the rug, because it is of a different kind or order, but to embrace it as it is and as it comes. And while the queer pleasure discussed throughout this chapter focuses squarely on queer youth sex, a different kind of queer pleasure also emerges in the interaction between Robbe and Sander: the pleasure of the mess, of the trouble.

But when we consider both shows together, *Generation* and *wtFOCK*, we are also presented with a queer pleasure and sexual project made banal. The sudden transition to Nathan's masturbation scene may be done to shock the audience, but it is equally done to make mundane queer youth sex—everyone masturbates, so why should we be shocked at the depiction of it? Even the oral sex that Nathan attempts to perform on Jake may seem sudden, but the quickness with which Nathan gets to his knees again makes this moment banal in its explicitness, especially given that the entire show is about the exploration of sex and sexuality. The show's broader aim, then, is to make mundane all forms of youth sex, including queer sex.

The explicit anal sex scene between Robbe and Sander is also stitched into the broader hotel scene as an expected moment—what else were they to do in a hotel but have sex? The presence of partial nudity, the lack of discussion about sex, again makes their sex an ordinary part of both their relationship and society writ large. Everyone is having sex, so why not queer youth? In both *Generation* and *wtFOCK*, what seems explicit and shocking is in fact done in order to routinize queer youth sex itself. And similar to *Young Royals* and *Shadow and Bone*, the remarkability of these scenes lies in the unremarkable framing of the sex—it just sort of happens.

Don't Panic, It's Just Sex!

What, then, might be the significance of pleasure's ascendancy for queer youth? Considering that these are scenes of scripted sex, we must recognize the intentionality behind the queer pleasure found in them. These are not scenes of actual queer sex—or even ideal queer sex, for who wishes that their mother would walk in while engaged in anal sex? Rather, these are scenes of what might be, what could be, not insofar as a deferment of sex—these, again, are not queer utopian visions of some sought after future (Muñoz 2009)—but instead a recognition that queer sex for some youth is ordinary and legitimate, and thus it could be (or should be) for other queer youth as well. Despite being scripted, these are unscripting moments of impromptu sex and scenes of when plans go awry, moments of when sex exists without optimism.

These scenes of scripted sex are not instructional; they are not teaching queer youth how to have sex or even insisting that they have sex. Instead, they are aspirational of a present—a radical present, even—where queer youth consider their pleasures legitimate and ordinary, though not necessarily (hetero)normative. These shows do not "obsess" over normality—or where "normality itself becomes a fetish, an excessive fantasy staging rather than a position of narrative coherency or viewer stability" (Joyrich 2014, 138)—but rather exist and operate within the messiness of being and doing queer, including the messiness of queer sex. This contributes to the ascendancy of queer pleasure and a belief and insistence that queer sex is a legitimate form of pleasure for queer youth, and that as such, this pleasure is ordinary. But even more fundamental, this particular ascendancy, one focused on queer youth sex and pleasure, gives credence to the fact that queer youth sex and pleasure are not to be panicked over, even if they are still taboo (at least to talk about). Instead, queer youth sex ought to be considered on par with all other sex despite thinking that because queer sex is outlawed it is somehow "hotter" (Amin 2017, 6).

On one hand, I am making a rather simple argument that representation matters. And it does, certainly, affect how queer youth perceive and understand themselves (e.g., Craig et al. 2015; Pullen 2014; Sarkissian 2014; McInroy and Craig 2015). How are we to expect queer youth to feel comfortable with their sex(uality) if there are no representations of their sex(uality) in popular culture? To thus represent queer sex is to give voice to a population either co-opted by adult voices or essentially voiceless (Talburt 2004, 2018). It is also meant, then, to counteract or complicate the barrage of panic and policies that restrict queer youth and identities mentioned throughout this book.

But on the other hand, the ascendancy of queer pleasure is more than a matter of representation. It is a call to consider queer youth sex(uality) and pleasure within conceptions of (queer) theory. This mirrors, to a certain extent, Driver's (2008) insistence on including the youth perspective in critical theory, paralleling also Susan Talburt's (2004, 2018) ongoing championing of the youth perspective that moves beyond the intelligibility and expectations of adults. However, in focusing on scenes of queer youth sex—some implicit and others more explicit—I hope to expand the interplay of sex and self/identity to one always already incoherent and "ruptured" (Berlant and Edelman 2014; Weiss 2020). Sex, like the self, is messy and never actually complete. Lingering feelings, fluids, and intensities remain—the sweat on the brow, the racing heart, the flashes of remembrance (Stewart 2007)—and so how can we even consider a moment when we are not "undone by each other" (Butler 2004, 23)? Perhaps, by supplanting panic—even momentarily so—pleasure may glimpse not only a horizon of queer youth legitimacy and ordinariness but also the actual ways some queer youth live and experience their sex and sexualities in unscripted ways.

Chapter Five

The American Security Apparatus

> It's always open season on gay kids.
>
> —Eve Kosofsky Sedgwick, "How to Bring Your Kids Up Gay"

> The time of LGBT inclusion is also a time of trans/queer death.
>
> —Eric A. Stanley, *Atmospheres of Violence*

Writing in the early 1990s, when reports of queer youth suicide revealed significant problems with abuse, bullying, and discrimination, feminist and queer theorist Eve Kosofsky Sedgwick proclaimed, "It's always open season on gay kids," as if to shake us into noticing. The 2023 film adaptation of the novel *Aristotle and Dante Discover the Secrets of the Universe* features one such moment. The film tells the story of the friendship and eventual romantic feelings of Mexican American boys Aristotle and Dante in 1987 El Paso. Dante is portrayed as carefree, thoughtful, emotional, and kind, while Aristotle is introspective and avoids associating with others, except for Dante. In the middle of the film, while the two boys are separated for the year, Dante confesses to Aristotle in a letter that he wants to marry a boy and hopes that Aristotle will not get angry or desert him. Late in the film, once Dante and his family return to El Paso, Dante is beaten up in an alley because he is caught kissing another boy, and while the other boy ran away, Dante chose to stay. When Dante's mother repeatedly asks aloud "Why didn't he run?" Aristotle simply responds, "Because he's Dante." While we do not see the actual assault, we witness as Aristotle sits on the hospital bed, Dante's hand in his own, a breathing tube is affixed to

Dante's face, which is nearly unrecognizable because of the bruises. It was certainly open season on Dante, and so a distraught and angry Aristotle laments that he should have been there to protect Dante.

More than twenty years later and I cannot help but wonder if it is still the case, if it is still open season on gay kids. But not all gay kids, right? When developmental psychologist Ritch C. Savin-Williams (2005, 3) begins his book on the "new gay teenager" by claiming that "they're adapting quite well, thank you," is he speaking of all teenagers that "resist or refuse to identify themselves as gay and are living ordinary adolescent lives" or of particular queer teens? And besides, what constitutes an "ordinary" life for adolescents, particularly queer adolescents? Savin-Williams is certainly not wrong, but then again, neither is Sedgwick, more than twenty years on. They both point us toward a rather crowded and complicated terrain that finds renewed sex panics in the form of antiqueer and trans laws sweeping the United States, colliding with a similar spread of progressive politics in schools that focus on niceness, diversity, and inclusion. This Janus-faced characteristic of American society engenders rather stark tension between incommensurable discourses and practices that pertain to queer youth—they are either a risk to the future of society or in need of protection against bullying and discrimination.

It really is open season on gay kids, but which ones and for what reason? Throughout this book I have called attention to the renewed sex panics sweeping the United States—from Don't Say Gay laws and antitrans bathroom laws to book banning and drag show restrictions. These sex panics operate within a particular form of security temporality that sees panic as a reaction to the potential arrival of an uncertain and risky future. Panic preempts the future in the present whereby the present moment exists to script desirable futures, heteronormatively so. Panic interprets the present world through a future normativity, rendering queer youth risky to normativity—but not all queer youth. While contemporary sex panics do discursively envelop all queer youth within their clutches, this seemingly totalizing effect erases the differential experiences queer youth have within contemporary society. Queer youth of color, trans youth, and disabled and neurodiverse queer and trans youth have been experiencing panic and discrimination long before the contemporary moment; the current moment does less to bring their experiences to the fore than it does to hide their experiences in the background, under rug swept.

As a discourse of security, sex panics are meant to include all but they actually target specific bodies—security may have become banal, but the result is laser-focused attention on bodies deemed threats. These threats are no doubt racialized (e.g., Puar 2007; Grewal 2017), but when sex panics are sieved through such racialized security, those oppressed and discriminated against become doubly so. This hides within the present moment, buried under an orientation toward an uncertain future. That uncertainty holds limitless potential, but such potential also means security institutions, including schools, work to govern uncertainty through risk and threat making. Such threat making likens to Sara Ahmed's (2012, 3) notion of "stranger making" insofar as "the stranger reappears as the one who is always lurking in the shadows" and such stranger experience "can be an experience of becoming noticeable, of not passing through or passing by, of being stopped or being held up."[1] Those being stopped and being held up—those lurking—are interpreted as threats, no doubt indexical of the violent, murderous treatment of Black folks by the police.

In her ethnography of the LGBTQ+ youth organization Spectrum, sociologist Mary Robertson (2018) makes an analogous observation regarding the bifurcation of experiences of queer youth: some, invoking Savin-Williams (2005), have normalized their sexualities, even within a broader youth culture, while others continue to be policed.[2] Robertson (2018, 9) rightly argues that "treating all so-called LGBTQ youth as one collapsible category results in over-simplifying the normalization of homoeroticism and obscuring the nuanced difference between homonormative and queer LBTQ-identified kids." I agree that difference in experiences matters, that collapsing folks into a single category not only oversimplifies the narrative but actively works to erase the nonnormative—and even nonhomonormative—experiences.

However, both sets of experiences and the institutional mechanisms that work to shape queer youth experiences operate within a security discourse and ideology that displaces the present for the navigation and even control of the future. Such security temporality stitches to the very notion of "growing up," as it sees adolescence as a time one must work to prepare oneself for an uncertain, albeit neoliberal, future. Even college students, many of whom are not yet separate from their parents, work to craft the best neoliberal self possible to be marketable for future employment. We could very well treat adolescence, writ large, as part of security ideology, and we would be right to do so. Yet doing so would also require additional steps to draw attention to the violence manifested toward queer youth—particularly queer youth of color and trans youth—within such a security ideology.

This chapter, like this book, moves laterally within the present moment, not to displace it for the future but to excavate it as a moment overflowing with meaningful experiences, affective connections, and relationalities not capturable in a security diagnostic. It explores moments when security is made visible, when queer youth actively encounter the American security apparatus,[3] be that through militarization or school shootings and lockdowns. Making security visible, drawing it into the light of day and interrogating the security logic behind particular moments, enables multiple interpretations. On the one hand, the work security does to hide violence is not locatable in a single entity or institution; in fact, we are all in some regard complicit with the securitization of American society—some more than others, of course. The dispersal of responsibility and compulsion to participate (Masco 2014) leaves those of us who notice—if we notice—intentionally ambivalent at our participation. But on the other hand, the elision of violence for the sake of the future leaves the present moment open for living, surviving, and maneuverability. While neither is unique to queer youth, queer youth are objects of both risk/threat and protection, securitized bodies pulled in different directions.

My focus, therefore, is on the ambivalence of queer youth navigating through the American security apparatus. I build on my earlier research into what I call *queer states of security* (Gitzen 2023), the participation of queer folks in policing and security practices to safeguard against physical violence at the expense of structural insecurity. Queer states of security are an ambivalent feeling queer folks have as they seek to protect themselves from institutions that are responsible for their continued insecurity. Expanding on this ambivalence also invites contemplation into moments of what Jasbir Puar (2007, 39) refers to as homonationalism, "a collusion between homosexuality and American nationalism that is generated both by national rhetorics of patriotic inclusion and by gay and queer subjects themselves." Puar argues that homonationalism relies on figures like the terrorist, as it "disaggregates U.S. national gays and queers from racial and sexual others" (Puar 2007, 39). But more than a decade after Puar's book—more than twenty years since 9/11 and more than fifteen years since the invasion of Afghanistan and Iraq—ambivalence has grown surrounding perpetual war and the American security apparatus (Kapadia 2019). Queer states of security work to foreground ambivalence, to "inspire scholarly nausea and unease" through what Kadji Amin (2017, 10) innovatively calls "deidealization," a way to "deexceptionalize queerness in order to analyze queer possibility as inextricable from relations of power, queer deviance as intertwined with normativity, and queer alternatives as not necessarily just alternatives."

Part of this "scholarly nausea and unease" emerges from the recent turn in some schools toward a type of progressivism that sees attention paid to antibullying, inclusivity, and diversity—what has been dubbed by multiple scholars as a politics of niceness (Pascoe 2023; Castagno 2014, 2019). These scholars have explored in detail the pitfalls of niceness and how it actually perpetuates institutional discrimination and violence. In this chapter I explore these debates about niceness, tolerance, and progressivism in schools as a context or setting for queer youth: how are they being treated within progressive security institutions, even as sex panics rage elsewhere? This dovetails into a broader conversation around the participation of citizens—particularly young queer citizens—in practices and discourses of security. I then transition into a deep textual analysis of two popular culture artifacts—Showtime's *Shameless* and HBO Max's *Generation*—that see queer characters interacting with the American security apparatus, attending to queer youth participation and simultaneous maneuverability with/in the apparatus. These are not clear-cut instances of participation and resilience; how, for instance, are we to positively spin a school lockdown due to a potential shooter? Rather, I sift through the layers of these encounters to complicate the American security apparatus and queer youth participation. I end by revisiting queer states of security and the ambivalence that funnels through the entire book.

Security Participation

Security ideologies and practices saturate our culture and society in ways that tie daily living to the perpetuation of an American security apparatus. Whether we are consciously aware or not, we are part and parcel of a security apparatus that works to make us all discernable and intelligible as vectors and nodes of information. We exist in relation to other nodes, the lines drawn instantiating knowledge of that relationality—we may believe our lives to be individuated, but we are made known through our relations (Amoore 2013; Gitzen 2023). In this way, we are participating in the making and even unmaking of security: we are the data for the machine.

To return to Joseph Masco (2014, 18) from chapter 1, he notes that "the goal of a national security system is to produce a citizen-subject who responds to officially designated signs of danger automatically, instinctively activating logics and actions learned over time through drills and media indoctrination." Inderpal Grewal (2017, 2), like Masco, argues that "constructs of security have come to dominate everyday life in the US imperial state." Taking Masco and Grewal seriously also requires what Ronak Kapadia (2019, 10) calls a "queer calculus," one that "advances an account of both dominant knowledge apparatuses and data logics of the US security state as well as alternative logics, affects, emotions, and affiliations of diasporic subjects living and laboring in the heart of empire." While I do not profess to do all this—Kapadia's work is testament enough to the reach of a queer calculus—I do suggest that attending to both dominant and alternative logics of the American security apparatus reveals the elision of queer violence within the apparatus and its ideologies and practices. This is a form of unscripting, itself a queer calculus that works to disentangle the normative scripts that comprise the American security apparatus while also offering alternative interpretations and possibilities. A queer calculus, considering Masco's national security affect (2014, 18), also draws attention to the ways we are all, in some capacity, pulled into national security participation. Elsewhere I discuss this as a sort of compulsion to participate given a context of what I refer to as *banal security* (Gitzen 2023), a context that may not directly correlate to the American security apparatus and US empire but nonetheless speaks to a compulsion to participate. We are educated to do so, Masco contends.[4]

Such participation also speaks to what both Puar (2007) and Grewal (2017) refer to as a form of American or US exceptionalism. As Grewal (2017, 3) notes, "The exceptional American citizen trying to save the security state is the product of the self-empowerment regime that is central to neoliberalism in the United States." The connection for Grewal between the security state and neoliberalism engenders an American exceptionalism that sees American citizens mobilize their "neoliberal agency" (Gershon 2011) to participate in the security apparatus in order to *save* the security state—or, I suggest, the apparatus itself.[5] Grewal tells the story, for instance, of "security moms" and "security feminists," the former idealized through the conservative white woman and her heterosexual family, while the latter is a patriotic and liberal white feminist that works for the military and state (Grewal 2017, 120). The example of the security mom in particular taps into a broader concern over the protection of the heterosexual, middle-class family (usually white), for "insecurity is also a gendered project, as forms of sexual, economic, social, and psychological violence produce subjects who work unceasingly as exceptional citizens to protect themselves, their families, the state, and nation" (Grewal 2017, 120).

A similar form of US exceptionalism appears in Puar's (2007) *Terrorist Assemblage*. She writes that "exceptionalism gestures to narratives of excellence, excellent nationalism, a process whereby a national population comes to believe in its own superiority and its own singularity" (2007, 5). For Puar, US exceptionalism now includes "certain homosexual bodies," namely white (often middle-class) gays and lesbians. Yet as both Grewal and Puar argue, the inclusion of some within the American security apparatus requires the exclusion of others from it—not everyone can be exceptional, despite Americans' fundamental belief in their exceptionality. This, for Grewal, is the effect of American neoliberalism.

I concur that the inclusion of some within the American security apparatus requires the exclusion of others, but I also take seriously the *compulsion* to participate, even at one's own expense. If protection is granted only by the apparatus working actively to interpret and treat one as a threat, what is one to do? Does one participate and seek protection from the apparatus, or does one live in continued insecurity? Is there even a choice for some? There is no single answer, but what I am suggesting is that even if security is not for everyone, the compulsion to participate, to belong to the security apparatus or security state, is strong. This is certainly not a zero-sum game—the compulsion may be strong, but one's sense of worth or one's dignity may be stronger.

My point is that this compulsion also manifests as ambivalence in some who recognize that their participation is counterproductive, contributing to continued violence, or ineffective. The gays and lesbians Puar (2007) discusses are considered active participants in the American security apparatus, which relies on the exclusion and targeting of other queer bodies (namely queers of color) to operate. But were all participants on board with the totality of US (sexual) exceptionalism and the security apparatus? Was there no deviation, no room for questioning or even simple ambivalence in one's participation? Again, there is no zero-sum game to be played within queer politics.

Refocusing attention on the ambivalence, what I am calling *queer states of security*, allows for interpretations that may contradict one another, that work to either uncover or hide violence, and that do not quite fit into any one box. "Embodying the dual meaning of 'state' as a polity and a mode of being, queer states of security index both the collaborations of [queer] organizers and police to use security technologies . . . and the simultaneous feeling of contingent and provisional safety and structural (or institutional) insecurity" (Gitzen 2023, 64).[6] We could compare queer states of security to Lauren Berlant's (2011, 24) notion of "cruel optimism . . . the condition of maintaining an attachment to a significantly problematic object." Attachment to the American security apparatus is certainly problematic, given the daily imperial violence carried out in its name (or secretly, behind closed doors). Yet it is the quality of the attachment that I wish to call into question, that I wish to interrogate, for not all attachments are the same for everyone; experiences and feelings of attachment may certainly differ from one another in ways that make the attachment in question ambivalent and even icky. The attachments I discuss below—one to the US military and the other to school lockdowns—are punctuated by decidedly insecure or nonsecure practices: gay sex between two high schoolers, discussions of vulnerability, and watching YouTube videos. These attachments are formed at school, as are the punctuating moments that seek to either rupture or maneuver within the American security apparatus. As such, I first turn to the school and the ways a politics of nice—indexical of a general push for diversity and inclusion—frame practices and ideologies through securitized discourse. Doing so will bring the scenes and queer states of security that follow into starker clarity, making the ambivalence and potentially cringe-worthy feelings that much more palpable.

Neoliberally Nice

"We are living," Eric A. Stanley (2021, 5) writes, "in a time of LGBT inclusion." Marriage equality, gays and lesbians serving openly in the military, and, as I have attempted to demonstrate throughout this book, the proliferation of queer characters in popular culture—sexual and gender diversity seems to be the norm, especially for young people (Savin-Williams 2005; Robertson 2018). At the start of season four of the Netflix show *Sex Education*, the remaining students of the now-closed Moordale Secondary School begin at Cavendish College. As main best friends Otis and Eric arrive on campus and begin walking around, Eric comments on just how gay Cavendish is, particularly compared to Moordale. Throughout the episode, attention is paid to the progressivism of the school—from a gossip jar where students must put money in if they are caught gossiping to intense recycling and environmental actions. And while *Sex Education* is set in the United Kingdom, the emphasis on progressive schools—overly progressive in comparison to others—resonates not only with some schools in the United States but with a neoliberal politics of diversity and inclusion rooted in the twin concepts of niceness and whiteness (Ahmed 2012; Castagno 2014).

The veil of inclusion, Stanley (2021, 5) quickly adds, is not so much a "precondition of safety" but rather "most properly names the state's violent expansion." While I agree that diversity and inclusion more broadly—indeed, a politics of niceness, as I explore below—hide "the state's violent expansion," I am not quick to dismiss their discursive power to instantiate a feeling of safety and security *for some*. In what follows, I trace the connections between diversity, inclusion, and niceness to both neoliberal agency and the American security apparatus, arguing that as a discourse of neoliberal security, the elements of diversity, inclusion, and niceness not only prepare young people for an uncertain future but also mask how these uncertain futures make precarious certain bodies, namely queer and trans youth of color.

In many ways, "neoliberalism often creates the illusion of LBTQ acceptance through visibility of these identities as consumers while leaving the underlying oppressive structure (e.g., hierarchical notions of sexual and gender differences in US society that ultimately create symbolic and material harm) unexamined and untouched" (Elia and Yep 2012, 880). This is precisely what Stanley (2021, 6) is also arguing, but he takes it a step further by drawing attention to acts of violence as individuated rather than systematic: "Thinking violence as individual acts versus epistemic force works to support the normative and normalizing structure of public pain." Such individualizing of violence works because of neoliberal agency, because we conceive of the self as individuated from others, autonomous subjects beholden only to self-responsibility and thus violence, too, is experienced by the individual as an isolated case rather than a systemic or "epistemic force."

Such attention to individuated violence versus systemic violence dovetails into broader regimes of kindness that attempts to bolster tolerance, acceptance, and inclusion by erasing a *politics* of difference. This is done, C. J. Pascoe (2023) argues, through what she calls a *politics of protection*, "the securitization of individual bodies at the expense of the structural changes necessary to actually keep *everyone* safe" (Gitzen 2024, 227). As a result, "systemic inequalities get made to look like individual ones" (Pascoe 2023, 29). Attention to potential bullying of queer and trans students, for instance, locates the bullying in the individual student—the student is homophobic, transphobic, or simply "not nice"—and thus the solution to the problem of bullying is to advocate for niceness. In short, the politics of protection operates as a security discourse that mobilizes the present as a way to preempt future uncertainty. The potential for bullying in the future necessitates a need for protection in the present—we must protect queer and trans students from the possibility of bullying—and this is done through zero-tolerance policies for bullying, signage that advocates for love over hate, and queer student organizations that advocate for antidiscrimination and LGBTQ+ inclusion (Pascoe 2023).

While Pascoe (2023) sidesteps any discussion of neoliberalism as one of the root causes of such an individuated approach to protection and problems such as bullying or racism,[7] she does recognize that such a politics of protection erases systemic forms of inequality, discrimination, and violence. Such regimes of kindness or niceness are intimately tied to the education of whiteness, Angelina Castagno (2014, 8) argues, for "whiteness works through nice people" (see also Castagno 2019). Castagno gestures toward the importance of neoliberal agency in such a politics of niceness/whiteness given the "assets-based approaches to education" that sees youth as a collection of assets—or skills and traits—whereby "focusing on one's assets is supposed to facilitate greater resilience, optimism, and confidence in the person" (Castagno 2014, 9). Optimism, Berlant (2011) teaches us, may be a cruel attachment we form, one that, on the surface, seems like a net good but underneath may be incredibly problematic. Given that the problem (of racism, for instance) is disaggregated from the system—that the problems are with the individual, not the institution—the solution, too, must also lie with the individual, not only in reforming the bully but in uplifting the bullied as well. Pascoe (2023) makes a similar observation with the sexual harassment of high school girls, for despite the overwhelming number of sexual harassment experiences by Pascoe's interlocutors, the school's solution was to prepare young women to protect themselves or know how to report harassment rather than tackle the systemic and institutional problem of toxic masculinity.

Attention to whiteness, however, must not be overlooked. Even though "diversity and inclusion, in the logic of neoliberalism, become commodities people can gain through training that they can then cash in for institutional political capital" (Spencer and Patterson 2017, 299), they are only commodities for some. Indeed, "when queer and trans resources *are* available, they largely benefit White, gender-normative students by reifying gender binaries and ignoring or undervaluing intersectionality" (Spencer and Patterson 2017, 298). As Leland Spencer and G. Patterson (2017) demonstrate through a university LGBTQ+ student organization, those most active and vocal in the organization, and those who occupy most of the leadership positions in the organization, are cisgender white allies. Spencer and Patterson contend that in this way, affiliation with organizational diversity becomes a commodity for these allies—the organization focused on acts of kindness and social events rather than social justice actions. This comes at the expense, however, of queer and trans students, particularly queer and trans students of color.

Therefore, the spread of liberalism and even progressivism in schools, including higher education, through the language of diversity and inclusion may seem like a net good, but, as I have discussed, it usually hides recurring systemic and institutional violence. As neoliberal discourses, diversity and inclusion are part of the repertoire of the self that are used to market the individual as a brand, while also marking the school or institution as progressive or, at the very least, accepting of difference (Urciuoli 2022; Bourassa 2021).[8] As a security discourse, diversity and inclusion aim to protect individual difference from potential harm without attending to either systemic or institutional violence or those left out of protection. Not everyone is deserving of protection; some must be sacrificed or left out for others to get ahead. As such, I favor Savannah Shange's (2019, 11) notion of "progressive dystopia," in which a school or a place is a "perpetually colonial place that reveals both the possibilities and limits of late liberal imaginary." Shange is speaking specifically of San Francisco and Robeson as a school, detailing seemingly progressive policies on racial difference that in fact reify, but also hide, institutional forms of racism.

My attention to the regimes of kindness, diversity, and inclusion within liberal and even progressive schools attempts to contextualize this seeming rise in LGBTQ+ inclusion. It sits uncomfortably next to, or interconnected with, the sex panics saturating the contemporary moment. Yet speaking of both in relation to one another, and recognizing the limits of kindness, diversity, and inclusion, similarly manifests ambivalence and even "scholarly nausea" at the possibility that good intentions may do more harm than good. On the one hand, protecting against bullies, for instance, is necessary—queer and trans students ought to be included and kept safe. But on the other hand, the system that gives rise to bullying and other forms of discrimination and violence is overlooked for the sake of a neoliberal approach that takes the individual as solely responsible. The effect, in Ahmed's (2012) calculation, is a making of strangers of those included but only with half measures.

In the sections that follow, I move into popular culture artifacts that complicate the politics of niceness, diversity, and inclusion with direct invocation of security contexts, ideologies, and practices. Here queer states of security prove useful, for the interpretive layers of the following scenes instantiate queer bodies as part of the American security apparatus in rather uncomfortable and even cringe-worthy ways. These scenes are reflective of militarized and securitized realities for youth more broadly, but queer youth—especially queer youth of color—more specifically. While niceness and kindness are not directly invoked, those regimes tied so intimately to diversity and inclusion and rooted in neoliberal agency are present in rather subtle forms. That these scenes bear witness to queer youth encounters with security means that they also speak to the deflation of other forms of discrimination and violence that are part and parcel of inclusivity and niceness. This amalgamation of interpretations and experiences thus engenders ambivalence in both the characters and us readers of such cultural texts.

Bullies, Sex, War

A central aspect to the American security apparatus, and securitization more broadly, is the mobilization of the military into everyday life, or *militarization*. The relationship of militarization to security and securitization is one of part to whole, where all iterations of militarization are part of security, but not all security practices and ideologies are necessarily forms of militarization. Elsewhere I define militarization as "more than the military reaching into society; it is the excess of military ideologies seeping into daily life and making those ideologies ordinary and even natural" (Gitzen 2021, 1007). It is a "process in which civil society organizes itself for the production of violence" (Geyer in Lutz 2007, 320). I refer to this as the "banality of military service and soldiering," as a method of "not only making the spectacular ordinary, but by signaling itself" (Gitzen 2021, 1013), what Michael Billing (1995) calls "flagging."[9] The emphasis on violence is important because attention to militarization is simultaneously a recognition that by organizing the production of violence through civil society, civil society becomes responsible and even perpetrators of said violence. More insidious, however, is the way militarization works to justify the spread of, in particular, the US empire through not only military bases (Lutz 2009) but also war, military occupation, and settler colonialism (e.g., Kapadia 2019; Puar 2017).

According to anthropologist Catherine Lutz (2007), militarization is both a tense and a contradictory process. On the one hand, "militarization is a tense process, that is, it can generate conflict between social sectors, and most importantly between those who might benefit from militarization" (Lutz 2007, 322). On the other hand, "militarization also sets contradictory processes in motion, for example, accentuating both localism and federalism" (Lutz 2007, 323).[10] I wish to stay with the tense and contradictory feelings of militarization—the process as itself tense and contradictory. The affectiveness of militarization relies both on the spread of military ideologies into daily life—the saturation of daily living with militarized practices, ideologies, and discourses—and the feelings that arise in their saturation.

Schools, be they high schools or postsecondary institutions, that have junior reserve officer training corps (JROTC) and reserve officer training corps (ROTC) programs, respectively, exemplify the contours of militarization, of the ways military and civil society intermingle in tense and contradictory ways.[11] Such programs not only bring the military into the hallways, thoroughfares, and classrooms of schools but also mobilize the infrastructure of the school to educate future soldiers. If we take seriously the way militarization works to normalize and spread both violence and US empire building, then the militarization of schools recasts schools as potential nodes of empire building along with militarized (and securitized) iterations of violence. Such a recognition is no doubt fraught with tense and contradictory feelings: how can our bastions of education be simultaneously operators of violence and empire building?[12] Such tense and contradictory feelings likewise instantiate queer states of security for those queer youth caught in the webs of militarization.

Building on this introductory discussion of militarization and empire building, I will examine one such tense and contradictory scene of militarization in schools. In particular, the scene I interrogate narrates the interconnections between militarization, empire building, race, and queer sexuality among high school students. It bears witness to those tense and contradictory processes and feelings that emerge in instances of militarization but are made particularly salient and palpable given the queerness of the characters and their acts. The scene is taken from the second episode of the third season of the long-running Showtime show *Shameless* (2011–21), the episode appropriately titled "The American Dream." The show tells the story of the Gallagher siblings as they learn to navigate life in the South Side of Chicago with an alcoholic and absent single father.

In the scene we find Ian, one of the siblings who is gay and bipolar, having sex with his friend with benefits, Ralph, under their high school bleachers. Both are in JROTC and are required to wear their JROTC uniforms. The scene begins with a brief montage of students on the field, presumably in gym class, and quickly moves to under the bleachers. We can see, through the rafters, the pair having sex: Ian is without a shirt and his pants and are boxers pulled down, and Ralph, bent over one of the rafters, is wearing his JROTC uniform and his pants are also pulled down. We can hear the grunts and moans as Ian, white with a shaved head, thrusts into his friend. Ralph then calls out, as the scene focuses in on the pair from the front—Ralph glancing back at Ian, lost in his thrusts: "Come on GI, pound me like an Iraqi soldier." A confused look washes over Ian's face as he then promptly replies, "Okay, you need to shut the fuck up." We eventually hear a voice call out—"Hey, what's going on under there?"—to which the two began to swear as they quickly dress. Ian chastises Ralph for "being too loud," as Ralph, now completely dressed in his JROTC uniform with his hat and backpack, replies, "I can't get expelled, my parents will kill me." Ian quips back, "Hearing about the gay sex will kill them sooner."

We eventually learn that the voice is not that of a teacher but of Mickey, Ian's on-again, off-again sex partner and romantic interest throughout most of the series, who had recently been released from juvenile detention. As Mickey walks up to the pair, Ralph says, "I thought you were still in juvie." Mickey replies, "Not anymore" before he kicks Ralph in his crotch, sending the boy down to the ground, and continues to kick Ralph while asking, "Are you having some sort of queer-bo sex under here?" Ian simply watches as Mickey continues to kick Ralph, saying that, despite Ian also engaging in the queer sex, "You're the one taking it in the ass, right? You're the one I gotta kick straight." Ralph eventually runs away before Mickey turns to Ian and asks, "You got any fuck left in you, or you dump it all in that faggot's ass?" Ian grins as the two make their way back to the rafters that Ralph and Ian had been pressed up against, Ian unbuckling his belt as Mickey, standing in front of Ian, begins doing the same as he bends over, insinuating that Mickey will, in fact, get fucked by Ian.[13]

While likely meant as a form of dirty talk to excite himself or Ian further, Ralph's sudden utterance—"Come on GI, pound me like an Iraqi soldier"—hums with ambivalence and ickiness. My initial observation is that the American invasion and war in Iraq ended in 2011, and while a new war in Iraq took place from 2013 to 2017, the US involvement amounted to roughly five thousand troops (Cronk 2016). This episode of *Shameless* aired in the early part of 2013, *after* the "GI's" presence in Iraq and encounters with the "Iraqi soldier" took place. While the invasion and war in Iraq remain, to this day, in America's cultural memory and even quintessential to the American security apparatus, it is somewhat odd for Ralph to invoke the war in Iraq when neither Ralph nor Ian—let alone any JROTC member or soldier—would have encountered an Iraqi soldier. The utterance perhaps illustrates, then, the pervasiveness of the war in Iraq and America's continued presence in the Middle East in America's cultural memory.

However, initial observation aside, the utterance does signal a racial and power divide between the white American GI and the Iraqi soldier. The fact that it is the Iraqi soldier that is to be "pounded" by the GI instantiates the analogy and reality of, to put it crassly, America fucking Iraq. The invasion of Iraq saw the US military enter the country and topple its government. That the Iraqi soldier was to bottom for the American GI implies that the Iraqi soldier is somehow subservient to the GI, that his existence is simply for the pleasure of the GI. It may very well be that the Iraqi soldier derives pleasure from bottoming for the GI—it is implied that Ralph certainly finds pleasure in his bottoming status. But Ralph's invocation of the GI pounding the Iraqi soldier does not carry the same implication of pleasure for the Iraqi soldier. In fact, the double meaning of the GI pounding the Iraqi soldier stands in stark contrast to the Iraqi soldier's pleasure. On the one hand, Ralph is demanding that Ian fuck him in the way that an American GI may sexually dominate an Iraqi soldier—the analogy connects one sexual act with another sexual act. But on the other hand, as described above, Ralph is also demanding that Ian fuck him the way the US military and government physically dominated Iraq and its people. My point is that in both instances, sexual domination and military domination are synonymous with one another.

This observation builds on Puar's (2007, 79) discussion of the torture of Iraqi prisoners at Abu Ghraib and the photos that arose of US military guards forcing the Iraqi prisoners to "mimic sexual acts closely associated with deviant sexuality or sexual excess such as sodomy and oral sex, as well as S/M practices of bondage, leashing, and hooding." Puar argues that simulated gay sex mutates gay sex into not only deviance but a disgusting act—the outrage over these pictures that people, including many gays and lesbians, felt and expressed cast gay sex as the problem rather than the torture. As Puar (2007, 81) writes, "Homonationalism is consolidated through its unwitting collusions with nationalist sentiment regarding 'sexual torture' in general and 'Muslim sexuality' in specific." Puar continues: "This homonationalism works biopolitically to redirect the devitalizing incident of torture toward a population targeted for death into a revitalizing life-optimizing event for the American citizenry for whom it purports to securitize." The Iraqi soldier Ralph mentions could very well be an Iraqi prisoner subjected to "sexual torture," and thus his very invocation of such a sexual encounter between the American GI and Iraqi soldier is part and parcel of Puar's homonationalism. His utterance "consolidates" that "collusion with nationalist sentiment" in a way that not only elides torture tout court but casts the sex with which Ralph is currently engaged as disgusting. But perhaps that is Ralph's point, the salacious, even torturous encounter between the American GI and Iraqi soldier is to be pleasurable for Ralph. Stated alternatively, Ralph may very well have a kink that extends beyond soldiers and uniforms and involves militarization and "sexual torture." This manifests a queer state of security, for while Ralph derives pleasure from the encounter, the encounter itself plays off a violent and costly invasion, expansion of US empire, and even the possibility (and, with the case of Abu Ghraib, reality) of "sexual torture." And while Ian's reply—"You should really shut the fuck up"—may very well be a response to both the absurdity of Ralph's statement and his verbal nature during a sexual practice that needed to stay hidden while at school, I also like to think it is Ian's way of telling Ralph that what he said was inappropriate and out of line. In other words, Ralph really should "shut the fuck up."

Complicating Ralph's utterance further, however, is Ralph's race as Asian American. We learn nothing specific about Ralph's background, only the offhand comment that his parents would "kill him" if he was suspended, and given Ian's retort that it would be the gay sex that would upset his parents, we can assume that his parents are not (or probably would not be) pleased with their son's sexuality. The utterance that Ralph, an Asian American gay high school student, makes ties Ralph's racialized experience as Asian American and his sexualized experience as gay to the experience of an Iraqi soldier. Perhaps, in Ralph's mind, being Asian

American is like being an Iraqi soldier getting fucked by an American GI, or perhaps it is akin to whiteness dominating his life in ways that he feels like he is being "fucked." I am not suggesting the two experiences *are* commensurable, but for a queer of color high school student surrounded by whiteness—including the whiteness perpetuated by the US military, JROTC, and the US empire (Darda 2018)[14]—the two experiences may *feel* similar. The fact that Mickey kicks Ralph—and then continues to kick Ralph—manifests that comparison between the assaulted, maimed, tortured, and killed Iraqi soldier and the bullied, harassed, assaulted, and even tortured queer Asian American student.

And yet, the fact that Ralph is in the JROTC—that he is getting fucked in his uniform—complicates the utterance and Ralph's racialized and sexualized experience as a queer Asian American high school student even further. For he is, in Puar's (2007) estimation, "colluding with nationalist sentiment" given his JROTC status, not to mention his utterance. But we also cannot erase his race and the whiteness saturating the scene, first with Ian and then with Mickey's toxicity. His race is further indexed with his bottom position in the sexual encounter with Ian, for as Tan Hoang Nguyen (2014) demonstrates, the association between "the bottom position and Oriental passivity" is common within American popular culture, including gay porn. However, Nguyen (2014, 2) wishes to complicate this association by deploying "bottomhood as a tactic that undermines normative sexual, gender, and racial standards . . . that articulates a novel model for coalition politics by affirming an ethical mode of relationality." My point is not to favor one interpretation of Ralph's utterance over another, but, like Nguyen, to complicate the utterance, Ralph's race, and Ralph's sexual experience (especially as a bottom). I am also drawing much needed attention to the ambivalence in the utterance and its racialized and sexualized, not to mention geopolitical, context.

Surrounding the utterance and Ralph's positionality is the problem of whiteness. Not only is Ian's enveloping presence over a bent over Ralph a material manifestation of the spread and dominance of whiteness, but Mickey's eventual presence and foul mouth make the whiteness literally more violent. Mickey's homophobic words and slur combined with his physical beating of Ralph for being a bottom—for being an Asian American bottom—are meant to enhance Mickey's toxic masculinity while drawing a stark contrast between Ralph and Mickey. While both will bottom for Ian, Mickey's whiteness safeguards against attacks to his masculinity—Ralph's race thus becomes synonymous with femininity and emasculation (Eng

2001; Nguyen 2014). Rather than locatable within Mickey alone as the supposed bully, I am arguing that Mickey's actions fit within a broader whiteness-homophobia matrix that washes over both the school and American society. This is further evidenced by Ian's disregard of Mickey's bullying and assault of Ralph, as Ian continues to wear a smirk and say nothing in Ralph's defense. Despite the two having been engaged in anal sex moments earlier, Ian's ignoring the assault speaks to not only his feelings for Mickey—a topic explored in future episodes—but also to his own whiteness-sexuality-gender matrix. His whiteness, like Mickey's, justifies his sexuality without threatening his manhood or his masculinity. Queer students of color, like Ralph, are thus disregarded or neglected—even bullied—for being gay while not being white. Their gender is called into question, which is what necessitates the assault of whiteness: "You're the one taking it in the ass, right? You're the one I gotta kick straight."

One final note I wish to make resonates with the previous chapter on queer pleasure and sex. In that chapter I argued that queer pleasure supplants sex panics, displacing a future-oriented look toward uncertainty with pleasure in the here and now. I contend that an analogous practice is taking place in Ralph and Ian's sexual encounter. The panic of getting caught is displaced by the "hotness" of the sex, until, of course, getting caught turns into a reality and panic returns. But perhaps more powerful is the fact that both Ralph and Ian are in JROTC and wearing parts (or all) of their uniforms. Having sex in uniform not only indexes the then-recent repeal of Don't Ask, Don't Tell in 2011,[15] but it supposedly disrupts military discipline and military time—a temporality where every minute must be accounted for—as they are hiding under the bleachers having sex rather than engaged in whatever JROTC duties that they ought to be doing. There is no doubt a sort of homoeroticism associated with soldiers (Gitzen 2021), but that eroticism, despite no longer being illegal in the military, still relies on normative practices of gender and whiteness. Ralph may desire to be "pounded" by an American GI—Ian—but we never hear Ian's desire until Mickey arrives and the latter asks Ian if he has any "fuck" left in him. That elicits a grin from Ian, his desire coming into focus as the epitome of (toxic) masculinity and whiteness.

Lockdown

I remember the teacher locking the door as we high school students hid under our desks. Having grown up in Florida, where the potential for hurricanes and tornadoes were part of daily life, from a young age we had plenty of practice hiding under our desks for drills. The teacher turned off the lights and instructed us to remain quiet as we heard footsteps ascend the stairs of the portable classroom and knock on the door, asking to be let in. We knew that we were not supposed to let anyone inside once the door was locked and the lights were turned off, for it could very well be a ruse, and letting anyone in could put all our lives in danger. Eventually a voice called over the loudspeaker "All clear!" and we climbed from under our desks back to our seats as the teacher turned the lights back on and unlocked the door. This was one of multiple active shooter trainings with which we engaged in the early 2000s, after Columbine in 1998 and both prior to and after September 11, 2001.

While the active shooter trainings are hard to forget, especially as more school shootings have proliferated the US education landscape in recent years, I also remembered an incident when the entire school evacuated to the football field. Apparently, a bomb threat had been called in—later reported as a fake threat—and the response was the complete evacuation of the school to the football field. This was not the only bomb threat we had experienced, and in years to come, it certainly would not be our—or any school's—last.

In Pascoe's (2023) book *Nice Is Not Enough*, Pascoe also details an active shooter training with real cops, teachers, students, and nerf guns.[16] This simulated active shooter training couples with practice lockdown procedures that involve synchronized slide show presentations in the classroom that follow along with instructions given over the loudspeakers. As Pascoe (2023, 33) notes of one of these procedures, "the emotional weight in the [class]room grew heavy." These training exercises and procedures were meant to unify the response and turn what would be an incredibly traumatic moment into a security exercise: "[T]he disjuncture between robotic instructions and the terrifying possibilities for which it was training us left the class somber, exhausted, and, perhaps, dehumanized" (Pascoe 2023, 35). For Pascoe, the impetus behind describing the active shooting training and procedures was to juxtapose them with student-led walkouts and initiatives that focused on gun control. While school administrators favored and engaged with the former, they actively discouraged and even penalized students who engaged in "political" actions because "politics in the school house is not okay" (Pascoe 2023, 36).

That the focus was on training and procedures and *not* "political" actions or discussions regarding gun control pivots on what Pascoe (2023, 38) calls a "logic of securitization . . . that focuses on securing the material and discursive borders of an organization against external, unpredictable, often unclear, and sometimes mysterious threats." The active shooter training is a telling example, for the point of the training is to preempt future catastrophes (i.e., school shootings) by training students, faculty, and staff in what to do if (or when) such catastrophes take place. Notice, however, how the logic of securitization is to preempt—not *prevent*—the catastrophe from occurring. Preventing, such as with gun control, would fall within the realm of the political and not be welcomed in the school. Therefore, a "politics of protection" locates the "dangers, threats, or harms to young people" as "external, random, and individual, not necessarily as preventable, systemic, or related to inequalities" (Pascoe 2023, 39). My point is that the focus on preempting the future rather than preventing it takes place in the present and thus obscures the actual causes of catastrophes like school shootings along with the violence done in the present to predict and prepare for the uncertainty of the future, such as penalizing students participating in a walkout in protest over lax gun control laws and policies.

Part of Pascoe's (2023) intention in detailing the active shooter training and procedures is to draw attention to just how mundane—and yet, incredibly heavy, and even traumatic—such trainings and procedures have become in the wake of rising gun violence in schools. School lockdowns due to suspected shooters in or near the school have equally become common practice. In what follows, I examine one such lockdown in the HBO Max show *Generation* (2021). The second episode, titled "Dickscovery," has several moving parts; I will interrogate the interactions of students and staff in a Gay-Straight Alliance (GSA) gathering that takes place during the lockdown.

Prior to the lockdown, the school's various organizations and clubs, including the GSA, had set up tables throughout the school and its outdoor spaces to gain student interest. We find best friends Nathan and Riley roaming the halls and outdoor spaces, moving from table and meeting to table and meeting, collecting stickers and eating the food provided. Openly gay black student Chester texts Riley to attend the GSA meeting, and so Nathan and Riley make their way to the meeting. Once inside, the students sit in chairs set up in a circle and one of the faculty mentors opens the meeting by asking students to introduce themselves and share a fun fact. After a few introductions, Chester introduces himself as a Scorpio and says, "If you hurt me, I'll pretend to be unbothered and then literally kill you." Once Chester finishes, an alarm rings out throughout the school followed by an announcement that the school is in lockdown. A title flashes across the screen that reads "Lockdown" followed by a timer.

The two faculty mentors instruct the students to stay calm, to help close the blinds, and to write their names in the notebook being passed around. The students move to the floor as one of the faculty mentors, the guidance counselor, tells students that if anyone needs to talk about anything, there is a spot next to him. Most of the students seem unphased by the lockdown—annoyed that they are indefinitely stuck in the room, but not scared or panicked over the lockdown itself. Chester, however, crawls over to Sam, the guidance counselor, and begins to talk about random deaths that have happened. Elsewhere in the room, we learn that Riley struggles with anxiety as she bonds with fellow student Greta, who is a lesbian and admits her mother was wrongly deported.

As "Lockdown 03:18:27" flashes across the screen, we can hear Chester talking about how the shooter would likely go to the Black Student Union first while fellow student Arianna is playing a shooting game on her phone. Chester continues to talk to no one in particular about the violence committed against black folks before hypothesizing who the shooter may be and which student group he might go to first, including groups that focus on Latinx students, Jewish students, and women, including the intersectionally oppressed GSA, and so "maybe for efficiency they'd just come here, multiple birds, one stone." Nathan eventually asks Chester to stop, noting, "It's not funny," to which Chester bites back, "What are you talking about? It's fucking hilarious. Also that the meaning of life is that it stops." Sam steps in and suggests listening to music, and when the music switches on Chester turns the speaker off before declaring that he does not want to listen to something "basic." At this point Sam instructs Chester to talk to him, and when he does, we learn that since his mother died of cancer, Chester has had a fear of dying. The students of the GSA eventually gather around Riley to watch the popping of a cyst on her phone, then an alarm rings throughout the school followed by a voice over the loudspeaker informing the school that the lockdown has ended.

Despite the uncertainty surrounding the lockdown, and whether it is a drill or an actual lockdown, the characters' behaviors combined with the ticking clock that flashes across the screen make the event rather mundane. Naomi, Nathan's twin sister, who is stuck in the bathroom, screams "Fuck!" right as the siren rings and the voice instructs faculty and students that the school is in lockdown, indicating her annoyance with the entire incident. This is made more apparent as she begins taking photos of her legs and sends them to her friend Arianna to help her select the best one to send to her boyfriend. Furthermore, given that Sam instinctively begins instructing the students to close the blinds and write their names in the notebook he is to pass around demonstrates that this is likely not the first lockdown or drill that Sam or the students have experienced.[17]

That Arianna spends part of the lockdown playing a shooting game on her phone further routinizes not only the lockdown but (school) shootings more broadly. She is unphased by the lockdown or the possibility that there might be an active shooter on or around campus. We learn throughout the show that Arianna is foul-mouthed and in her jokes usually resorts to bigotry, despite being black and the daughter of two fathers, to mask her own insecurities. Therefore, her engagement with the shooting game fits within a broader characterization that sees her push the envelope of acceptable behavior. This also mirror's Chester initial statement about killing anyone who hurts him—jokes about killing others are similarly made banal by Chester's statement, the lockdown, and Chester's pontification on what kind of person might be responsible and who that person is likely after.

Chester's hypothesizing as to the potential shooter's identity and possible target student group illustrates that school shootings and gun violence in America are suffused by whiteness on all sides. I am certainly not suggesting that all gun violence is committed by white people, but roughly 60 percent of all mass shootings committed from 1966 to the present were committed by white people, the vast majority of whom were male (Violence Project 2022). Furthermore, Joshua Gregory (2020, 157) theorizes how whiteness is a contributing factor to school shootings, writing, "Why might gun availability, mental illness, and bullying—among and in concert with other etiological forces—catalyze school shootings in the presence, but not the absence, of whiteness? Because socialization into whiteness imbues the white subject—to varying degrees depending on intersecting identities and the specificities of context and temporality—with a view of the world and their relationship to that world characterized by relational negation, circumscribed humanity, and presumed superiority."

While relational negation makes whiteness "more illusory, more precarious than other racial identities" and circumscribed humanity means that "whites experience only a diminished affinity toward global humankind," presumed superiority is reinforced by schools and society so that "white students invest in a belief that they must attain, and by nature deserve, inordinate success" (Gregory 2020, 158–59). Even Chester recognizes the dilemma of whiteness with regard to school shootings, but he also indexes a more violent problem of presumably male white supremacy. Each of the groups Chester mentions as being a target for the potential shooter—black students, Latinx students, Jewish students, women, and LGBTQ+ students—all face the real threat of male white supremacy, as the shooter's actions are not rooted solely in individual hatred but also in the systemic infiltration of white supremacy in schools, institutions, and society more broadly.

Chester's growing hostility, as we learn, is due to his general fear of death, and so his agitation is meant to be thought of as a coping mechanism for such a fear. His retort to Nathan's insistence that the lockdown "is not funny"—"It's fucking hilarious. Also that the meaning of life is that it stops"—works to shore up hostility to hide his actual fear of death. However, Chester's retort also embodies both the complacency with which society has come to regard school shootings—"It's fucking hilarious"—and the seeming telos of youth's lives: to stop. But not all youth, as Chester reminds us, only queer, black, Latinx, Jewish, and female students. Therefore, it is perhaps more accurate to say that the telos of minority students' lives in the world of white supremacy is for it to stop.

Whether the lockdown is the result of an active shooter or simply a drill, the remainder of the students of the GSA are only mildly agitated. Riley's anxiety is slowly calmed by her interactions with Greta, the two growing closer as a result. Here we see the lateral movement taken in the present, for while the immediate moment is supposed to be scary—or, if it is a drill, preparatory for an actual active shooter incident—Riley and Greta can sidestep the intention of the moment and carve their own lateral path as queer students. Their lives are punctuated by school shootings and violence, but they maneuver within that reality to find something else, something meaningful and relational. Chester engages in a similar maneuver, for while he is becoming more hostile as the lockdown continues, he eventually confesses his fear of death to Sam, not only creating a bond between the two but also helping Chester move through his fear without letting the fear completely overtake him. Fear is how he is supposed to experience the moment, as he sees death always in the immediate future, but by discussing this fear with Sam, Chester works to not preempt his inevitable future—the telos of life stopping—but instead to experience the present moment.

Such routinization of school shootings and gun violence—not to mention violence toward queer youth more broadly—coupled with the lateral maneuvers multiple GSA members make during the lockdown culminates in the final interaction of all the students being huddled around Riley watching a video. They find a sort of comfort in the grossness of the video, as the grossness of popping cysts and pimples counters the fear and anxiety of the lockdown. Watching this video is thus how the lockdown ends, for we do not know for how long the students have been watching videos, but that is the point: one form of ordinariness supplants another, as grossness overtakes fear. We might also read the grossness and popping of cysts and pimples as a queer student rejoinder to school shootings in general, for by paying no attention and focusing their attention on the ridiculousness of the videos, the queer students are in some ways saying, as Chester first opined, that school shootings and their collective precarity are "fucking hilarious." Watching these videos is a method for queer youth to unscript the security expectations of the moment, to displace the preparation and fear implicitly woven through the moment and instead watch impromptu videos that ground them in the present moment as not fearful but passable, even enjoyable.

Queer States of Security

The refocus of the GSA members from the fear and anxiety of the lockdown to the grossness of Riley's video and subsequent disregard for the lockdown itself is meant to be a coping mechanism, a way for students to maneuver within a precarious and preparatory moment. While the video itself, which is briefly shown, may elicit actual nausea, the situation—including Chester's ramblings throughout the lockdown—sits uncomfortably within the scenes. The room gets heavier, with the other queer students not responding to Chester's outward ramblings until Nathan finally asks Chester to stop because the lockdown is "not funny." Nathan's insistence that Chester stop renders the room too heavy to stay afloat, and is the moment when the discomfort became too much to bear.

These are queer states of security, the moments—be them instantaneous or prolonged[18]—when rooms get too heavy to bear, when discomfort, awkwardness, or ambivalence reigns supreme and the stuckness we feel can be only momentarily sidestepped. Ralph's utterance in *Shameless* similarly contributes ambivalence to an already precarious situation, annoying Ian and making the entire encounter uncomfortable. This is only further enhanced by Mickey's arrival and assault of Ralph, particularly Ian's disregard for Ralph's well-being despite having moments prior been sexually engaged with the boy. Making the entire situation even more awkward is Ralph's JROTC uniform, as though both the sex and the assault are meant to disrespect or call into question the authority of the uniform, JROTC, and the military itself. Such disregard compares to the disregard that several students, such as Arianna, show for the supposed seriousness of the lockdown and potential active shooter. Both the military and school shootings are not considered serious or worthy of contemplation—they are afterthoughts or institutions that ought to actively be pushed against.

These scenes ultimately detail the ways queer youth (and adults) encounter and participate in the American security apparatus. As demonstrated above, security compels citizens' participation to the point of instinctual response, as evidenced by Sam's immediate call for the students to close the blinds, to remain calm, and to write their names in the notebook. We are trained to respond, Masco (2014) theorizes, to particular signs and situations of danger and threat with learned behavior. That the students move from their chairs to the floor also indicates that they have been socialized with a national security affect, proper citizens tasked with the safety of themselves and others.

While both scenes bear witness to queer youth's encounters with the American security apparatus, both also work to dislodge the seriousness, authority, or pull of the apparatus and security more broadly. The sex in which Ian and Ralph, and later Ian and Mickey, engage is a direct afront to the JROTC and to militarization, not because homosexuality is illegal in the military but because sex becomes a way to downplay the discipline and authority embodied in the uniform itself. Soldiers ought not be fucking while on duty (or in uniform), we might imagine, and Ralph's invocation of GIs and Iraqi soldiers further downplays both the interaction of these soldiers and the soldier and the military more broadly. Comparatively, the GSA members watching Riley's video takes away from the seriousness of the situation, but if the lockdown is actually a drill, it takes away from the preemptive goal of the drill—the students should not be gathered together, some sitting in chairs and others standing, but instead spread out throughout the room on the floor, out of sight of a potential shooter.

Queer states of security may draw attention to the ambivalence and awkwardness of the situation for and with queer youth, but they also work to emphasize that the present moment is more important than the future's uncertainty. In other words, queer states of security are a method of unscripting expectations of security and youth more broadly. In both scenes, the future is precarious and uncertain—whether it be getting caught having sex at school or being caught by a potential school shooter—and should thus be preempted with actions that prepare queer youth for that possibly inevitable outcome. The present is thus predicated on preparation for the future. But Ralph and Ian continue to have sex, and the GSA members bond over a gross video; neither scene engages in such preparatory practices. Rather, both sets of queer youth work to displace the uncertainty of the future with either queer pleasure or queer relationality in the here and now. Such attention to the here and now balks at the supposed supremacy and omnipresence of the American security apparatus. For both sets of queer youth recognize, encounter, and even interact with the apparatus but choose to move laterally through the moment—to unscript the present—rather than stay scripted to an uncertain and precarious future. The future is still there; displacing the future is not a forever action. But when one is radically present, an infinite number of things can transpire.

Coda

World Ending

> I didn't know if the world was going to end tomorrow, nor did I care.
>
> —Shaun David Hutchinson, *We Are the Ants*

Henry Denton haunts this book as he does me. In many ways, Henry was the impetus for my writing, even before Shaun David Hutchinson's *We Are the Ants* began getting banned throughout the country. Henry was certainly braver than I was at his age in high school, but his experiences still resonate with me and my theoretical formulation around queer youth sexuality. His aversion to gravity, as discussed at the end of the introduction, indexes his more personal aversion to the stringent, normative orientation of growing up, while his eventual disinterest in the end of the world at the end of the book, as captured by this coda's epigraph (Hutchinson 2016, 448), embodies a broader concern with the present and maneuverability within the present moment. Not knowing if the world was to end the following day no longer interested Henry, only the present did: "We remember the past, live in the present, and write the future" (Hutchinson 2016, 451). This is a radical state to be in, especially after mildly obsessing over the future and end of the world throughout much of the book. But it also perfectly captures an anxiety that queer youth themselves have about the future: it could very well be world-ending and all that is left for queer youth is the present.

The present is scripted with future uncertainty, anxiety, fear, and insecurity. Sex panics work to script fear and anxiety about future sexual catastrophes into the present through laws, policies, media, and broader social discourse, tapping into securitization ideologies and practices as a hallmark of a post-9/11 American zeitgeist. Proponents of these sex panics, which they feel to be parents' rights, mobilize fear about the future by anticipating catastrophe and preempting or preparing for such uncertainty and insecurity in the present. The regulation of what can and cannot be said in classrooms, as explored in chapter 1, aligns with what ought to be reported to authorities regarding suspicious objects, peoples, and actions. In other words, security weaves through sex panics in ways that often go unnoticed or ignored, an unconscious erasure of security ideologies and practices that work to embed sex panics into the American security apparatus and thus heighten the fear and anxiety induced by sex panics. For this reason, as I have argued, sex panics are forms of security panics, enabling a securitization of sex in ways that make nonnormativity threatening, dangerous, and an afront to the security of the nation.

And yet, Henry is no longer concerned with the end of the world. He finds more solvency in the present, in a weightless, horizontal movement rather than the gravity-infused trudge toward the future. This is not to say that queer youth are unconcerned with the deluge of sex panics sweeping the country—youth across the country have been protesting the slew of anti-LGBTQ laws that target schools as ground zero for parents' rights (GLAAD 2022; Olmos 2023; Chavez 2023; Alfonseca 2022). Rather, if the future is not for queer youth, if growing up precludes one from being queer or acting queer, then the present becomes where one must maneuver, within the sieving scripts that work to disassociate one from normativity.

This book has explored representations of the different lateral movements queer youth take amid growing sex panics. These representations and maneuvers of queer youth unscript the expectations of youth more broadly, as my own approach aims to do the same; both are a queer methodology that seeks to unseat the primacy and normativity of the future in favor of attention to the present. In chapter 2 I called this a form of radical presentism as representations of queer youth, though concerned about their futures in general, took to worrying more about the immediate present, the minute-to-minute lives they must lead to navigate an uncertain here and now. For the members of TK in *Teenage Kiss*, as discussed in the preface, such a concern with the present matters because the future and adulthood lead to monochromatism and apathy. Queer sex similarly works to unscript normative expectations set in the present for a type of "reproductive futurism" (Edelman 2004) and thus supplants panic with queer pleasure, as discussed in chapter 4.

The series of unscripted—unplanned, impromptu—experiences of the queer youth represented throughout this book also feature moments of when plans go awry. The scene of Victor and Benji's sexual encounter in Victor's room is one such moment, as discussed in chapter 4, for their plan certainly was derailed the moment Victor's mother walked in on the two of them having sex. This unscripted moment led to a rather heated argument between Benji and Victor's mother, which led then to arguments between Benji and Victor and Victor and his mother. This was the turning point in both relationships, for until then Victor's mother had all but ignored Victor's admission at the start of season two that he is gay, given her own religious misgivings about queerness. Unscripted though it may be, witnessing her son's queerness in such spectacular fashion meant that Victor's mother could no longer keep hidden his sexuality; the child's innocence was shattered and there was no piecing it back together.

Unpacking this moment, then, draws further attention to not only the loss of childhood innocence for the adult (i.e., Victor's mother) but also to the failed normative expectations of Victor to be both heterosexual and thus oriented toward growing up. Such failure is also a failure to secure the child's future, the family's future, and, by extension, the nation's future. Victor's queerness is the root of this set of failures, for his queer youth sexuality flies in the face of youth expectations, of what it means (to adults) to be a child. He is therefore the epitome of sex panics, the fear and anxiety that his mother feels for her child's future as potentially queer only verified when she walks in on him having sex. The fear about Victor's future, of every child's future, is actualized in the present through panicked discourse, laws, and policies. Yet the unscripted moments of sex, such as Ian's sexual rendezvous underneath the bleachers with Ralph as discussed in chapter 5, challenges future expectations of youth, unraveling the child's innocence and insisting that the present moment of the sex is where attention ought to be paid.

Yet Henry's disinvestment from the future surfaces in these moments as well. Ian's on-campus, in-uniform sex embodies this quite well, for there is great risk to be had having sex on campus and in uniform, and yet he does not seem to care. Ralph's admission that his parents would kill him if they found out indexes the potential world-ending effect of their sex, and despite that, they still fucked. Neither cared because the present pleasure mattered more than future consequences, than the potential catastrophe of the future. Their own divestment from the future underlines my point that the present has the power to unravel the sieving scripts of the future, and challenge security more broadly by outwardly and consciously sidestepping the future. Queer youth throw caution to the wind because the alternative is unobtainable—their queerness precludes them from future security and so they say fuck the future, the present is all they need.

The future is of immense concern to queer youth and their allies. But it is a different sort of concern, one that is concrete and rooted in data rather than misplaced fear and sensationalized anxiety. As discussed in chapter 5, participating in future-oriented practices invokes a securitized discourse and ideology that compels citizens to participate in their securitization, but that does not mean queer youth are not uncomfortable in doing so. The awkwardness and ambivalence manifest queer states of security, I argued, for the concern over one's physical safety may come at the expense of further structural insecurity. A concern for the future may require participation in security, but queer youth do so by sidestepping the panic placed upon them by adults. All contemporary sex panics may be security panics, but not all iterations of security are sex panics, so queer youth can participate in security without reducing it to a panic about their sexualities. This may be a form of what José Esteban Muñoz (2009) refers to as "educated hope," invoking Ernst Bloch, which sees utopic visions of the future as actionable and achievable, queer as the not-yet realized of the present moment.

It is certainly my hope that this book provides some reprieve for queer youth navigating their precarious presents, to assure them that they are enough, yes, but that they need not wait for a future that may or may not come to pass and instead they can carve out a piece of the present for themselves. It is also my hope that in the pages of this book resides an alternative to the securitization of sex, a wrench thrown in the seemingly totalizing machine of the American security apparatus that demands accounting for the insecurities, injuries, and discriminations perpetrated against queer youth. Might attention to queer youth sexuality in the present work to slowly disentangle and even disassemble the logic of securitization? I may be a realist—and my continued work in critiquing security certainly sobers my expectations—but I am hopeful. Mark Maguire and Setha Low (2024) are also hopeful that securitization can be thwarted, at least in piecemeal, by opening the gates of communities, taking back the city from racial and classist discrimination, reimagining policing by removing capitalism from public safety, countering counterterrorism by divesting from private contractors, and reclaiming the homeland from the security-industrial complex. While I am not as lofty as Maguire and

Low, I do think attention to how queer youth survive among the security panics inundating their daily lives draws much needed attention to the securitization of sex and may work to critique, challenge, and even chip away at the American security apparatus.

However, I wish to end by cutting the present moment a bit of slack, by giving it some breathing room. Allowing for queers to have a future, to imagine a future, is important, no doubt, but we must also consider the ways queer youth maneuver within the present despite the sex panics that target them and their sexualities. Can we see Victor and Benji's sex—Ian and Ralph's sex—as not more than the moment, more than the sex, but the moment of sex itself? Could we take Isak's word and let him and Even take things "completely chill," to experience their relationship minute by minute rather than adorn it with labels and expectations? In short, could we let queer youth fuck the future by living in the present?

I admit, alongside Henry, that it would be disappointing to find gravity on an alien spaceship because life is heavy enough as it is, and queer youth could do with some weightlessness, even if just for a moment.

Notes

Introduction

1. There are over thirty thousand students in KISD, and in August 2022, the school district removed forty-one books from its libraries, including several books that address gender fluidity and LGBTQ+ characters and themes (Lopez 2022).

2. C. J. Pascoe (2023) makes a similar observation about liberalizing schools, namely that "politics" has no place in schools and is better left for the confinement of the home to be discussed with parents and family members. I discuss this in more detail in chapter 5.

3. Bouie (2023) continues: "The reality of the 'parents' rights' movement is that it is meant to empower a conservative and reactionary minority of parents to dictate education and curriculums to the rest of the community. It is, in essence, an institutionalization of the heckler's veto, in which a single parent—or any individual, really—can remove hundreds of books or shut down lessons on the basis of that one person's political discomfort. 'Parents' rights,' in other words, is when some parents have the right to dominate all the others."

4. Some scientists and news reports contend that the next global pandemic will emerge from melting glaciers, that anthropogenic climate change will lead to melting glaciers and release ancient viruses trapped within (Geddes 2022).

5. Lauren Berlant (2011, 100) refers to this as "slow death" and contends that agency exists within it: "[I]n the scene of slow death, a condition of being worn out by the activity of reproducing life, agency can be an activity of maintenance, not making; fantasy, without grandiosity; sentience, without full intentionality; inconsistency, without shattering; and embodying, alongside embodiment."

6. Weeks mobilizes the concept of moral panic from Stan Cohen's 1972 book *Folk Devils and Moral Panics*. Rubin (2011, 168) provides the examples of "the white-slavery hysteria of the 1880s, the antihomosexual campaigns of the 1950s, and the child pornography panic of the late 1970s" as types of moral panics.

7. Erica R. Meiners (2016), for instance, follows discourse surrounding the innocence of the child and keeping children safe as intimately tied to the

carceral state and the prison industrial complex, focusing specifically on the school-to-prison pipeline.

8. Rubin (2011, 168–69) adds that "the criminalization of innocuous behaviors such as homosexuality, prostitution, obscenity, or recreational drug use is rationalized by portraying them as menaces to health and safety, women and children, national security, the family, or civilization itself."

9. Edelman is not after actual experiences of children but the figure of the Child as a foreclosure of queer futures—the future is not for queer folks, and thus the Child represents all that queer folks lack.

10. As Stockton (2016, 507) later writes, "[T]he gay child was precisely ghostly because it could not live in the present tense, even though it often consciously, secretly had a relationship with the *word* gay—or with the word's vague associations and connotations, without the word itself."

11. Brown (1995, 170) writes of women who seek protection from the state: [I]indeed, to be 'protected' by the same power whose violation one fears perpetuates the very modality of dependence and powerlessness marking much of women's experience across widely diverse cultures and epochs."

12. They do recognize that marginalization and discrimination emerge from within security practices and ideologies, that security, caught in webs of power, engender marginalization. But I am specifically making a point about security targeting marginalized and dispossessed individuals, that even if their marginalization emerges from security practices, those security practices target them specifically.

13. See Ronak K. Kapadia's (2019) discussion of "queer calculus" within forever wars as an illustration of how queer theory might extend beyond gender and sexuality.

14. As a result, sex offender registries are also populated with these teens charged with possession and distribution of their own naked pictures.

15. I interchange the usage of "artifact" and "text" throughout this book.

16. I stress popular here to indicate that I am focusing on popular culture that is popular, not only made for mass consumption.

17. I revisit the importance of textual approaches in chapter 4, specifically with the interrogation of queer youth sex and the ways pleasure supplants panic in the scenes described in that chapter.

18. The child as sexual subject juxtaposes with the child as sexual object, whereby the child is sexual rather than others sexualizing the child (Angelides 2019).

19. Other words for "sieves," Kockelman (2017, 139) writes, "include filters, strainers, and sifters."

20. Kockelman (2017, 140) continues: "[W]e apperceive through our sieves as much as we sieve through our apperception . . . we are our sieves."

21. Lynne Joyrich (2014, 136) makes an analogous claim, but suggests that television "might help us think outside the binaries of queer theory itself—binaries

like those of being . . . too straight-forward-looking or too stuck in the past, too focused on the positive or too mired by the negative, too mainstream or too oppositional, too socialized or too antisocial, too commonsensical or too dismissive of the commons."

22. See also Erica R. Meiners (2016, 194).

23. David Valentine (2017) writes about the ways gravity exists as a universal context for humankind, and that when humans go to space and gravity is no longer a given context, the concept of human similarly changes.

Chapter One

1. This often leads, Grossberg (2005, 30) demonstrates, to the imprisonment of kids: "[A]s a nation we spent $4.2 billion building prisons for kids in 2000, significantly more than we spent on child care." See also Erica R. Meiners (2016) on the connections between children, innocence, and the carceral state.

2. Adrienne Rich (1980) famously referred to this as compulsory heterosexuality as an explanation for understanding the lesbian experience in the United States.

3. Puar (2007, 3) borrows from Giorgio Agamben's notion of state of exception, noting "the sanctioned and naturalized disregard of the limits of state juridical and political power through times of state crisis, a 'state of exception' that is used to justify the extreme measures of the state." This manifests, in some ways, as a national population coming to believe "in its own superiority and its own singularity" (5). To speak of US sexual exceptionalism is thus to not only posit a heteronormative exceptionalism, but one that is also homonormative: "[H]omosexual sexual exceptionalism does not necessarily contradict or undermine heterosexual sexual exceptionalism; in actuality it may support forms of heteronormativity and the class, racial, and citizenship privileges they require" (9).

4. President Truman's 1948 Executive Order 9981 desegregated the US military. Yet in response to a piece of legislation in 1940 that would have desegregated the military, the secretary of war claimed that this legislation would "demoralize and weaken the effect of military units by mixing colored and white soldiers in closely related units, or even in the same units" (Dalfiume 1969, 46).

5. See also feminist historian Margot Canaday (2009) on how the rise of the US bureaucratic state in the twentieth century relied on the systemic targeting of homosexuality within institutions of the military, welfare, and immigration.

6. Frank (2023) quickly notes that "in reality, it did the opposite, heightening division, undermining trust, hampering morale and driving capable people away."

7. While each of the laws that disallow the teaching or inclusion of sexual orientation and gender identity all have their own individual names and bill numbers, I refer to them as Don't Say Gay laws given that this is their colloquial

nomenclature. Using this draws links between different states' laws and indexes what the laws are attempting to do: silence students and educators from even saying words that represent nonnormative sexualities and gender variance. I also use this nomenclature to draw a much-needed comparison between these types of laws and other kinds of laws that also restrict what is *said* about sexuality, including the military's Don't Ask, Don't Tell law and the older no homo promo law, which I shall discuss later in the chapter. Most of these Don't Say Gay laws, however, are associated with some sort of Parents' Rights or Parents' Bill of Rights, thus framing the discussion of gender identity and sexual orientation as not only a concern of the family but as directed and managed by parents' own (often scientifically inaccurate or ignored) beliefs regarding gender and sexuality.

8. Gilbert (2014, 25) writes, "[T]his relation of non-relation—the repudiation of the adolescent who lives on in the adult—is the underside of sex education, defended against thorough assertions of pedagogical authority, assertions that forget the impossibility of positioning oneself as an 'expert on sex.'" She refers to adolescence and adulthood as "a psychical relation."

9. Here, Balzacq is borrowing from Pierre Bourdieu's (1977, 72) notion of the *habitus*, or "systems of durable, transposable *dispositions*, structured structures predisposed to function as structuring structures, that is, as principles of the generation and structuring practices and representations which can be objectively 'regulated' and 'regular' without any way being the product of obedience to rules, objectively adapted to their goals without presupposing a conscious aiming at ends or an express mastery of the operations necessary to attain them and, being all this, collectively orchestrated without being the product of the orchestrating action of a conductor."

10. Penal Code 21.06 is the same antisodomy law that Lawrence and Garner were charged and convicted under, and that was then brought to the Supreme Court and ruled unconstitutional in 2003 (Hoshall 2013).

11. Both Mississippi and Oklahoma now have Don't Say Gay laws that target lower grades (typically elementary schools) (Movement Advancement Project 2023).

12. The *Diagnostic and Statistical Manual of Mental Disorders* 1, published in 1952, included homosexuality as a "sociopathic personality disturbance." Yet the *Diagnostic and Statistical Manual of Mental Disorders* 2, published in 1974, no longer included homosexuality as a disorder.

13. Furthermore, the bill "prohibits trans school employees from sharing their pronouns with students" (Yurcaba 2023).

14. DeSantis commented that "there's these adult performances, these drag shows, sexually explicit [. . .] what they're doing is adult entertainment. People can do what they want with some of that, but to have minors there, I mean, you'll have situations where you'll have like an 8-year-old girl there, where you have these like really explicit shows, and that is just inappropriate" (Yurcaba 2023).

Notes to Chapter One | 173

15. The bill would also "bar the use of public health funds to cover such care for anyone, including adults. Health care providers who violate the measure could face a felony punishable by up to five years in prison" (Yurcaba 2023).

16. See Jabir Puar (2017) on mutilation and debility.

17. Johnson is cosponsor of the bill "The Stop the Sexualization of Children Act" that would "prohibit the use of Federal funds to develop, implement, facilitate, or fund any sexually-oriented program, event, or literature for children under the age of 10, and for other purposes" (Finley 2023, 199)

18. Some Don't Say Gay laws also would require that teachers and school employees "out" trans students to their parents (LaFrance 2023).

19. Most sexual abuse of minors takes place by someone the minor knows, especially family members, "a space that is conceptualized as both natural and safe" (Meiners 2016, 165). To then have parents regulate if students can even learn about sexual abuse provides no hope for children being abused in their very own homes.

20. North Carolina also has a 2023 law (SB49, the "Parent's Bill of Rights"), that bans the instruction of gender identity, sexuality, or sexual activity in grades 4 and below.

21. "The bill clarifies that recreational sexualization means 'any form of non-procreative sex'" (Finley 2023, 200).

22. Fox News—the name of the channel and not necessarily what they report (i.e., the news)—often decries the way schools and liberals are grooming children (Block 2022).

23. See also Meredith Johnson (2022) on legal consequences with regards to Florida's Don't Say Gay law.

24. See also Ashley Woo and Melissa Kay Diliberti's (2023) RAND survey of "national samples of educators to learn about how efforts, like those in Florida . . . restrict discussions of race, gender, and LGBTQ+ issues" and thus affect teaching and learning.

25. The lawsuit was filed against school districts in Indian River, Orange, Duval, and Palm Beach Counties by the Southern Poverty Law Center, Southern Legal Counsel, Lambda Legal, and private counsel Baker McKenzie. These groups represent "seven students and their parents, as well as CenterLink Inc., a nonprofit LGBTQ+ advocacy organization based in Fort Lauderdale, Florida" (SPLC 2022).

26. As I explore in chapter 5, this also contributes to a form of US exceptionalism that weaves through security practices.

27. Browne (2015, 137) pulls from Robin D. G. Kelley's explication of "'moving theaters'" of the Jim Crow South during World War II, namely segregated buses and other public transportation spaces.

Chapter Two

1. Puar (2017, 10) continues: "'It Gets Better' circulates as a projection of bodily capacity that ultimately partakes in slow death, even as it reforms the valence of debility—homosexual identity—through a white/liberal/male assemblage: a recapacitation machine."

2. Puar (2017, 11) is concerned with "what kinds of slow deaths have been ongoing that a suicide might represent an escape from." Puar borrows the notion of slow death from Lauren Berlant (2011, 100), noted as "a condition of being worn out by the activity of reproducing life."

3. Some may argue that we are living in a post–queer-shame world, that we have "won" against homophobia because folks can live out and proud lives. But these claims and beliefs are akin to the It Gets Better campaign, for certain folks may have "won," but not all folks. As Sally Munt (2019) notes, this framing is steeped in neoliberal discourse and posits a prideful West compared to a shameful East. Such a distinction, one that Munt is quick to criticize, also recalls the early 2000s' insistence of a global gay paradigm that saw gay discourse spread across the world and take hold, rooting out traditional systems and institutions of family that saw the oppression of gay folks (Altman 2001).

4. Dana Luciano (2007, 9) calls this chronobiopolitics, or "the sexual arrangements of the entire time of life" for the whole of the population (see also Freeman 2010, 3).

5. Krüger and Rustad (2019, 76) elaborate on this point: "Overly idealistic as it may sound, this claim aligns with Trine Syverstenʼs . . . observation that NRK employees usually are more values than ratings oriented compared to commercial broadcasters." And, therefore, "the conceptualization and production of *Skam* should be read in a context of value-driven television production."

6. Susan Talburt (2004, 18) interrogates the ways "dominant narratives about queer youth make youth intelligible—to others and to themselves in narrowly defined ways . . . the narrative character of the knowledge adults have created in defining the means and ends of building the young."

7. As Evan Novrup Redvall (2018, 144) writes, "[T]he aim was to explore their main need in relation to fictional content and create stories and characters of relevance to them, based on this need." The needs, approach, benefits, and competition model was developed by the Stanford Research Institute.

8. Most of the actors were unknowns—not professional actors—while some were even students at the school at which they filmed the series.

9. As Sundet (2020, 75) writes, "In-depth insider knowledge is obviously useful for serving one's audience in a relevant and attractive way; however, it is also a great advantage in an increasingly globalized television market [. . .] NRK would never be able to compete with the budgets or production values of US drama series, especially not in an online teen drama such as SKAM, which

had a relatively small budget of 10 million NOK (1.15 million Euro) in total for seasons two and three [. . .] NRK has unique knowledge on Norwegian (teen) culture, and precisely local familiarity and relevance were considered key advantages in a globalised market, reflecting, as they did, the power of 'cultural proximity.'"

10. Part of this format carries into current NRK shows aimed at teens, namely the show *Rykter* (2022–present), which translates to "Rumors." In particular, short eight- to nine-minute clips/episodes are uploaded to the show's website—sometimes multiple clips uploaded on the same day.

11. Ilana Gershon (2010, 5) would refer to this as remediation: "the ways people interlink media, suggesting that people define every technology in terms of other communicative technologies available to them."

12. Youthification, for Sundet (2021a, 146), relies on a double meaning: "First, it refers to the *strategic focus* that television producers, executives and decision-makers bring to the production of youth content in the interest of answering the 'youth challenge' . . . or 'missing audience' problem [. . .] second, 'youthification' refers to the way in which producers, scholars and audience members *conceptually* make sense of television as an always-changing medium that must, to stay relevant, perpetually 'youthify' itself—through innovation involving genres, formats, platforms, storytelling techniques and distribution models."

13. Lindtner and Dahl (2019, 64–65) refer to this as a "democratic aesthetic of melodrama" whereby it "makes sense to read *Skam* as a classic melodrama with a moral lesson rather than [a] soap." This, however, seems to contradict Magnus's insistence that *Skam* was not created to engage in moralizing practices.

14. In Sundet's (2020, 78) estimation, double liveliness amounts to the fact that "an audience member watched the characters' lives 'as they happened' but also at the same time as other audience members."

15. Furthermore, Gershon (2010, 6) notes that the rules about how to use a specific medium, or "idioms of practice," are agreed upon by the group of people who use that medium. This does not mean that all users of Instagram, for example, use Instagram the same way. But rather, a group of friends may agree to use Instagram in a particular way, such as sharing memes with one another.

16. Lepselter (2016, 24) invites readers to think of narrative resonance "as an intertextual half-rhyme, which in poetry produces a more ambiguous sense of structure than does a fully rhyme [. . .] resonance produces aesthetic intensity and the poetic pleasure of repetition with variation not only in consciously artful stories but also in the lived and embodied metaphors and the felt, discursive practices that compose phenomenological realities."

17. Counterpublics was famously theorized by Michael Warner (2002, 56): "A counterpublic, against the background of the public sphere, enables a horizon of opinion and exchange; its exchanges remain distinct from authority and can have a critical relation to power; its extent is in principle indefinite, because it

is not based on a precise demography but mediated by print, theater, diffuse networks of talk, commerce, and the like."

18. Kursell (2010, 220) continues, noting that "even a shifter itself does not require a person who is in a particular place at a particular time at the moment they say something and who guarantees that words such as 'I,' 'now' and 'here,' appearing in their utterance, can be understood."

19. This also resonates with Elliott's admission that he has medication to help him but will not always take it because he likes the way he is feeling; he does not want things to change.

20. Viveiros de Castro (2011, 141) notes that the "arrow is a universal symbol of the index (look where the arrow is pointing and you will get somewhere) as well as the elemental vector of the 'distributed person' (look to where the arrow came from and you will find someone)." He continues by stating that "every arrow is magical: while it paradoxically transforms the far into the near and vice versa—as skepticism transforms itself into belief, aggressivity into generosity, and reciprocally so on—no arrow that we see arriving is exactly the one we saw leaving."

21. Bergson (2004, 248) continues: "[A]nd by the very fact that you represent the movement to yourself successively in these different points, you necessarily arrest it in each of them; your successive positions are, at bottom, only so many imaginary halts."

22. This is certainly not representative of all manic states, as hypomanic states are typically less intense.

Chapter Three

1. Margot Weiss (2011, 6) makes an analogous point in her work on S/M culture in the United States, arguing that "sexuality—indeed, all sexuality—is a social relation, linking subjects . . . to socioeconomics."

2. I discuss this normalization effect more fully in chapter 4.

3. Muñoz (2009) focuses on "educated hope," invoking theorist Ernst Bloch, but with regard to the future. I contend that we may operationalize a similar form of hope in the present.

4. For a more detailed exploration of the multimodal, transmedia format, see chapter 2's discussion of *Skam*.

5. GLAAD reported that of the 596 LGBTQ+ characters found on television between 2022 and 2023, 140 characters will not be returning because the series was cancelled (Deerwater and Townsend 2023).

6. This point about contracts and its application in this chapter was initially spurred by a conversation with Ilana Gershon in May 2023 while strolling through a Tom of Finland exhibit in Helsinki.

7. For a further explication on the differences between Hobbes's and Locke's conception of the social contract, see John Michael Sasan's (2021) analysis.

8. It is important to note, as both Foucault (1990) and Butler (1993) contend, that sexual identities are also categories of regulation and even discrimination at both the individual and especially the institutional level.

9. Butler (1997, 3) continues: "The illocutionary speech act is itself the deed that it effects; the perlocutionary merely leads to certain effects that are not the same as the speech act itself."

10. For instance, a teenager that comes out to one's parents and friends is likely not yet thinking about marriage. But when that teenager does think about marriage, the declaration that the teenager is gay not only indexes a specific marriable partner but invokes the Supreme Court's 2015 marriage equality decision, *Obergefell v. Hodges*.

11. Following both Gray (2009) and Michael Warner (2002), we may even consider coming out as a move into the counterpublic sphere. For more on counterpublics and queer identity formation, refer to chapter 2.

12. Bacon (1998, 151) continues: "To tell the story of your life is to demand self-definition, and at the same time to trap oneself within a specific definition of self based in sexual identity."

13. Foucault (1990) demonstrates how truth resides within the individual to be discovered, often by a facilitator (i.e., psychiatrist). As he writes, confessions were thus the "most highly valued techniques for producing truth" as truth is "driven from its hiding place in the soul, or extracted from the body" (Foucault 1990, 59).

14. "Confession frees, but power reduces one to silence; truth does not belong to the order of power, but shares an original affinity with freedom: traditional themes in philosophy . . . would have to overturn by showing that truth is not by nature free . . . but that its production is thoroughly imbued with relations of power" (Foucault 1990, 60)

15. "Pleasure in the truth of pleasure, the pleasure of knowing that truth, of discovering and exposing it, the fascination of seeing it and telling it, of captivating and capturing others by it, of confiding it in secret, of luring it out in the open—the specific pleasure of the true discourse on pleasure" (Foucault 1990, 71).

16. Reddy (1979) refers to this as the toolmaker's paradigm.

17. "Discourse finds the object at which it was directed already overlain with qualifications" (Bakhtin in Bacon 1998, 257).

18. And as Bacon (1998, 256) also notes, "[O]ur cultural logic, and our language do not necessarily have to reflect a tendency toward closure." Even with energy spent, communication is rather messy and requires work to succeed in meaning making.

19. Here Vainiomäki is indexing the field of semiotics.

20. Antonia Cava (2023, 116) similarly writes that "silence is the space that words invade [. . .] and silence is a perpetual background around words. All

conversations inescapably come up against the need for silence between their origin and their conclusion. Knowing how to speak involves knowing how to keep silence."

Chapter Four

1. *Druck* is an adaptation of the Norwegian show *Skam*, though after season four, *Druck* has produced original content and is no longer adapting storylines from *Skam* given that *Skam* only ran for four seasons.

2. I refer to Isi as genderqueer, not because they refer to themselves as genderqueer, but rather because throughout the season, Isi grapples with how to understand their gender identity and, near the end, admits that all pronouns are fine to use when addressing them.

3. Berlant (2022, 40) notes how anxious sex is, even panicked, because "our modern training in erotophobic subjectivity, which casts sex as an overwhelming object of fear and threat, tends to make us frame its pleasures as good luck and its pains as the real."

4. In some ways, this compares to Michel Foucault's (1990) explication of the truth of sex ascertained through confessional, through the verbalization of desire and practice, as explored in the previous chapter. But where Foucault posits that a truth of sex is sexuality, I am suggesting that another truth is relationality.

5. Stockton (2016, 508) cheekily continues: "one can almost hear a collective plea from parents, at least these parents, who are crying out: is there a child somewhere who is innocent and, yes, maybe sexual, and *wants* our protections?"

6. As Driver writes (2008, 3), "queer youth are frequently cast as victims of homophobic violence or heterosexist exclusion in ways that inscribe them with tropes of victimization and risk."

7. Interestingly, Driver (2008, 4) channels Susan Talburt's (2004) notion of queer youth intelligibility, writing that "the very languages that render queer youth intelligible and unified create pathos toward sexual minority youth while at the same time undermining possibilities for questioning the very terms of normality that abject queer youth differences in the first place."

8. Driver (2008, 2) also notes that "the goal is not to encapsulate queer youth once and for all but rather to initiate provisional and detailed analysis of the ways they precariously make and unmake sense of their lives in relation to the world around them."

9. For further discussion of the narrative resonance of queer youth popular culture and stories, see chapter 2.

10. Michel Foucault (1990) is crucial for Rubin's (2011, 146) theorization of sex and sexuality, namely that desires "are not preexisting biological entities, but rather that they are constituted in the course of historically specific social practices."

11. As such, Rubin (2011, 156) contends, "contemporary sexual politics should be reconceptualized in terms of the emergence and ongoing development of this system, its social relations, the ideologies that interpret it, and its characteristic modes of conflict."

12. Speaking of sexuality as an adult possession indexes Rubin's (2011) notion of sexual essentialism as sex is considered to be an individual possession rather than a social and historical construct.

13. Hirsch and Khan (2020, 93) continue: "The sex that students have to accumulate experience, or to demonstrate that they can be modern people, highlights one risk built into impersonal sex: not caring if the other person has a bad experience, sexually or otherwise."

14. For discussion on speech act theory and the distinction between perlocutionary and illocutionary speech acts, see chapter 3.

15. See chapter 3 for a parallel discussion of *Love, Victor* and *Love, Simon*.

16. Wilhelm and Simon have sex in the third episode in the third season as well, this time in celebration of their status as out boyfriends, their sex momentarily sidestepping the pressure Wilhelm faces as crowned prince.

17. When Chester arrives at school in the first episode of the series, he is reprimanded and written up for a dress code violation because of the top he is wearing.

18. *wtFOCK* is the Belgian adaptation of the Norwegian show *Skam*, discussed in chapters 2 and 3.

19. A version of this scene is replicated in the different adaptations of *Skam/wtFOCK*, though none are as explicit as the scene in *wtFOCK*.

Chapter Five

1. Ahmed (2012) is speaking specifically to institutional forms of stranger making within the turn toward diversity in institutions of higher education.

2. Here, Robertson (2018, 9) is invoking C. J. Pascoe's (2007) ethnography on masculinity and sexuality within high schools, whereby "fag discourse is used by adolescent boys as a tool to police masculinity."

3. Others refer to this as a "security state" (Grewal 2017), but I favor "apparatus," as it draws attention to the moving parts, techniques, mechanisms, and constructedness of security.

4. The original context of banal security is South Korea, and the ways national security has become so mundane that it is often ignored or not even seen, an image or object just to the right of one's perception (Gitzen 2023).

5. Stephen Collier and Andrew Lakoff (2021) make a similar argument about the protection of "vital systems" in this new set of security logics and practices.

6. I am specifically referencing in this passage the ways Korean queer folks worked with police to set up a barricade and checkpoint entrance/exit for the annual Korean Queer Culture Festival (now called the Seoul Queer Culture Festival).

7. Racism, for instance, is perceived as a problem with the individual—an individual is racist—rather than a systemic problem of institutional racism (Pascoe 2023).

8. Urciuoli (2022, 12) contends that "the notion of diversity dominating higher education was imported from the corporate world."

9. For Billing (1995), flagging is a process whereby nationalism calls attention to itself as a way to reify a nationalism predicated on "us versus them" that works to make nationalism ordinary. Cindi Katz (2007, 350) operationalizes this notion of banality to explicate what she calls "banal terrorism," or the "everyday, routinized, barely noticed reminders of terror or the threat of an always already presence of terrorism in our mind." I combine both into a broader notion of "banal security" (Gitzen 2023, 4), or the "making of security—and the destruction it professes to prevent—a natural and normative part of daily living to the extent of its unconscious erasure."

10. Militarism, though related to militarization, is not the same thing. For Lutz (2007, 321–22), militarism involves "identifying a society's emphasis on martial values" while militarization "draws attention to the simultaneously material and discursive nature of military dominance."

11. Reserve officer training corps aim to prepare students as commissioned officers in the US Armed Forces.

12. This is also part of Shange's (2019) point about schooling—and a much broader point that social scientists make regarding school-to-prison pipelines, particularly for black students.

13. Mickey is typically the one who bottoms in his sexual encounters with Ian throughout the show.

14. As Joseph Darda (2018, 79) writes, "[M]ilitary whiteness also drew on the discourse of liberal multiculturalism by casting the white veteran as himself a voice of minoritized difference."

15. Don't Ask, Don't Tell was a policy implemented by President Clinton in 1993 that disallowed openly gay and lesbian individuals to serve in the military. The policy was that the military would not ask, and as such the soldier would not tell. President Obama repealed the law in 2011.

16. It is debatable if such training is effective, particularly given "the emotional toll it exacts on many who participate" (Pascoe 2023, 31).

17. Sam is new to the school, so it is unlikely that he has experienced a lockdown at this particular school.

18. Alternatively, we might say that the moment is durational, a series of individual moments strung together ad infinitum, as discussed in chapter 2.

References

Abu-Lughod, Lila. 2005. *Dramas of Nationhood: The Politics of Television in Egypt.* Chicago: University of Chicago Press.

Ahmed, Sara. 2004. *The Cultural Politics of Emotion.* New York: Routledge.

———. 2006. *Queer Phenomenology: Orientations, Objects, Others.* Durham: Duke University Press.

———. 2010. *The Promise of Happiness.* Durham: Duke University Press.

———. 2012. *On Being Included: Racism and Diversity in Institutional Life.* Durham: Duke University Press.

———. 2016. "Queer Fragility." *Feminist Killjoys*, April 21. https://feministkilljoys.com/2016/04/21/queer-fragility/.

———. 2017. "Queer Fatalism." *Feminist Killjoys*, January 13. https://feministkilljoys.com/2017/01/13/queer-fatalism/.

Alexander, Jonathan, and Elizabeth Losh. 2010. "'A YouTube of One's Own?': 'Coming Out' Videos as Rhetorical Action." *LGBT Identity and Online New Media*, 37–50. https://doi.org/10.4324/9780203855430.

Alfonseca, Kiara. 2022. "Students Challenge 'Don't Say Gay' Laws amid Wave of Anti-LGBTQ Legislation." *ABC News*, June 10. https://abcnews.go.com/US/students-challenge-dont-gay-laws-amid-wave-anti/story?id=85256706.

Allen, David J., and Terry Olseon. 1999. "Shame and Internalized Homophobia in Gay Men." *Journal of Homosexuality* 37 (3): 33–43.

Altman, Dennis. 2001. *Global Sex.* Chicago: University of Chicago Press.

Amin, Kadji. 2017. *Disturbing Attachments: Genet, Modern Pederasty, and Queer History.* Durham: Duke University Press.

Amoore, Louise. 2013. *The Politics of Possibility: Risk and Security beyond Probability.* Durham: Duke University Press.

Angelides, Steven. 2019. *The Fear of Child Sexuality: Young People, Sex, and Agency.* Chicago: University of Chicago Press.

Anzaldúa, Gloria. 2009. *The Gloria Anzaldua Reader.* Durham: Duke University Press.

Asmar, Axelle, Tim Raats, and Leo Van Audenhove. 2023. "Streaming Difference(s): Netflix and the Branding of Diversity." *Critical Studies in Television* 18 (1): 24–40. https://doi.org/10.1177/17496020221129516.

Aubrey, Jennifer Stevens, Kun Yan, Larissa Terán, and Lindsay Roberts. 2020. "The Heterosexual Script on Tween, Teen, and Young-Adult Television Programs: A Content Analytic Update and Extension." *Journal of Sex Research* 57 (9): 1134–45. https://doi.org/10.1080/00224499.2019.1699895.

Austin, J. L. 1975. *How to Do Things with Words*. Cambridge: Harvard University Press.

Avila-Saavedra, Guillermo. 2009. "Nothing Queer about Queer Television: Televized Construction of Gay Masculinities." *Media, Culture and Society* 31 (1): 5–21. https://doi.org/10.1177/0163443708098243.

Bacon, Jen. 1998. "Getting the Story Straight: Coming Out Narratives and the Possibility of a Cultural Rhetoric." *World Englishes* 17 (2): 249–58. https://doi.org/10.1111/1467-971X.00098.

Bakhtin, Mikhail. 1981. *The Dialogic Imagination: Four Essays*. Austin: University of Texas Press.

Ball, Christopher, and Shunsuke Nozawa. 2016. "Tearful Sojourns and Tribal Wives: Primitivism, Kinship, Suffering, and Salvation on Japanese and British Reality Television." *American Ethnologist* 43 (2): 243–57. https://doi.org/10.1111/amet.12302.

Balzacq, Thierry. 2011. "A Theory of Securitization: Origins, Core Assumptions, and Variants." In *Securitization Theory: How Security Problems Emerge and Dissolve*, edited by Thierry Blazacq, 1–30. New York: Routledge.

Barnard, Ian. 2020. *Sex Panic Rhetorics, Queer Interventions*. Tuscaloosa: University of Alabama Press.

Basso, Keith. 1970. " 'To Give Up on Words': Silence in Western Apache Culture." *Southwestern Journal of Anthropology* 26 (3): 213–30.

Beauchamp, Toby. 2019. *Going Stealth: Transgender Politics and U.S. Surveillance Practices*. Durham: Duke University Press.

Becker, Ron. 2006. *Gay TV and Straight America*. New Brunswick, NJ: Rutgers University Press.

Beirne, Rebecca Clare. 2006. "Embattled Sex: Rise of the Right and Victory of the Queer in Queer as Folk." In *The New Queer Aesthetic on Television: Essays on Recent Programming*, edited by James R. Keller and Leslie Stratyner, 43–58. Jefferson, NC: McFarland.

Bengtsson, Emelie, Rebecka Källquist, and Malin Sveningsson. 2018. "Combining New and Old Viewing Practices." *Nordicom Review* 39 (2): 63–77. https://doi.org/10.2478/nor-2018-0012.

Bergson, Henri. 2004. *Matter and Memory*. Mineola, NY: Dover Publications.

Berlant, Lauren. 2011. *Cruel Optimism*. Durham: Duke University Press.

———. 2022. *On the Inconvenience of Other People*. Durham: Duke University Press.

Berlant, Lauren, and Lee Edelman. 2014. *Sex, or the Unbearable*. Durham: Duke University Press.

Berliner, Lauren S. 2018. *Producing Queer Youth: The Paradox of Digital Media Empowerment*. New York: Routledge.

Bernini, Lorenzo. 2018. "Gay Orgies under the Big Top Re-Sexualising the Queer Debate." *Whatever* 1:93–103. https://doi.org/10.13131/2611-657X.whatever.v1i1.5.

Bernstein, Elizabeth. 2017. "Carceral Politics as Gender Justice? The 'Traffic in Women' and Neoliberal Circuits of Crime, Sex, and Rights." In *The War on Sex*, edited by David M. Halperin and Trevor Hoppe, 297–322. Durham: Duke University Press.

Berridge, Susan. 2013. "'Doing It for the Kids'? The Discursive Construction of the Teenager and Teenage Sexuality in Skins." *Journal of British Cinema and Television* 10 (4): 785–801. https://doi.org/10.3366/jbctv.2013.0175.

Bible, Jacqueline, Alejandra Kaplan, Lisa Lieberman, and Eva Goldfarb. 2022. "A Retrospective Analysis of Sex Education Messages Received by LGB Youth." *Journal of LGBT Youth* 19 (3): 287–306. https://doi.org/10.1080/19361653.2020.1819509.

Billing, Michael. 1995. *Banal Nationalism*. London: Sage.

Bilmes, Jack. 1994. "Constituting Silence: Life in the World of Total Meaning." *Semiotica* 98 (1/2): 73–87.

Block, Melissa. 2022. "Accusations of 'Grooming' Are the Latest Political Attack—with Homophobic Origins." *NPR*, May 11. https://www.npr.org/2022/05/11/1096623939/accusations-grooming-political-attack-homophobic-origins.

Boellstorff, Tom. 2008. *Coming of Age in Second Life: An Anthropologist Explores the Virtually Human*. Princeton: Princeton University Press.

Boellstorff, Tom, Bonnie Nardi, Celia Pearce, and T. L. Taylor. 2012. *Ethnography and Virtual Worlds: A Handbook of Method*. Princeton: Princeton University Press.

Borgogna, Nicholas C., Ryon C. McDermott, Stephen L. Aita, and Matthew M. Kridel. 2019. "Anxiety and Depression across Gender and Sexual Minorities: Implications for Transgender, Gender Nonconforming, Pansexual, Demisexual, Asexual, Queer, and Questioning Individuals." *Psychology of Sexual Orientation and Gender Diversity* 6 (1): 54–63. https://doi.org/10.1037/sgd0000306.

Bouie, Jamelle. 2023. "What the Republican Push for 'Parents' Rights' Is Really About." *The New York Times*, March 28. https://www.nytimes.com/2023/03/28/opinion/parents-rights-republicans-florida.html?auth=login-google1tap&login=google1tap.

Bourassa, Gregory. 2021. "Neoliberal Multiculturalism and Productive Inclusion: Beyond the Politics of Fulfillment in Education." *Journal of Education Policy* 36 (2): 253–78. https://doi.org/10.1080/02680939.2019.1676472.

Bourdieu, Pierre. 1977. *Outline of a Theory of Practice.* Cambridge: Cambridge University Press.
Brennan, Teresa. 2004. *The Transmission of Affect.* Ithaca: Cornell University Press.
Brown, Wendy. 1995. *States of Injury: Power and Freedom in Late Modernity.* Princeton: Princeton University Press.
Browne, Katelyn R. 2020. "Reimagining Queer Death in Young Adult Fiction." *Research on Diversity in Youth Literature* 2 (2): 3.
Browne, Simone. 2015. *Dark Matters: On the Surveillance of Blackness.* Durham: Duke University Press.
Bruhm, Steven, and Natasha Hurley. 2004. "Curiouser: On the Queerness of Children." In *Curiouser: On the Queerness of Children*, edited by Steven Bruhm and Natasha Hurley, ix–xxxviii. Minneapolis: University of Minnesota Press.
Burnichon, Magali Claudine Dominique. 2018. "Queer TV? The Case of Showtime's Queer as Folk and The L Word." PhD thesis, University College London.
Butler, Judith. 1993. "Imitation and Gender Insubordination." In *The Gay and Lesbian Studies Reader*, edited by Henry Abelove, 307–20. New York: Routledge.
———. 1997. *Excitable Speech: A Politics of the Performative.* New York: Routledge.
———. 2002. "Is Kinship Always Already Heterosexual?" *Differences* 13 (1): 14–44. https://doi.org/10.1215/10407391-13-1-14.
———. 2004. *Precarious Life: The Powers of Mourning and Violence.* New York: Verso.
Byron, Paul. 2021. *Digital Media, Friendship, and Cultures of Care.* New York: Routledge.
Canaday, Margot. 2009. *The Straight State: Sexuality and Citizenship in Twentieth-Century America.* Princeton: Princeton University Press.
Caraway, Rebecca. 2022. "'I Am an Adult with a Mature Brain': How Texas Parents Lobbied to Get Books on Gender Identity Banned from Schools." *Daily Hot*, December 2. https://www.dailydot.com/debug/keller-texas-school-ban-gender-fluid-books/.
Castagno, Angelina E. 2014. *Educated in Whiteness: Good Intentions and Diversity in Schools.* Minneapolis: University of Minnesota Press.
———, ed. 2019. *The Price of Nice: How Good Intentions Maintain Educational Inequality.* Minneapolis: University of Minnesota Press.
Cava, Antonia. 2023. "Silence as a Meaning Framework." In *Exploring Contextualism and Performativity: The Environment Matters*, edited by Alessandro Capone and Assunta Penna, 115–25. New York: Springer. https://doi.org/10.1007/978-3-031-12543-0_7.
Cavalcante, Andre. 2015. "Anxious Displacements: The Representation of Gay Parenting on Modern Family and the New Normal and the Management of Cultural Anxiety." *Television and New Media* 16 (5): 454–71. https://doi.org/10.1177/1527476414538525.

Chambers, Samuel A. 2009. *The Queer Politics of Television*. New York: I. B. Tauris.
Chavez, Roby. 2023. "Why Youth Activists in Louisiana Say They'll 'No Longer Stay Quiet.'" *PBS News Hour*, May 18. https://www.pbs.org/newshour/nation/why-youth-activists-in-louisiana-say-theyll-no-longer-stay-quiet.
Chiang, Howard, and Alvin K. Wong. 2016. "Queering the Transnational Turn: Regionalism and Queer Asias." *Gender, Place and Culture* 23 (11): 1643–56. https://doi.org/10.1080/0966369X.2015.1136811.
———. 2017. "Asia Is Burning: Queer Asia as Critique." *Culture, Theory and Critique* 58 (2): 121–26. https://doi.org/10.1080/14735784.2017.1294839.
Chinn, Sarah, and Anna Mae Duane. 2015. "Introduction." *WSQ: Women's Studies Quarterly* 43 (1 & 2): 14–26.
Christian, Aymar Jean. 2020. "Beyond Branding: The Value of Intersectionality on Streaming TV Channels." *Television and New Media* 21 (5): 457–74.
Clark, Caroline T., and Mollie V. Blackburn. 2016. "Scenes of Violence and Sex in Recent Award-Winning LGBT-Themed Young Adult Novels and the Ideologies They Offer Their Readers." *Discourse* 37 (6): 867–86. https://doi.org/10.1080/01596306.2014.936713.
Collier, Stephen J., and Andrew Lakoff. 2021. *The Government of Emergency: Vital Systems, Expertise, and the Politics of Security*. Princeton: Princeton University Press.
Cortvriend, Jack. 2018. "Stylistic Convergences between British Film and American Television: Andrew Haigh's Looking." *Critical Studies in Television* 13 (1): 96–112. https://doi.org/10.1177/1749602017746115.
Craig, Shelley L., Lauren McInroy, Lance T. McCready, and Ramona Alaggia. 2015. "Media: A Catalyst for Resilience in Lesbian, Gay, Bisexual, Transgender, and Queer Youth." *Journal of LGBT Youth* 12 (3): 254–75. https://doi.org/10.1080/19361653.2015.1040193.
Cronk, Terri Moon. 2016. "Carter: 600 Troops to Deploy to Enable Iraqis to Retake Mosul from ISIL." *US Central Command*, September 28. https://www.centcom.mil/MEDIA/NEWS-ARTICLES/News-Article-View/Article/958881/carter-600-troops-to-deploy-to-enable-iraqis-to-retake-mosul-from-isil/.
Cummings, Kelsey. 2022. "Queer Seriality, Streaming Television, and She-Ra and the Princesses of Power." *Global Storytelling: Journal of Digital and Moving Images* 2 (1): 3.
Dajches, Leah, and Jennifer Stevens Aubrey. 2020. "Defining the Relationship: An Examination of Sexual Behaviors and Relational Contexts across Tween, Teen, and Young Adult U.S. Television." *Communication Reports* 33 (3): 136–47. https://doi.org/10.1080/08934215.2020.1803389.
Dajches, Leah, Larissa Terán, Kun Yan, and Jennifer Stevens Aubrey. 2021. "Not Another Teen Show: Exploring the Impact of Sexual Scripts in Sexually Oriented Teenage Television on Adolescent Girls' Romantic Relationship

and Sexual Expectations." *Journal of Broadcasting and Electronic Media* 65 (4): 575–94. https://doi.org/10.1080/08838151.2021.1981903.

Dalfiume, Richard M. 1969. "Military Segregation and the 1940 Presidential Election." *Phylon* 30 (1): 42–55.

Daniel, Tallie Ben, and Hilary Berwick. 2020. "Queer In/Security: An Introduction." *GLQ: A Journal of Lesbian and Gay Studies* 26 (1): 129–40.

Darda, Joseph. 2018. "Military Whiteness." *Critical Inquiry* 45 (1): 76–96. https://doi.org/10.1086/699574.

Davis, Charles L. 1993. "Lifting the Gay Ban." *Society* 31 (1): 24–28.

Davis, Glyn, and Kay Dickinson, eds. 2000. *Teen TV: Genre, Consumption, and Identity*. London: British Film Institute.

Davis, Nick. 2008. "The View from the Shortbus. Or All Those Fucking Movies." *Glq* 14 (4): 623–37. https://doi.org/10.1215/10642684-2008-010.

De Goede, Marieke. 2008. "Beyond Risk: Premediation and the Post-9/11 Security Imagination." *Security Dialogue* 39 (2–3): 155–76. https://doi.org/10.1177/0967010608088773.

De Orio, Scott. 2017. "The Creation of the Modern Sex Offender." In *The War on Sex*, edited by David M. Halperin and Trevor Hoppe, 247–67. Durham: Duke University Press.

De Ridder, Sander, and Sofie Van Bauwel. 2015. "The Discursive Construction of Gay Teenagers in Times of Mediatization: Youth's Reflections on Intimate Storytelling, Queer Shame and Realness in Popular Social Media Places." *Journal of Youth Studies* 18 (6): 777–93.

Deerwater, Raina, and Townsend, Megan. 2023. "Where We Are on TV, 2022–2023." GLAAD Media Institute. https://glaad.org/whereweareontv22/.

Dhaenens, Frederik. 2012. "Gay Male Domesticity on the Small Screen: Queer Representations of Gay Homemaking in Six Feet Under and Brothers & Sisters." *Popular Communication* 10 (3): 217–30. https://doi.org/10.1080/15405702.2012.682936.

Driver, Susan. 2008. "Introducing Queer Youth Cultures." In *Queer Youth Cultures*, edited by Susan Driver, 1–18. Albany, NY: State University of New York Press.

Edelman, Lee. 2004. *No Future: Queer Theory and the Death Drive*. Durham: Duke University Press.

Edwards, Natalie. 2009. "From Minority to Mainstream: Channel 4's Queer Television." *Journal of E-Media Studies* 2 (1). https://journals.dartmouth.edu/cgi-bin/WebObjects/Journals.woa/xmlpage/4/article/325.

Elia, John P., and Mickey Eliason. 2010. "Discourses of Exclusion: Sexuality Education's Silencing of Sexual Others." *Journal of LGBT Youth* 7 (1): 29–48. https://doi.org/10.1080/19361650903507791.

Elia, John P., and Gust A. Yep. 2012. "Sexualities and Genders in an Age of Neoterrorism." *Journal of Homosexuality* 59 (7): 879–89.

Eng, David L. 2001. *Racial Castration: Managing Masculinity in Asian America*. Durham: Duke University Press.
Eng, David L., Judith Halberstam, and José Esteban Muñoz. 2005. "Introduction: What's Queer about Queer Studies Now?" *Social Text* 23 (3–4): 1–17.
Eng, David L., and Jasbir K. Puar. 2020. "Introduction: Left of Queer." *Social Text* 38 (4): 1–24.
Ewald, Francois. 2002. "The Return of Descartes' Malicious Demon: An Outline of a Philosophy of Precaution." In *Embracing Risk: The Changing Culture of Insurance and Responsibility*, edited by Tom Baker and Jonathan Simon, 273–301. Chicago: University of Chicago Press.
Fields, Jessica. 2008. *Risky Lessons: Sex Education and Social Inequality*. New Brunswick, NJ: Rutgers University Press.
Finley, Laura. 2023. "LGBTQ Activism to Counter 'Don't Say Gay,' Trans Athlete Bans and Other Attacks on Affirming Education in US Public Schools." In *Global LGBTQ Activism: Social Media, Digital Technologies, and Protest Mechanisms*, edited by Paromita Pain, 198–214. New York: Taylor & Francis.
Fisher, Christopher Micheal. 2009. "Queer Youth Experiences with Abstinence-Only-until-Marriage Sexuality Education: 'Can't Get Married So Where Does That Leave Me?'" *Journal of LGBT Youth* 6 (1): 61–79. https://doi.org/10.1080/19361650802396775.
Fleming, Luke. 2014. "Australian Exceptionalism in the Typology of Affinal Avoidance Registers." *Anthropological Linguistics* 56 (2): 115–58. https://doi.org/10.1353/anl.2014.0006.
Flores, Dalmacio, Sharron L. Docherty, Michael V. Relf, Ross E. McKinney, and Julie V. Barroso. 2019. "'It's Almost Like Gay Sex Doesn't Exist': Parent-Child Sex Communication According to Gay, Bisexual, and Queer Male Adolescents." *Journal of Adolescent Research* 34 (5): 528–62. https://doi.org/10.1177/0743558418757464.
Foucault, Michel. 1990. *The History of Sexuality: An Introduction*. Vol. 1. New York: Vintage Books.
Frank, Nathaniel. 2023. "What the Science Says about 'Don't Say Gay' and Young People." *The New York Times*, April 20. https://www.nytimes.com/2023/04/20/opinion/dont-say-gay-bill-florida.html.
Fraser, Suzanne. 2006. "Poetic World-Making: Queer as Folk, Counterpublic Speech and the 'Reader.'" *Sexualities* 9 (2): 152–70. https://doi.org/10.1177/1363460706063117.
Freeman, Elizabeth. 2010. *Time Binds: Queer Temporalities, Queer Histories*. Durham: Duke University Press.
Fuller, Danielle. 2019. "The Multimodal Reader: Or, How My Obsession with NRK's Skam Made Me Think Again about Readers, Reading and Digital Media." *Participations: Journal of Audience & Reception Studies* 16 (1): 496–509.

Garg, Namrata, and Anna Volerman. 2021. "A National Analysis of State Policies on Lesbian, Gay, Bisexual, Transgender, and Questioning/Queer Inclusive Sex Education." *Journal of School Health* 91 (2): 164–75. https://doi.org/10.1111/josh.12987.

Geddes, Linda. 2022. "Next Pandemic May Come from Melting Glaciers, New Data Shows." *The Guardian*, October 18. https://www.theguardian.com/science/2022/oct/19/next-pandemic-may-come-from-melting-glaciers-new-data-shows.

Gershon, Ilana. 2010. *The Breakup 2.0: Disconnecting over New Media*. Chicago, IL: University of Chicago Press.

———. 2011. "Neoliberal Agency." *Current Anthropology* 52 (4): 537–55. https://doi.org/10.1086/660866.

———. 2014. "Selling Your Self in the United States." *Political and Legal Anthropology Review* 37 (2): 281–95. https://doi.org/10.1111/plar.12075.

———. 2016. "'I'm Not a Businessman, I'm a Business, Man': Typing the Neoliberal Self into a Branded Existence." *HAU: Journal of Ethnographic Theory* 6 (3): 223–46. https://doi.org/10.14318/hau6.3.017.

———. 2017. *Down and Out in the New Economy: How People Find (or Don't Find) Work Today*. Chicago: University of Chicago Press.

———. 2019. "Undercover Boss's Travels: Comparing the US and UK Reality Shows." *Visual Anthropology Review* 35 (2): 176–86. https://doi.org/10.1111/var.12190.

———. 2024. *The Pandemic Workplace: How We Learned to Be Citizens in the Office*. Chicago: University of Chicago Press.

Gilbert, Jen. 2014. *Sexuality in School: The Limits of Education*. Minneapolis: University of Minnesota Press.

Gill-Peterson, Julian. 2015. "The Value of the Future: The Child as Human Capital and the Neoliberal Labor of Race." *WSQ: Women's Studies Quarterly* 43 (1–2): 181–96. https://doi.org/10.1353/wsq.2015.0023.

Ginsburg, Faye D., Lila Abu-Lughod, and Brian Larkin, eds. 2002. *Media Worlds: Anthropology on New Terrain*. Berkeley: University of California Press.

Gitzen, Timothy. 2021. "Narratives of the Homoerotic Soldier: The Fleshiness of the South Korean Military." *Cultural Studies* 36 (6): 1005–32. https://doi.org/10.1080/09502386.2021.1919166.

———. 2023. *Banal Security: Queer Korea in the Time of Viruses*. Helsinki: Helsinki University Press.

———. 2024. "Review of Nice Is Not Enough: Inequality and the Limits of Kindness at American High by C. J. Pascoe." *Anthropology & Education Quarterly* 55 (2): 227–28. https://doi.org/10.1111/aeq.12492.

Gitzen, Timothy, and Ilana Gershon. 2024. "Fictitious Folklore and World Making in Popular Culture." In *Möbius Media: Popular Culture, Folklore, and the Folkloresque*, edited by Jeffery A. Tolbert and Michael Dylan Foster, 137–54. Salt Lake City: Utah State University Press.

GLAAD. 2022. "Students Fight Anti-LGBTQ Policies with Nationwide Walkouts." *GLAAD*, September 28. https://glaad.org/students-fight-anti-lgbtq-policies-nationwide-walkouts/.

Goddard, Michael N., and Christopher Hogg. 2019. "Streaming Intersectionality: Queer and Trans Television Aesthetics in Post-Medium Transformation." *Critical Studies in Television* 14 (4): 429–34. https://doi.org/10.1177/1749602019875846.

Goldberg, Abbie E. 2023. "Impact of HB 1557 (Florida's Don't Say Gay Bill) on LGBTQ+ Parents in Florida." Los Angeles: UCLA Williams Institute. https://williamsinstitute.law.ucla.edu/publications/impact-dont-say-parents/.

Grandio, M., and J. Bonaut. 2012. "Transmedia Audiences and Television Fiction: A Comparative Approach between Skins (UK) and El Barco (Spain)." *Participations* 9 (2): 558.

Gray, Mary L. 2009. *Out in the Country: Youth, Media, and Queer Visibility in Rural America*. New York: New York University Press.

Greene, Doyle. 2012. *Teens, TV, and Tunes: The Manufacturing of American Adolescent Culture*. Jefferson, NC: McFarland.

Gregory, Joshua R. 2020. "Whiteness and School Shootings: Theorization toward a More Critical School Social Work." *Children and Schools* 42 (3): 153–60. https://doi.org/10.1093/cs/cdaa017.

Grewal, Inderpal. 2017. *Saving the Security State: Exceptional Citizens in Twenty-First-Century America*. Durham: Duke University Press.

Grossberg, Lawrence. 2005. *Caught in the Crossfire: Kids, Politics, and America's Future*. Boulder: Paradigm.

Grusin, Richard. 2004. "Premediation." *Criticism* 46 (1): 17–39.

Guy Emerson, R. 2022a. "Vigilant Subjects, Risky Objects: 'If You See Something, Say Something.'" *Theory and Event* 25 (3): 614–38. https://doi.org/10.1353/tae.2022.0030.

Halberstam, Judith (Jack). 2005. *In a Queer Time and Place: Transgender Bodies, Subcultural Lives*. New York City: New York University Press.

———. 2011. *The Queer Art of Failure*. Durham: Duke University Press.

Halperin, David M. 2017. "Introduction: The War on Sex." In *The War on Sex*, edited by David M. Halperin and Trevor Hoppe, 1–61. Durham: Duke University Press.

Halperin, David M., and Trevor Hoppe, eds. 2017. *The War on Sex*. Durham: Duke University Press.

Hanckel, Benjamin, Son Vivienne, Paul Byron, Brady Robards, and Brendan Churchill. 2019. "'That's Not Necessarily for Them': LGBTIQ+ Young People, Social Media Platform Affordances and Identity Curation." *Media, Culture & Society* 41 (8): 1261–78.

Heim, Julia. 2020. "Italian LGBTQ Representation in Transnational Television." *Journal of Italian Cinema and Media Studies* 8 (2): 189–203. https://doi.org/10.1386/jicms_00016_1.

Hiller, Lynne, and Lyn Harrison. 2004. "Homophobia and the Production of Shame: Young People and Same Sex Attraction." *Culture, Health & Sexuality* 6 (1): 79–94.

Hirsch, Jennifer S., and Shamus Khan. 2020. *Sexual Citizens: Sex, Power, and Assault on Campus*. New York City: W. W. Norton.

Hoshall, Leora. 2013. "Afraid of Who You Are: No Promo Homo Laws in Public School Sex Education." *Texas Journal of Women & the Law* 22 (2): 219–39.

Howes, Sarah Alex. 2019. "Digital Replicas, Performers Livelihoods, and Sex Scenes: Likeness Rights for the 21st Century." *Columbia Journal of Law and Arts* 42 (3): 345–50.

Hughes, Katherine. 2014. "Boy Wizards: Magical and Homosocial Power in Harry Potter and the Goblet of Fire and The Covenant." In *Queer Youth and Media Cultures*, edited by Christopher Pullen, 158–69. New York: Palgrave Macmillan.

Human Rights Watch. 2022. "'I Became Scared, This Was Their Goal': Efforts to Ban Gender and Sexuality Education in Brazil." Human Rights Watch. https://www.hrw.org/report/2022/05/12/i-became-scared-was-their-goal/efforts-ban-gender-and-sexuality-education-brazil.

Hunt, Cynthia. 2023. "'They Were Trying to Scare Us': College Students' Retrospective Accounts of School-Based Sex Education." *Sex Education* 23 (4): 464–77. https://doi.org/10.1080/14681811.2022.2062592.

Hutchinson, Shaun David. 2016. *We Are the Ants*. New York: Simon Pulse.

Irvine, Janice M. 2002. *Talk about Sex: The Battles over Sex Education in the United States*. Berkeley: University of California Press.

———. 2007. "Transient Feelings: Sex Panics and the Politics of Emotions." *GLQ: A Journal of Lesbian and Gay Studies* 14 (1): 1–40.

Izaguirre, Anthony. 2022. "WATCH: Governor Ron DeSantis Gives Remarks as He Signs into Law Florida's 'Don't Say Gay' Bill." *PBS News Hour*, March 298. https://www.pbs.org/newshour/politics/watch-governor-ron-desantis-gives-remarks-as-he-signs-into-law-floridas-dont-say-gay-bill.

Izaguirre, Anthony, and Brendan Farrington. 2023. "Florida Expands 'Don't Say Gay'; House OKs Anti-LGBTQ Bills." *AP*, April 19. https://apnews.com/article/desantis-florida-dont-say-gay-ban-684ed25a303f83208a89c556543183cb.

Jakobson, Roman. 1971. "Shifters, Verbal Categories, and the Russian Verb." In *Selected Writings II: Word and Language*, edited by Roman Jakobson, 130–47. The Hague: Mouton.

Javaid, Aliraza. 2020. "The Haunting of Shame: Autoethnography and the Multivalent Stigma of Being Queer, Muslim, and Single." *Symbolic Interaction* 43 (1): 72–101.

Jenner, Mareike. 2014. "We Need to Talk about Jack! On the Representation of Male Homosexuality in American Teen Soaps." In *Queer Youth and Media Cultures*, edited by Christopher Pullen, 131–44. New York: Palgrave Macmillan.

Johnson, Meredith. 2022. "The Dangerous Consequences of Florida's 'Don't Say Gay' Bill on Lgbtq+ Youth in Florida." *Georgetown Journal of Gender and Law* 23 (3): 25–27.

Joyrich, Lynne. 2014. "Queer Television Studies: Currents, Flows, and (Main) Streams." *Cinema Journal* 53 (2): 133–39.

Kapadia, Ronak K. 2019. *Insurgent Aesthetics: Security and the Queer Life of the Forever War*. Durham: Duke University Press.

Katz, Cindi. 2007. "Banal Terrorism." In *Violent Geographies: Fear, Terror, and Political Violence*, edited by Derek Gregory and Allan Pred, 349–62. New York: Routledge.

Kelly, Maura. 2010. "Virginity Loss Narratives in Teen Drama Television Programs." *Journal of Sex Research* 47 (5): 479–89. https://doi.org/10.1080/00224499 0903132044.

Kendall, Nancy. 2013. *The Sex Education Debates*. Chicago: University of Chicago Press.

Kockelman, Paul. 2017. *The Art of Interpretation in the Age of Computation*. New York: Oxford University Press.

Kondo, Dorinne K. 1990. *Crafting Selves: Power, Gender, and Discourses of Identity in a Japanese Workplace*. Chicago: University of Chicago Press.

Krüger, Steffen, and Gry C. Rustad. 2019. "Coping with Shame in a Media-Saturated Society: Norwegian Web-Series Skam as Transitional Object." *Television and New Media* 20 (1): 72–95. https://doi.org/10.1177/1527476417741379.

Kumar, Deepa. 2018. "See Something, Say Something: Security Rituals, Affect, and US Nationalism from the Cold War to the War on Terror." *Public Culture* 30 (1): 143–71. https://doi.org/10.1215/08992363-4189203.

Kursell, Julia. 2010. "First Person Plural: Roman Jakobson's Grammatical Fictions." *Studies in East European Thought* 62 (2): 217–36. https://doi.org/10.1007/s11212-010-9115-x.

LaFrance, Samantha. 2023. "It's Not Just Florida: 4 New 'Don't Say Gay' Laws Passed in 2023." *Pen America*, August 31. https://pen.org/4-new-dont-say-gay-laws-passed-in-2023/.

Lakoff, Andrew. 2017. *Unprepared: Global Health in a Time of Emergency*. Berkeley: University of California Press.

Lancaster, Roger N. 2011. *Sex Panic and the Punitive State*. Berkeley: University of California Press.

Lepselter, Susan. 2016. *The Resonance of Unseen Things: Poetics, Power, Captivity, and UFOs in the American Uncanny*. Ann Arbor: University of Michigan Press.

Levine, Judith. 2003. *Harmful to Minors: The Perils of Protecting Children from Sex*. New York: Thunder's Mouth Press.

Lindtner, Synnøve Skarsbø, and John Magnus Dahl. 2019. "Aligning Adolescents to the Public Sphere: The Teen Serial Skam and Democratic Aesthetic." *Javnost* 26 (1): 54–69. https://doi.org/10.1080/13183222.2018.1529471.

Lindtner, Synnøve Skarsbø, and John Magnus Ragnhildson Dahl. 2020. "The Romantic Fantasy of Even and Isak—An Exploration of Scandinavian Women Looking for Gratification in the Teen Serial SKAM." *Feminist Media Studies* 22 (2): 291–305. https://doi.org/10.1080/14680777.2020.1830146.

Lopez, Brian. 2022. "Texas School Officials Remove 41 Books from Library Shelves, Including the Bible." *United Press International*, August 16. https://www.upi.com/Top_News/US/2022/08/16/texas-school-board-removes-books-libraries/8301660688071/.

Luciano, Dana. 2007. *Arranging Grief: Sacred Time and the Body in Nineteenth-Century America*. New York: New York University Press.

Lukacs, Gabriella. 2010. "Iron Chef around the World: Japanese Food Television, Soft Power, and Cultural Globalization." *International Journal of Cultural Studies* 13 (4): 409–26. https://doi.org/10.1177/1367877910369980.

Lutz, Catherine. 2007. "Militarization." In *A Companion to the Anthropology of Politics*, edited by David Nugent and Joan Vincent, 318–31. Malden, MA: Blackwell.

———, ed. 2009. *The Bases of Empire: The Global Struggle against U.S. Military Posts*. New York: New York University Press.

Macintosh, Paige. 2022. "Transgressive TV: Euphoria, HBO, and a New Trans Aesthetic." *Global Storytelling: Journal of Digital and Moving Images* 2 (1): 2.

Maguire, Mark, and Setha Low. 2024. *Trapped: Life under Security Capitalism and How to Escape It*. Stanford, CA: Stanford University Press.

Malakaj, Ervin. 2023. "Queer Time and the Cinematic Pleasures of the Locus Amoenus in Free Fall." *Glq* 29 (2): 237–60. https://doi.org/10.1215/10642684-10308521.

Mankekar, Purnima. 1999. *Screening Culture, Viewing Politics: An Ethnography of Television, Womanhood, and Nation in Postcolonial India*. Durham: Stanford University Press.

Manserus, Laura. 2017. "For What They Might Do: A Sex Offender Exception to the Constitution." In *The War on Sex*, edited by David M. Haplerin and Trevor Hoppe, 268–90. Durham: Duke University Press.

Manuel, Sheri L. 2009. "Becoming the Homovoyeur: Consuming Homosexual Representation in Queer as Folk." *Social Semiotics* 19 (3): 275–91. https://doi.org/10.1080/10350330903072656.

Maris, Elena. 2016. "Hacking Xena: Technological Innovation and Queer Influence in the Production of Mainstream Television." *Critical Studies in Media Communication* 33 (1): 123–37. https://doi.org/10.1080/15295036.2015.1129063.

Martin, Emily. 1991. "The Egg and the Sperm: How Science Has Constructed a Romance Based on Stereotypical Male-Female Roles." *Signs* 16 (3): 485–501.

———. 1994. *Flexible Bodies: The Role of Immunity in American Culture, from the Days of Polio to the Age of AIDS*. Boston: Beacon Press.

Masco, Joseph. 2014. *The Theater of Operations: National Security Affect from the Cold War to the War on Terror*. Durham: Duke University Press.

Mason, Derritt. 2021. *Queer Anxieties of Young Adult Literature and Culture*. Oxford: University of Mississippi Press.

McDavitt, Bryce, and Matt G. Mutchler. 2014. "'Dude, You're Such a Slut!' Barriers and Facilitators of Sexual Communication among Young Gay Men and Their Best Friends." *Journal of Adolescent Research* 29 (4): 464–98. https://doi.org/10.1177/0743558414528974.

McDermott, Elizabeth, Katrina Roen, and Jonathan Scourfield. 2008. "Avoiding Shame: Young LGBT People, Homophobia and Self-Destructive Behaviours." *Culture, Health & Sexuality* 10 (8): 815–29.

McInroy, Lauren B., and Shelley L. Craig. 2015. "Transgender Representation in Offline and Online Media: LGBTQ Youth Perspectives." *Journal of Human Behavior in the Social Environment* 25 (6): 606–17. https://doi.org/10.1080/10911359.2014.995392.

McNeill, Tanya. 2013. "Sex Education and the Promotion of Heteronormativity." *Sexualities* 16 (7): 826–46. https://doi.org/10.1177/1363460713497216.

Meiners, Erica R. 2016. *For the Children? Protecting Innocence in a Carceral State*. Minneapolis: University of Minnesota Press.

Mikdashi, Maya, and Jasbir K. Puar. 2016. "Queer Theory and Permanent War." *GLQ* 22 (2): 215–22.

Mitchell, Alice. 2018. "Allusive References and Other-Oriented Stance in an Affinal Avoidance Register." *Journal of Linguistic Anthropology* 28 (1): 4–21. https://doi.org/10.1111/jola.12174.

Mitchell, Danielle. 2005. "Producing Containment: The Rhetorical Construction of Difference in Will & Grace." *Journal of Popular Culture* 38 (6): 1050–68. https://doi.org/10.1111/j.1540-5931.2005.00175.x.

Movement Advancement Project. 2023. "Equality Maps: LGBTQ Curricular Laws." 2023. https://www.lgbtmap.org/equality-maps/curricular_laws.

Muñoz, José Esteban. 2009. *Cruising Utopia: The Then and There of Queer Futurity*. New York City: New York University Press.

Munt, Sally. 2007. *Queer Attachments: The Cultural Politics of Shame*. Abingdon, UK: Taylor & Francis.

———. 2019. "Gay Shame in a Geopolitical Context." *Cultural Studies* 33 (2): 223–48.

Nardi, Bonnie A. 2010. *My Life as a Night Elf Priest: An Anthropological Account of World of Warcraft*. Ann Arbor: University of Michigan Press.

Ng, Eve. 2021. "The 'Gentleman-like' Anne Lister on Gentleman Jack: Queerness, Class, and Prestige in 'Quality' Period Dramas." *International Journal of Communication* 15:2397–417.

———. 2023. *Mainstreaming Gays: Critical Convergences of Queer Media, Fan Cultures, and Commercial Television*. New Brunswick, NJ: Rutgers University Press.

Nguyen, Tan Hoang. 2014. *A View from the Bottom: Asian American Masculinity and Sexual Representation*. Durham: Duke University Press.

Obadia, Julienne. 2022. "Contracts, Polyamory, and Late Liberalism: The Relational Production of Unrelationality." *Theory and Event* 25 (3): 509–35. https://doi.org/10.1353/tae.2022.0026.

Olmos, Sergio. 2023. "Protests against LGBTQ Inclusivity in Schools Have Turned Violent in LA County." *NPR*, June 28. https://www.npr.org/2023/06/28/1184726301/protests-against-lgbtq-inclusivity-in-schools-have-turned-violent-in-la-county.

Owens, Andrew J. 2019. "Hold Me, Thrill Me, Kiss Me, Kill Me: The Ambivalent Queer of Post-Network Television." *New Review of Film and Television Studies* 17 (2): 131–47. https://doi.org/10.1080/17400309.2019.1602981.

Papacharissi, Zizi, and Jan Fernback. 2008. "The Aesthetic Power of the Fab 5: Discursive Themes of Homonormativity in Queer Eye for the Straight Guy." *Journal of Communication Inquiry* 32 (4): 348–67. https://doi.org/10.1177/0196859908320301.

Pascoe, C. J. 2007. *Dude You're a Fag: Masculinity and Sexuality in High School.* Berkeley: University of California Press.

———. 2023. *Nice Is Not Enough: Inequality and the Limits of Kindness at American High.* Berkeley: University of California Press.

Pedersen, Morten Axel, and Martin Holbraad. 2013. "Introduction: Times of Security." In *Times of Security: Ethnographies of Fear, Protest and the Future*, edited by Martin Holbraad and Morten Axel Pedersen, 1–27. New York: Routledge.

Peeren, Esther. 2006. "Queering the Straight World: The Politics of Resignification in Queer as Folk." In *The New Queer Aesthetic on Television: Essays on Recent Programming*, edited by James R. Kellery and Leslie Stratyner, 60–74. Jefferson, NC: McFarland.

Perkins, Claire. 2014. "Dancing on My Own: Girls and Television of the Body." *Critical Studies in Television* 9 (3): 33–43. https://doi.org/10.7227/CST.9.3.4.

Plummer, Ken. 1991. "Understanding Childhood Sexualities." *Journal of Homosexuality* 20 (1–2): 231–49.

Povinelli, Elizabeth. 2011. *Economies of Abandonment: Social Belonging and Endurance in Late Liberalism.* Durham: Duke University Press.

Prasse-Freeman, Elliott. 2022. "Resistance/Refusal: Politics of Manoeuvre under Diffuse Regimes of Governmentality." *Anthropological Theory* 22 (1): 102–27. https://doi.org/10.1177/1463499620940218.

Promise, Sandy Hook. 2023. "Say Something." Sandy Hook Promise. 2023. https://www.sandyhookpromise.org/our-programs/say-something/.

Puar, Jasbir. 2007. *Terrorist Assemblages: Homonationalism in Queer Times.* Durham: Duke University Press.

———. 2017. *The Right to Maim: Debility, Capacity, Disability.* Durham: Duke University Press.

Pullen, Christopher. 2014. "Media Responses to Queer Youth Suicide: Trauma, Therapeutic Discourse and Co-Presence." In *Queer Youth and Media Cultures*, edited by Christopher Pullen, 63–85. New York: Palgrave Macmillan.

Queen, Carol, and Penelope Saunders. 2017. "California's Proposition 35 and the Trouble with Trafficking." In *The War on Sex*, edited by David M. Halperin and Trevor Hoppe, 323–246. Durham: Duke University Press.

Quinlivan, Kathleen. 2012. "Popular Culture as Emotional Provocation: The Material Enactment of Queer Pedagogies in a High School Classroom." *Sex Education* 12 (5): 511–22. https://doi.org/10.1080/14681811.2011.627728.

Reddy, Michael J. 1979. "The Conduit Metaphor: A Case of Frame Conflict in Our Language about Language." In *Metaphor and Thought*, edited by Andrew Ortony, 284–324. Cambridge: Cambridge University Press.

Redvall, Eva Novrup. 2018. "Reaching Young Audiences through Research: Using the NABC Method to Create the Norwegian Web Teenage Drama SKAM/Shame." In *True Event Adaptation: Scripting Real Lives*, edited by Davinia Thornley, 143–61. London: Palgrave Macmillan.

Reeves, Joshua. 2012. "If You See Something, Say Something: Lateral Surveillance and the Uses of Responsibility." *Surveillance and Society* 10 (3–4): 235–48. https://doi.org/10.24908/ss.v10i3/4.4209.

Rich, Adrienne. 1980. "Compulsory Heterosexuality and Lesbian Existence." *Signs* 5 (4): 631–60. https://doi.org/10.4324/9780203966105-24.

Robertson, Mary. 2018. *Growing Up Queer: Kids and the Remaking of LGBTQ Identity*. New York: New York University Press.

Ross, Sharon Marie, and Louisa Ellen Stein, eds. 2008. *Teen Television: Essays on Programming and Fandom*. Jefferson, NC: McFarland.

Rubin, Gayle. 2011. *Deviations: A Gayle Rubin Reader*. Durham: Duke University Press.

Rubinsky, Valerie, and Angela Hosek. 2020. " 'We Have to Get Over It': Navigating Sex Talk through the Lens of Sexual Communication Comfort and Sexual Self-Disclosure in LGBTQ Intimate Partnerships." *Sexuality and Culture* 24 (3): 613–29. https://doi.org/10.1007/s12119-019-09652-0.

Rustad, Gry. 2018. "Skam (NRK, 2015–17) and the Rhythms of Reception of Digital Television." *Critical Studies in Television* 13 (4): 505–9. https://doi.org/10.1177/1749602018796755.

Sarkissian, Raffi. 2014. "Queering TV Conventions: LGBT Teen Narratives on Glee." In *Queer Youth and Media Cultures*, edited by Christopher Pullen, 145–47. New York: Palgrave Macmillan.

Sasan, John Michael V. 2021. "The Social Contract Theories of Thomas Hobbes and John Locke: Comparative Analysis." *Shanlax International Journal of Arts, Science and Humanities* 9 (1): 34–45. https://doi.org/10.34293/sijash.v9i1.4042.

Savin-Williams, Ritch C. 2005. *The New Gay Teenager*. Cambridge: Harvard University Press.
Sedgwick, Eve Kosofsky. 1991. "How to Bring Your Kids Up Gay." *Social Text*, no. 29:18–27.
Shange, Savannah. 2019. *Progressive Dystopia: Abolition, Antiblackness, and Schooling in San Francisco*. Durham: Duke University Press.
Shannon, Barrie. 2016. "Comprehensive for Who? Neoliberal Directives in Australian 'Comprehensive' Sexuality Education and the Erasure of GLBTIQ Identity." *Sex Education* 16 (6): 573–85. https://doi.org/10.1080/14681811.2016.1141090.
Sheldon, Rebekah. 2016. *The Child to Come: Life after the Human Catastrophe*. Minneapolis: University of Minnesota Press.
Simon, William, and John H. Gagnon. 1986. "Sexual Scripts: Permanence and Change." *Archives of Sexual Behavior* 15 (2): 97–120.
Sinclair, G. Dean. 2009. "Homosexuality and the Military: A Review of the Literature." *Journal of Homosexuality* 56 (6): 701–18. https://doi.org/10.1080/00918360903054137.
Southern Poverty Law Center (SPLC). 2022. "Battling against Bigotry: Florida Families and Advocacy Groups Sue to Block State Law Known as 'Don't Say Gay.'" *Southern Poverty Law Center*, July 27. https://www.splcenter.org/news/2022/07/27/florida-families-sue-block-dont-say-gay-law.
Spencer, Leland G., and G. Patterson. 2017. "Abridging the Acronym: Neoliberalism and the Proliferation of Identitarian Politics." *Journal of LGBT Youth* 14 (3): 296–316. https://doi.org/10.1080/19361653.2017.1324343.
Stangl, Anne L., and Valerie A. Earnshaw. 2019. "The Health Stigma and Discrimination Framework: A Global, Crosscutting Framework to Inform Research, Intervention Development, and Policy on Health-Related Stigmas." *BMC Medicine* 17 (31): 1–13. https://doi.org/10.1186/s12916-019-1271-3.
Stanley, Eric A. 2021. *Atmospheres of Violence: Structuring Antagonism and the Trans/Queer Ungovernable*. Durham: Duke University Press.
Stewart, Kathleen. 2007. *Ordinary Affects*. Durham: Duke University Press.
Stockton, Kathryn Bond. 2009. *The Queer Child, Or Growing Sideways in the Twentieth Century*. Durham: Duke University Press.
———. 2016. "The Queer Child Now and Its Paradoxical Global Effects," *GLQ: A Journal of Lesbian and Gay Studies* 22 (4): 493–503.
Stout, Noelle M. 2014. *After Love: Queer Intimacy and Erotic Economies in Post-Soviet Cuba*. Durham: Duke University Press.
Strathern, Marilyn. 1988. *The Gender of the Gift*. Cambridge: Cambridge University Press.
Strub, Sean. 2017. "HIV: Prosecution or Prevention? HIV Is Not a Crime." In *The War on Sex*, edited by David M. Halperin and Trevor Hoppe, 347–52. Durham: Duke University Press.

Sundet, Vilde Schanke. 2020. "From 'Secret' Online Teen Drama to International Cult Phenomenon: The Global Expansion of SKAM and Its Public Service Mission." *Critical Studies in Television* 15 (1): 69–90. https://doi.org/10.1177/1749602019879856.

———. 2021a. *Television Drama in the Age of Streaming: Transnational Strategies and Digital Production Cultures at the NRK*. Cham, Switzerland: Palgrave Macmillan.

———. 2021b. "'Youthification' of Drama through Real-Time Storytelling: A Production Study of Blank and the Legacy of SKAM." *Critical Studies in Television* 16 (2): 145–62. https://doi.org/10.1177/17496020211005311.

Swidriski, Edward. 2022. "Florida's 'Don't Say Gay' Law Raises Serious Legal Questions." *American Bar Association*, November 22. https://www.americanbar.org/groups/labor_law/publications/labor_employment_law_news/fall-2022/florida-do-not-say-gay-law/.

Talburt, Susan. 2004. "Intelligibility and Narrating Queer Youth." In *Youth and Sexualities: Pleasure, Subversion, and Insubordination In and Out of School*, edited by Mary Louise Rasmussen, Eric Rofes, and Susan Talburt, 17–40. New York: Palgrave Macmillan.

———, ed. 2018. *Youth Sexualities: Public Feelings and Contemporary Cultural Politics*. Santa Barbara, CA: Praeger Press.

Tomso, Gregory. 2017. "HIV Monsters: Gay Men, Criminal Law, and the New Political Economy of HIV." In *The War on Sex*, edited by David Halperin and Trevor Hoppe, 353–77. Durham: Duke University Press.

Urciuoli, Bonnie. 2008. "Skills and Selves in the New Workplace." *American Ethnologist* 35:211–28.

———, ed. 2018. *The Experience of Neoliberal Education*. New York: Berghahn Books.

———. 2022. *Neoliberalizing Diversity in Liberal Arts College Life*. New York: Berghahn Books.

Vainiomäki, Tiina. 2004. "Silence as a Cultural Sign." *Semiotica* 150 (1/4): 347–61.

Valentine, David. 2017. "Gravity Fixes: Habituating to the Human on Mars and Island Three." *HAU: Journal of Ethnographic Theory* 7 (3): 185–209.

Van Wichelen, Thalia, and Alexander Dhoest. 2023. "Pink-Wearing Hairdressers to Manly Gay Men: LGBT+ in Flemish Children's Fiction." *Communications* 48 (1): 112–29. https://doi.org/10.1515/commun-2021-0013.

Vance, Carole S. 1992a. "Epilogue." In *Pleasure and Danger: Exploring Female Sexuality*, edited by Carole S. Vance, 431–39. London: Pandora Press.

———. 1992b. "More Danger, More Pleasure: A Decade after the Barnard Sexuality Conference." In *Pleasure and Danger: Exploring Female Sexuality*, edited by Carole S. Vance, xvi–xxxix. London: Pandora Press.

Vanlee, Florian, Frederik Dhaenens, and Sofie Van Bauwel. 2018. "Understanding Queer Normality: LGBT+ Representations in Millennial Flemish

Television Fiction." *Television and New Media* 19 (7): 610–25. https://doi.org/10.1177/1527476417748431.
The Violence Project. 2022. "Key Findings." The Violence Project. https://www.theviolenceproject.org/key-findings/.
Viveiros De Castro, Eduardo. 2011. "Zeno and the Art of Anthropology: Of Lies, Beliefs, Paradoxes, and Other Truths." *Common Knowledge* 17 (1): 128–45. https://doi.org/10.1215/0961754X-2010-045.
Wade, Lisa. 2017. *American Hookup: The New Cultures of Sex on Campus*. New York: W. W. Norton & Company.
Ward, Jane. 2023. "Sex Scenes, Television, and Disavowed Sex Work." *Signs* 48 (2): 371–93. https://doi.org/10.1086/722316.
Warner, Michael. 2002. *Publics and Counterpublics*. New York City: Zone Books.
Weeks, Jeffrey. 1981. *Sex, Politics, and Society: The Regulation of Sexuality since 1800*. London: Longman.
Weiss, Margot. 2011. *Techniques of Pleasure: BDSM and the Circuits of Sexuality*. Durham: Duke University Press.
———. 2016. "Always After: Desiring Queerness, Desiring Anthropology." *Cultural Anthropology* 31 (4): 627–38.
———. 2020. "Intimate Encounters: Queer Entanglements in Ethnographic Fieldwork." *Anthropological Quarterly* 93 (1): 1355–86. https://doi.org/10.1353/anq.2020.0015.
———. 2022. "Queer Theory from Elsewhere and the Im/Proper Objects of Queer Anthropology." *Feminist Anthropology*. 3(2): 315–35. https://doi.org/10.1002/fea2.12084.
Weston, Kath. 1991. *Families We Choose: Lesbians, Gays, Kinship*. New York: Columbia University Press.
———. 1995. "Get Thee to a Big City: Sexual Imaginary and the Great Gay Migration." *GLQ: A Journal of Lesbian and Gay Studies* 2 (3): 253–77.
What We Know. 2023. "What Does the Scholarly Research Say about the Effects of Discrimination on the Health of LGBT People?" What We Know. https://whatweknow.inequality.cornell.edu/topics/lgbt-equality/what-does-scholarly-research-say-about-the-effects-of-discrimination-on-the-health-of-lgbt-people/.
Wichelen, Thalia van, and Alexander Dhoest. 2023. "Pink-Wearing Hairdressers to Manly Gay Men: LGBT+ in Flemish Children's Fiction." *Communications* 48 (1): 112–29.
Williams, Raymond. 1978. *Marxism and Literature*. Oxford: Oxford University Press.
Woo, Ashley, and Melissa Kay Diliberti. 2023. "How Florida's Expansion of 'Don't Say Gay' Law Will Hurt Students and Teachers across the United States." *RAND Blog*, May 13. https://www.rand.org/blog/2023/05/how-floridas-expansion-of-dont-say-gay-law-will-hurt.html.

Woods, Faye. 2013. "Teen TV Meets T4: Assimilating *The O.C.* into British Youth Television." *Critical Studies in Television: The International Journal of Television Studies* 8 (1): 14–35. https://doi.org/10.7227/cst.8.1.4.

Wozolek, Boni, Lindsey Wootton, and Aaron Demlow. 2017. "The School-to-Coffin Pipeline: Queer Youth, Suicide, and Living the In-Between." *Cultural Studies—Critical Methodologies* 17 (5): 392–98. https://doi.org/10.1177/1532708616673659.

Wuest, Bryan. 2014. "Stories Like Mine: Coming Out Videos and Queer Identities on YouTube." In *Queer Youth and Media Cultures*, edited by Christopher Pullen, 19–33. New York: Palgrave Macmillan.

Yurcaba, Jo. 2023. "DeSantis Signs 'Don't Say Gay' Expansion and Gender-Affirming Care Ban." *NBC News*, May 17. https://www.nbcnews.com/nbc-out/out-politics-and-policy/desantis-signs-dont-say-gay-expansion-gender-affirming-care-ban-rcna84698.

Index

Ahmed, Sara, 63, 75, 79, 85, 145, 179n1
AIDS, 41–43, 65
AIDS crisis, 15
Alex Strangelove, 89, 94–96, 99–101, 106
American exceptionalism, 96–97, 142
American GIs, 151–54
American society, 3, 6, 28, 36, 83–85, 138, 154, 164; and individualism, 87; and nationalism, 140
Amin, Kadji, 61, 82, 98, 135, 140
Amoore, Louise, 13–14
Angelides, Steven, 8, 11, 23, 64
Aristotle and Dante Discover the Secrets of the Universe, 137–38

Bacon, Jen, 90, 92–94, 177n12, 177n17–18
Being 17, 89, 103, 106–107, 110
Berlant, Lauren, 29, 111–13, 115, 135, 146, 169, 174n2, 178n3
Butler, Judith, 34–36, 91, 112–13, 135, 177nn8–9

Chambers, Samuel, 22, 123
Charlie, 100–103, 107
Chester, 129–31, 156–60, 179n17
child abuse, 1, 46

childhood (children), 10, 18, 42, 54, 95; definition of, 19; development, 23, 65–66, 110; education, 33, 45, 48, 51; and gay children, 10, 30, 40; and growth of children, 5, 15; and heterosexuality, 115; and innocence, 2, 4, 7–8, 34, 37–38, 47, 64, 165; and maturing, 5; and parenting, 49, 57; protection of, 56–57, 169–70nn7–8; and protogay children, 11–12; and queerness, 19; and radical presentism, 61; and sex panics, 36, 39; and sexuality, 6, 8–9, 11, 25, 35, 59, 113, 120–21; and shame, 64; and teaching, 50
cultural anxiety, 44
cultural assumptions, 45
cultural figures, 12
cultural industries, 13
cultural memory, 151
cultural narratives, 64
cultural scenarios, 22
cultural scripts, 23, 26
cultural sign, 103
cultural texts, 148
cultural theory, 105
cultural values, 21
cultural wars, 44

Index

Damien, 103–105, 107–108
Don't Ask Don't Tell (DADT), 35–36, 55
Don't Say Gay Laws, 40–41, 43, 48–49, 52, 55, 57, 171n7, 173n18, 174n3; in Florida, 8, 15, 20, 24, 28, 36, 38, 44–46, 50–51, 56
Driver, Susan, 114–15, 178nn6–8
Druck, 111, 117, 178n1

Edelman, Lee, 10, 17, 19, 34, 40, 99, 111–13, 115, 135, 164, 170
Elliott, 63, 71, 76–79, 95–96, 100

fear, 2, 4, 6, 8, 12–15, 23, 25, 27, 34–37, 39, 41, 44–46, 48–51, 57; and anxiety, 163–66; of death, 157, 159–60; and insecurity, 102; and panic, 114; and sex, 113, 124
Foucault, Michel, 85, 90, 92, 94, 96, 106, 108, 177n8, 177n13, 178n4
Freeman, Elizabeth, 65–66, 131

gay, 35–36, 38, 140, 143–44, 156, 165; characters, 100–102, 118, 129; children, 137–38, 170n10; coming out as, 95–98, 132; experiences, 73–74, 83, 90–93, 105–106, 110; masculinity, 119; parenting, 119; porn, 153; "saying," 40, 48, 56; sex, 126–27, 144, 150, 152
gay boys, 30, 97
gay marriage, 60
gay men, 42, 64, 72
gayness, 72
gay soldiers, 28
gay youth, 62
gender, 4, 15, 18, 44, 60, 119, 144–45, 147, 153–54, 170n13
gender-affirming care, 45, 48
gender fluidity, 1, 5, 169n1
gender identity, 2, 8, 33, 36, 43–50, 55, 85, 171–72n7, 173n20, 178n2
gender ideology, 21
gender modification, 1
genderqueer, 178n2
gender variance, 40, 172n7
Generation, 86, 117, 129, 133–34, 141, 156
Gershon, Ilana, 70–71, 84, 87, 96, 175n11, 175n15
Gilbert, Jen, 11, 19, 38, 45, 172n8
global health data, 14
Gray, Mary L., 61–62, 73–74, 80, 84, 86, 92, 107, 109, 177n11
Grewal, Inderpal, 139, 142–43

Halberstam, Judith (Jack), 9, 16, 18, 25, 65, 68
Heartstopper, 89, 100, 102, 106–107, 110, 117
heterosexuality, 8, 30, 34, 45, 95, 98–99, 113–16, 121, 126; and characters, 118, 165; and choices, 5; compulsory, 171n2; and family dynamic, 33, 142; and heteronormativity, 10; and identity, 17; and institutions, 34; and romance, 99, 102, 124; and sex, 126, 171n3; and youth sexuality, 25, 44
higher education, 30, 84, 147, 179n1, 180n8
homosexuality, 28, 35, 41–43, 47, 140, 161, 170n8, 171n5, 172n12
Human Rights Watch, 21

innocence, 2, 4–5, 7–9, 19–20, 34, 37–38, 40, 47, 56, 64, 113–14, 121, 165
Irvine, Janice, 16, 23, 37–39, 55

Kockelman, Paul, 24, 170nn19–20

Lancaster, Roger N., 2, 7–8, 12
language, 23–24, 28, 36, 40, 42, 44, 66, 82, 90, 93–94, 103, 108, 147, 177n18; body, 104; of risk, 13–14, 38
Lepselter, Susan, 22, 72, 82, 175n16
LGBTQ+ community, 30, 37, 48–51, 60, 83, 118, 139, 146–47, 159, 164, 169n1, 173nn24–25
Love, Simon, 20, 22, 60–61, 83–84, 89, 97–99, 101–102, 106, 126, 128–29
Love, Victor, 60–61, 89, 97–99, 101–102, 106, 117, 124, 126–28, 165, 167
Low, Setha, 12, 166–67
Lucas, 63, 71–73, 75–78

Maguire, Mark, 12–13, 166
masculinity, 30, 72, 119, 146, 153–54, 179n2
media, 23, 29, 38, 52, 81–82, 88–89, 109, 116, 163; artifacts, 18, 22, 27–28, 30, 63, 90, 105, 120; culture, 7, 9; news, 13; queer, 12; representations, 106, 108; scripts, 26; social, 48, 64, 66–67, 70, 85–86
Meiners, Erica R., 20, 169n7, 171n1
mental health, 46, 62, 79, 133
Muñoz, José Esteban, 16–17, 62, 82, 86, 134, 166, 176n3
Munt, Sally, 63, 174n3

neoliberalism, 12, 29, 60, 84, 87–89, 96, 98, 112, 115, 139, 143–44, 147–48, 174n3; and American society, 83, 143; and European society, 85; and LGBTQ rights, 145; and protection, 146; and queerness, 21; and security state, 142

Ng, Eve, 118
Nick, 101–103, 107–108, 128
nonnormativity, 2, 8, 17–18, 24–25, 29, 34–35, 40, 43, 55–56, 113, 116, 119, 124, 127, 139, 172
normativity, 5, 18, 25–26, 119, 123, 134, 142, 145, 147, 153–54, 163–65, 180n9; and behavior, 24, 55; and expectations, 116; and gender, 55; and sexuality, 8, 118, 121

obscenity, 170n8
obscenity laws, 7

parents' rights, 2, 33–34, 43, 46–47, 57
Pascoe, C.J., 141, 145–46, 155–56, 169n2
physical health, 48
pleasure, 92, 112, 116–17, 120–22, 124–25, 127–30, 151–52, 165, 177n15; and panic, 170n17
Puar, Jasbir K., 16, 18, 34, 60–61, 96, 139–40, 142–43, 149, 152, 171n3, 173n16, 174nn1–2
public health, 41–43, 173n15

queer characters, 2, 29, 85, 90–91, 93, 99–102, 116–18, 122, 144
queer childhood, 8, 11, 19
queer feminism, 91
queer futures, 170n9
queer identity, 107–108
queer individualism, 98–99
queer men, 42
queer methodology, 26
queerness, 60–61; and communities, 60–63, 74; definition of, 17; and deviance, 141; and phenomenology, 80; and pleasure, 29, 126, 128–29, 131–33, 135, 154; and politics, 81–82, 143

queer pleasure, 29, 114–15, 117, 120, 123, 126, 128, 131–35, 154, 162, 164
queer relationality, 105
queer relationships, 1–2, 8, 10
queer rights, 45
queer romances, 8
queer sex, 121–28, 133–35, 150
queer sexuality, 8, 29, 82–85, 89, 95–96, 103, 107–109, 120, 149; and individuality, 86, 94, 106; and narratives, 100
queer soldiers, 35
queer spaces, 98
queer states of security, 30, 140–41, 143–44, 148–49, 160–61, 166
queer theory, 11, 16, 18, 22, 26, 65, 137, 170n21
queer time, 68–69
queer trauma, 98
queer violence, 142
queer young adult novels, 1, 3
queer youth, xiii, xv–xvi, 5–7, 10–13, 15, 47, 59, 64, 73, 135, 140, 161–62, 178nn6–9; of color, 85, 138–39, 145, 148, 153–54; and desire, 115; and discrimination, 55; and experience, 66–67; and healthcare laws, 37; and identity work, 75, 79–80, 84, 177n11; and inclusivity, 37; and legislation, 37, 40; maneuverability, 20, 27, 167; and marginalization, 18; and media, 30; narratives of, 86, 88–90, 96–99, 108, 164, 174n6; and pleasure, 114–15, 117, 120, 123, 164; representations, 116, 118; and sex, 113–15, 118–20, 123, 133–34, 167, 170n17; and sex education, 37; sexuality, 6, 8–9, 12, 20–22, 25, 27–28, 62, 70, 72, 82, 84, 86–89, 95, 99, 106, 108–109, 118, 163, 165–66; and students, 55, 146–47, 159–60; and suicide, 60, 137

radical gender ideology, 46
radical presentism, 28, 60–62, 66, 69–70, 75, 78–81, 115, 134, 164
Reddy, Michael, 93–94, 106–107
relationality, 75–76, 78–79, 85, 108, 122, 141, 153, 178n4; building of, 24, 65, 123–24; engaging with, 66; and happiness, 77; and individuality, 86–90; and intimacy, 59, 62; narratives of, 90–91; nonnormative, 113; and pleasure, 29, 112, 129, 133; queer, 74, 105, 162; representations of, 109–10; and sex, 113; and sexuality, 81; and shame, 21; and social situations, 103; teenage, 80
reproductive health, 44
rights, 51, 60, 88, 164, 169n3, 172n7
Robbe, 63, 71, 73–76, 132–34
Rubin, Gayle, 2, 7, 9, 17, 37, 120–21, 169n6, 170n8, 179n11

Sander, 63, 71, 73–74, 76, 132–34
school boards, 1, 4, 6–7, 56
school lockdowns, 141, 154–61, 180n17
schools, 1–2, 33, 38, 67, 76–77, 84, 99–100, 138–40, 159; boarding, 128; and curricula, 41–42, 44; and gender, 15, 21; and high schools, 20, 27, 30, 48, 61–62, 97–98, 102–104, 119–20, 125, 129, 149–50, 152–54, 163–64; and identity, 44–45; and LGBTQ issues, 49–50; and libraries, 2, 4, 47; private, 49; progressive, 144–45, 147; public, 8; and queerness, 127; and sex

education, 36–37; and shootings, 53–54, 155–58, 160–62; and students, 20, 54, 89, 94–95, 97, 100, 129, 146; and teachers, 45–46
scripts, 24; media, 26; normative, 26, 142; sexual, 22–23, 116; sieving, 25–27, 51, 115, 164–65; social, 22, 24
securitization, 21, 30, 57, 145, 148, 155–56, 164, 166–67; definition of, 12–13; discourse, 40; of education, 54; practices, 56; and preemptive action, 5; of sex, 6, 18, 27–28; and sex panics, 6, 14, 27; of society, 140; theory, 39–40, 56
security, 5, 21, 24–25, 38–40, 59, 84, 92, 138, 164; and American security apparatus, 51–52, 55, 140, 142–45, 148, 151, 160–62, 166; discourse, 146–47; feminism, 142; ideologies, 141; institutions, 141; logics, 29; national, 15, 46, 52, 55–56, 170n8, 179n4; panics, 6–7, 12, 18, 20, 27–28, 35–37, 41, 43, 56–57, 167; post-9/11, 12–14, 52; practices, 30, 56, 148, 155, 170n12, 173n26; racialized, 139; theater, 54; threats to, 13
security education, 53–54
Sedgwick, Eve Kosofsky, 19, 137–38
self, 10, 19, 22, 24, 71, 73, 83–84, 86–87, 90–94, 96, 106–10, 113, 147; contractual, 29, 88–89, 99, 103, 112; and identity, 115–16, 135; neoliberal, 29, 139; and relationality, 123
self-acceptance, 72
self-awareness, 64, 81
self-empowerment, 142
self-esteem, 64
self-harm, 60

self-making, 90
self-responsibility, 12, 21, 145
sex education, 19–20, 23, 33–34, 36–44, 46–47, 52, 172n8
Sex Education, 20, 117, 120, 124, 126–28, 144–45
sex panics, 2, 4–8, 14–16, 23, 29–30, 59, 123, 138–39, 141, 147, 154, 163–67; and children, 39; forming of, 34, 114; and laws, 9; and queerness, 21, 27–28, 117; and scripts, 25, 27–28; and security, 12, 18, 20, 28, 36–38, 41, 43, 56–57; and sex education, 52; and sexual practice, 121; and youth sexuality, 11
sexual agency, 11, 39, 94, 98–99, 123, 165
sexual attraction, 76
sexual banality, 129
sexual behavior, 24, 37–39, 48, 122; nonnormative, 35, 55
sexual development, 8
sexual difference, 40, 87, 145
sexual diversity, 118, 144
sexual exceptionalism, 34, 96, 143
sexual exploitation, 8
sexual expression, 63–64, 88, 153–54
sexual freedom, 57
sexual harassment, 146
sexual identity, 2, 4, 17, 33, 36, 38–39, 47, 49, 82, 91–92
sexual individuals, 94
sexual intimacy, 26
sexuality, 4, 17–18, 23, 28–29, 35, 40, 43, 47, 78, 115; adult, 8, 25; childhood, 9, 11, 59, 64, 113, 121; and community, 80; crafting of, 7, 71–74, 83, 85, 88, 90, 103–104; deviant, 151; and discrimination, 60; experiences of, 84, 91–101, 105–10, 129, 132; and gender, xiii,

sexuality *(continued)*
15, 18, 36, 44–45, 55, 170n13, 172n7; individual, 72, 84; and individualism, 112; and language, 108; nonnormative, 8; and pleasure, 120; presocial, 95; and public feelings, 16; representations of, 118; and sex, 56, 111, 117, 127, 134, 178n4; and sex panics, 6–8, 39; thingness of, 72–76, 79, 81; and whiteness, 154; youth, 8, 16, 25, 59, 62, 81–82, 116–17, 120–22, 165. *See also* queer sexuality, queer youth
sexual materials, 15
sexual minorities, 44, 46
sexual oppression, 121–22
sexual orientation, 36, 44, 46–48, 50, 55, 80
sexual pleasure, 112, 120, 126
sexual predators, 7, 12
sexual projects, 29, 121–23, 125–26, 128–29, 131, 133
sexual relationships, 104
sexual reproduction, 46
sexual scripts, 22–23, 116
sexual thought, 37–38
sexual torture, 151–52
sexual violence, 142
Shadow and Bone, 117, 123, 126, 129, 134
shame, 21, 62–65, 67, 72, 80, 119, 130, 174n3
Shameless, 141, 150–51, 160
Sheldon, Rebekah, 9–11, 15, 45
Skam, 20, 28, 64, 66–71, 73–74, 79–81, 89, 91, 99–100, 106–107, 110, 117, 174n5
Skam France, 62–63, 77
Skam Italia, 62–63
Stanley, Eric A., 137, 144–45
Stockton, Kathryn Bond, 9–11, 19, 34, 40, 66, 110–11, 113, 170n10, 178n5

Talburt, Susan, 15–16, 62, 67, 87–88, 114, 135, 174n6
Teenage Bounty Hunters, 26, 86
Teenage Kiss: The Future is Dead, 21, 59, 62, 132, 164
teens, 40, 64, 175n9; and bullying, 61; and sexuality, 117; and shame, 63; and suicide, 60; and television, 28, 62, 68, 116–17, 128, 174n9
television, 9, 12, 28, 62, 66–67, 69–71, 81, 85–86, 95–96, 114, 116, 118–20, 123, 170n21
trans rights, 45
trauma, 3–4, 8, 98

US military, 28, 36, 142, 144, 148–49, 151, 153–54, 161, 171n4; code, 35; and military metaphor, 53

Valterson, Isak, 62–63, 65–66, 68–69, 71–82, 91, 99–100, 106–108, 167
Victor, 61, 97–98, 101–102, 106, 126–28, 165, 167
violence, 3–4, 34, 36, 45–46, 52, 139–40, 143, 149; gun, 156–59; and homophobia, 132–33, 178n6; imperial, 144; individuated, 145–46; institutional, 147; production of, 148; and queer youth, 86, 98, 102, 141–42; systemic, 145

We Are the Ants, 1, 3–4, 8, 30–31, 33–34, 120, 163
Weiss, Margot, 16–18, 92, 107, 115, 135, 176n1
whiteness, 30, 60, 145–46, 153–54, 158, 180n14
wtFOCK, 62, 117, 129, 132–34, 179nn18–19

Young Royals, 128–29, 134

www.ingramcontent.com/pod-product-compliance
Ingram Content Group UK Ltd.
Pitfield, Milton Keynes, MK11 3LW, UK
UKHW041302090425
5406UKWH00002B/17

9 798855 801644